Commercial and Economic Law in the Czech Republic

Commercial and Economic Law in the Czech Republic

Second Edition

Jan Lasák

This book was originally published as a monograph in the International Encyclopaedia of Laws/Commercial and Economic Law.

Founding Editor: Roger Blanpain
General Editor: Frank Hendrickx
Volume Editors: Jules Stuyck & Evelyne Terryn

Wolters Kluwer

Published by:
Kluwer Law International B.V.
PO Box 316
2400 AH Alphen aan den Rijn
The Netherlands
E-mail: lrs-sales@wolterskluwer.com
Website: www.wolterskluwer.com/en/solutions/kluwerlawinternational

Sold and distributed by:
Wolters Kluwer Legal & Regulatory U.S.
7201 McKinney Circle
Frederick, MD 21704
United States of America
E-mail: customer.service@wolterskluwer.com

DISCLAIMER: The material in this volume is in the nature of general comment only. It is not offered as advice on any particular matter and should not be taken as such. The editor and the contributing authors expressly disclaim all liability to any person with regard to anything done or omitted to be done, and with respect to the consequences of anything done or omitted to be done wholly or partly in reliance upon the whole or any part of the contents of this volume. No reader should act or refrain from acting on the basis of any matter contained in this volume without first obtaining professional advice regarding the particular facts and circumstances at issue. Any and all opinions expressed herein are those of the particular author and are not necessarily those of the editor or publisher of this volume.

ISBN 978-94-035-0226-7

e-Book: ISBN 978-94-035-0436-0
web-PDF: ISBN 978-94-035-0446-9

The Author

Jan Lasák is Lecturer of Corporate Law at the Faculty of Law, Masaryk University in Brno, and at the Faculty of Law, Palacký University in Olomouc, the Czech Republic and Partner in Kocián Šolc Balaštík, advokátní kancelář, s.r.o. (www.ksb.cz). Jan received his Juris Doctor Degree and LLM Degree (Columbia Law School) in 2010 and PhD in 2015. Jan has advised and been actively involved in the development of the new Czech law on corporations (Corporations Act) and corporate transformations (Transformations Act). He focuses on company law, mergers and acquisitions, contract law, corporate restructuring and European Union Law. Jan regularly publishes in the field of corporate law and company reorganizations, having published commentary on the Czech Corporations Act (Wolters Kluwer Publishing) as the lead author and commentary on the Civil Code and Takeovers Act as a leading co-author (CH Beck publishing).

The author is extremely grateful for research assistance provided by Klára Dvorská, Daniel Marian, Ota Mach, Tomáš Trávníček, Filip Šperl, Lucie Patková, Ondřej Siška, Sabina Prokopová and David Línek.

The Author

Table of Contents

Table of Contents

List of Abbreviations

Accounting Act	Czech Act No. 563/1991 Coll., the Accounting Act, as amended
Act on Safety of Goods or ASG	Czech Act No. 102/2001 Coll., on General Safety of Goods and on Amendment to Certain Acts, as amended
ADA	Anti-discrimination Act
AIPL	Act on International Private Law
Arbitration Act	Czech Act No. 2016/1994 Coll., on Arbitration Proceedings and Enforcement of Arbitration Awards, as amended
Banking Act	Czech Act No. 21/1992 Coll., on banks, as amended
Bankruptcy Act	Czech Act No. 328/1991 Coll., on bankruptcy, as amended
Biotechnological Inventions Act	Czech Act No. 206/2000, on the Protection of Biotechnological Inventions and on the Amendment to Act No. 132/1989 of Coll., on the Protection of Rights to New Plant and Animal Varieties, as amended by Act No. 93/ 1996 of Coll.
Brussels 1 bis Regulation	Regulation (EU) No. 1215/2012 of the European Parliament and of the Council of 12 December 2012 on jurisdiction and the recognition and enforcement of judgments in civil and commercial matters
Bulletin	Official Bulletin of the Industrial Property Office
CAS	Czech Accounting Standards
Charter or CHRF	Charter of Fundamental Rights and Freedoms
CISG	Contracts for the International Sale of Goods
Civil Code	Czech Act No. 89/2012 Coll., Civil Code, as amended
CJEU	Court of Justice of the European Union
CMNI	Carriage of Goods by Inland Waterways
CNB	Czech National Bank
Commercial Code	Czech Act No. 513/1991 Coll., Commercial Code, as amended

List of Abbreviations

Competition Act or PCA	Czech Act No. 143/2001 Coll., the Competition Act, as amended
Consumer Protection Act or CPA	Czech Act No. 634/1992 Coll., on Consumer Protection as amended
Copyright Act	Czech Act No. 121/2000 Coll, on copyright, rights related to copyright and amendment to certain laws
Corporations Act	Czech Act No. 90/2012 Coll., Corporations Act, as amended
Credit Consumer Act	Czech Act No. 257/2016 Coll., on Credit Consumer, as amended
Criminal Code	Czech Act No. 40/2009 Coll., Criminal Code, as amended
ČSSD	Czech Social Democratic Party
Czech Trade Inspection Act or CTIA	Czech Act No. 64/1986 Coll., on the Czech Trade Inspection, as amended
ECHR	European Convention on Human Rights
EPO	European Patent Organization
IAdm	Czech Act 312/2006 Coll., on Insolvency Trustees, as amended
Incentives Act	Czech Act No. 72/2000 Coll., on Investment Incentives, as amended
Income Tax Act	Czech Act No. 586/1992 Coll., Income Tax Act, as amended
Industrial Designs Act	Czech Act No. 527/1990 of Coll., on Inventions, Industrial Designs and Rationalisation Proposals, as amended
Insolvency Act	Czech Act 182/2006 Coll., on Insolvency, as amended
IPO	Industrial Property Office
KDU-ČSL	Christian and Democratic Union – Czechoslovak People's Party
KSČM	Czech Communist Party
Merger Regulation	Council Regulation (EC) No. 139/2004 of 20 January 2004 on the control of concentrations between undertakings (the EC Merger Regulation)
NGO	Non-profit Organization
ODS	Civic Democratic Party
Patent Act	Czech Act No. 527/1990 Coll., on Inventions and Rationalisation Proposals, as amended
PIL	Private International Law
Plant Breeders Rights Act	Czech Act No. 408/2000 on the Protection of Plant Variety Rights, as amended

SICAR	Société d'Investissement en Capital à Risque
SICAV	Societe d'Investissement a Capital Variable
Small Privatization Act	Czech Act No. 427/1990 Coll., on the transfer of state ownership of certain entities to other legal entities and physical persons, as amended
SMEs	Small- and Medium-Sized Enterprises
Takeover Act	Czech Act No. 104/2008 Coll., the Takeover Act, as amended
Takeover Directive	*Directive 2004/25/EC of the European Parliament and of the Council o*f 21 April 2004 on *takeover* bids
TFEU	Treaty on the Functioning of the European Union
Trade Licensing Act	Czech Act No. 455/1991 Coll., on Trade Licensing, as amended
Trademark Act	Czech Act No. 441/2003 Coll., on Trademarks, as amended
Transformations Act	Czech Act No. 125/2008 Coll., on Company Transformations, as amended
TRIPS	Trade-Related Aspects of Intellectual Property Rights
Utility Models Act	Act No. 478/1992 Coll., on Utility Models as amended
VAT	Value Added Tax
VPI	Visegrad Patent Institute

List of Abbreviations

General Introduction

§1. General Background of the Country

I. Geography and History

A. Geography

1. Located in Central Europe, the Czech Republic is a landlocked country covering 78,867 km^2. It is bordered by Germany to the west, Austria to the south, Slovakia to the east, and Poland to the northeast. The total length of its borders is 2,303 km. The capital and the largest city of the Czech Republic is Prague, which has about 1.2 million inhabitants, while the second largest city of the Czech Republic, Brno, follows with about 380,000 inhabitants. Ostrava, Pilsen, Olomouc, Liberec, Ústí nad Labem and České Budějovice are other large cities in the Czech Republic.

2. The Czech Republic is divided into fourteen autonomous regions (*kraje*), with the capital city (Prague) also having regional status. The Czech regions are Jihocesky (South Bohemia), Jihomoravsky (South Moravia), Karlovarsky (Karlovy Vary), Kralovehradecky (Hradec Kralove), Liberecky (Liberec), Moravskoslezsky (Moravia-Silesia), Olomoucky (Olomouc), Pardubicky (Pardubice), Plzensky (Pilsen), Praha (Prague), Stredocesky (Central Bohemia), Ustecky (Usti), Vysocina (Highlands) and Zlinsky (Zlin). Each region has its own elected regional assembly (*krajské zastupitelstvo*) and a regional governor (*hejtman*). In Prague, executive powers are executed by the city council and the mayor, both of whom are elected by the directly elected municipal assembly.

3. Over time, the Czech Republic has become an increasingly popular tourist destination in Europe, although there has been a significant decrease in the number of incoming tourists in spring 2020 due to the COVID-19 pandemic. The most frequently visited place is no doubt Prague, followed by the Western Bohemian spa triangle of Karlovy Vary, Marianske Lázně, and Františkovy Lázně. Besides the United Nations Educational, Scientific and Cultural Organization cultural heritage sites in the Czech Republic, many historical castles and chateaux across the country are also popular among tourists, with the most popular being Karlštejn and Křivoklát, both of which are conveniently located in the vicinity of the capital city.

B. History

4. The documented history of the so-called Czech lands can be traced back to Samo's Empire (seventh century), followed by the Great Moravia empire in the eighth century and, most importantly, the Kingdom of Bohemia, which gained significant political (regional) power in the middle ages. Undoubtedly, the golden age of Czech history is universally associated with the reign of King Charles IV, who also became the King of the Romans, King of Italy and Holy Roman Emperor. During his reign, Charles University in Prague was founded (in 1348) and the construction of the famous Charles Bridge, a historic bridge with an avenue of thirty mostly baroque statues and statuaries situated on the balustrade that crosses the Vltava River in Prague was initiated. Many of the Prague castles and the cathedral of Saint Vitus were also completed during this era.

5. In the fifteenth century, the Bohemian lands became increasingly under the control of the Habsburg Empire. Nevertheless, during the reign of Rudolf II (1583–1611), Prague became the official seat of the Holy Roman Emperor. Following the so-called Defenestration of Prague, the European Thirty Years' War erupted. The rebellion in Bohemia against the Habsburgs was, however, crushed at the Battle of White Mountain in 1620. The following period beginning in 1620 (until the late eighteenth century) is often called colloquially as the 'Dark Age'. The population of the Czech lands declined by a third through the expulsion of Czech Protestants as well as due to war, a devastating plague, famine and the invasion of the Ottoman Turks and Tatars.

6. The 'Dark Age' was followed by a period characterized as 'enlightened absolutism' during the reign of Maria Theresa of Austria and her son Joseph II, the Holy Roman Emperor. However, the end of the Holy Roman Empire in 1806 consequently led to the degradation of the political status of the Kingdom of Bohemia. The Czech lands became an integral part of the Austrian Empire and later of the Austrian–Hungarian Empire.

7. The independent Czech state's modern history dates back to the end of World War I, when following the collapse of the Austro-Hungarian Empire, the Czech lands merged with the Slovaks to form Czechoslovakia in 1918 (with T. G. Masaryk as the first Czechoslovak's President). The independence of the Czechoslovak Republic was, however, suspended during World War II. German occupation during World War II was followed in 1948 by the rule of communism, and the country basically became a one-party communist state under Soviet influence for the next forty years.

8. In 1989, the communist regime in Czechoslovakia collapsed during the peaceful 'Velvet Revolution', which inaugurated a return to democratic rule (with Václav Havel as the President) and a market economy. In 1993, Czechoslovakia peacefully dissolved, with the Czech Republic becoming a single independent state. The Czech Republic joined NATO in 1999 and the European Union in 2004. As of April 2020, the Czech Republic has not joined the eurozone yet.

II. Cultural Composition

9. The Czech Republic has a relatively homogeneous population, with the majority of the 10.6 million inhabitants being ethnically and linguistically Czech. Most foreigners living in the country have Ukrainian citizenship; others are from Slovakia, Vietnam, Russia, Poland and Germany.

III. Political System

A. General Observations

10. The Czech Republic could be viewed as a pluralist multiparty parliamentary representative democracy in which executive power is exercised by the government and the President, legislative power is exercised by the bicameral Parliament, and a four-tier system of courts represents the Czech judiciary.

11. The predominant political parties in the Czech Republic are:

- The *Civic Democratic Party (ODS)*: formerly the leading right-wing party supporting economic liberalism; in contrast to TOP 09, ODS represents a rather Eurosceptic party in the Czech right-wing political spectrum.
- *ANO*: this party identifies itself as a political movement rather than a standard political party; ANO is difficult to label on the left-right political axis; nevertheless, according to its programme, it aims at '*cleansing the country of corruption, abolishing immunity for politicians, fighting unemployment and improving the transport infrastructure*'.
- *TOP 09*: a conservative party supporting fiscal conservatism; it is strongly in favour of European integration.
- The *Christian and Democratic Union – Czechoslovak People's Party (KDU-ČSL)*: this traditional party supports social conservatism, regionalism and Euro-federalism.
- *Mayors and Independents (STAN):* this liberal centre to centre-right political movement, originally focused mainly on localism and promoting community involvement of municipalities and regions.– *The Pirate Party (Pirates)*: liberal progressive political party founded in 2009.
- *Party of Direct Democracy (SPD)*; right-wing populist party supporting direct democracy.– *The Social Democratic Party (ČSSD)*: this traditional Czech party's political platform in economic matters is typical for Western European social democratic parties; ČSSD supports a mixed economy, a strong welfare state, progressive taxation, and European integration (including joining the eurozone).
- Other popular parties include the *Green Party (SZ) and the Communist Party (KSČM).*

B. The Parliament

12. Legislative power is vested in the Parliament. The bicameral Parliament consists of two houses; the Senate as the upper house (with eighty-one seats; members are directly elected in single-seat constituencies by an absolute majority vote in two rounds if needed; members serve six-year terms with one-third of the membership renewed every two years) and the Chamber of Deputies as the lower house (200 seats; members are directly elected in multi-seat constituencies by proportional representation vote with a 5% election threshold; there are fourteen voting districts, which are identical to the country's administrative regions; members of the Chamber of Deputies serve four-year terms).

13. The bicameral Parliament exercises standard legislative powers. The Parliament holds and passes bills, has the right to modify the Constitution, ratifies international agreements; if necessary, it declares a state of war, approves the presence of foreign military forces in the Czech Republic and the dispatch of Czech military forces abroad (Article 43 of the Czech Constitution).

C. The Government

14. Executive power is vested in the government and the President. The government is led by the Prime Minister, who is appointed by the President. The Prime Minister selects all the remaining ministers (typically based on the results of negotiations between the political parties which agreed to form the governing coalition) and wields considerable powers. The government is constitutionally responsible to the Chamber of Deputies. Within thirty days after the Prime Minister's appointment, his/her government shall present itself to the Chamber of Deputies and ask for a vote of confidence. If confidence is granted, the new government is created; otherwise, the President shall appoint another Prime Minister and other members of the government who shall then ask for a vote of confidence. If history repeats itself, the President shall, in the final attempt, appoint the Prime Minister according to the President of the Chamber of Deputies' proposal. If no confidence in such Prime Minister's cabinet is granted, the President shall dissolve the Chamber of Deputies and initiate new elections (Article 35 of the Czech Constitution).

15. The President of the Czech Republic is the directly elected head of state and (formally) the commander-in-chief of the Czech Military. Many of the President's powers are, however, rather ceremonial. Many powers can be exercised only with the government's assent, as expressed by the signature of the Prime Minister (such as foreign relations, use of the military, appointment of judges to lower courts or granting of amnesty – Article 63 of the Czech Constitution). The President has the power to appoint the Chief Justice of the Supreme Court and the Supreme Administrative Court (Article 62 of the Czech Constitution). With the Senate's approval, the President appoints Constitutional Court justices (Article 84(2) of the Czech Constitution). One of the President's most prominent powers is his veto right to adopted bills. The President's veto can, however, be overruled by the majority of all (not only present) members of the Chamber of Deputies (Article 50 of the Czech Constitution). The President also convenes sessions of the Chamber of Deputies, can dissolve the Chamber of Deputies when the Constitution so provides and can grant pardons, commute in-force sentences and order that a criminal record be expunged (Articles 62 and 63 of the Czech Constitution).

D. The Judiciary

16. The four-tier Czech judiciary system is represented by the district courts, regional courts, two High Courts and two Supreme Courts (the Supreme Court and Supreme Administrative Court). Typically, court proceedings are of a two-instance nature. The courts are divided by jurisdiction into courts of general jurisdiction, administrative courts and the Constitutional Court of the Czech Republic, which, as a matter of law, stands outside the structure of the general and administrative courts and is designed to protect fundamental human rights and freedoms. There are no special courts which hear disputes on commercial and corporate law. Such disputes are, in the first instance, heard by the regional courts.

IV. Population and Employment Statistics

17. As of 30 September 2016, the population of the Czech Republic was 10,572,400. Natural growth has been positive since 2005, with the most important influence being immigration (https://www.czso.cz/csu/czso/cri/pohyb-obyvatelstva-1-3-ctvrtleti-2016).

18. As of 2016, the manufacturing industry is the main source of employment, followed by the wholesale and retail trade sector and the construction industry. The unemployment rate for people 15 years old and older, as of the third quarter of 2016, was 4% of the labour force. According to the latest news, the registered unemployment rate is declining as of March 2017.

V. Enterprise, Corporations, and Partnerships Statistics

19. As of 31 December 2015, there were 2,768,953 registered entrepreneurs (in Czech: *podnikatelé*) in the Czech Republic, of which 1,825,627 were organized as sole entrepreneurs, and 455,588 as private legal persons. The predominant legal form of business in the Czech Republic remains a limited liability company (in Czech: *společnost s ručením omezeným*). As of 31 December 2015, the number of limited liability companies amounted to 415,047. Limited liability companies are (in terms of number) followed by joint-stock companies (in Czech: *akciová společnost)*, which have 25,710 entries in the Companies Register, Cooperatives (in Czech: *družstvo)* which have 14,831 entries, and state-owned enterprises (in Czech: *státní podnik*) which have 207 entries.

VI. Social and Cultural Values

20. The population in the Czech Republic is relatively homogeneous and shares a common language (Czech, *čeština*). Although historically dominated by Christianity until at least the first half of the twentieth century, the country is most likely one of the least religious populations in the world. According to the 2011 census, only 10.3% of the population stated they are Roman Catholic, and 10.2% followed other forms of religion. However, it is part of the Czech culture to celebrate Christian feasts such as Christmas, Easter, Three Kings and others.

VII. Privatization Efforts

21. During the communist regime (1948–1989), essentially no private sector economy existed. Following the so-called Velvet Revolution, previously nationalized property was privatized after 1989 on several levels. In the beginning, small-scale businesses and stores were offered to the general public under the Small Privatization Act (1990); 'small privatization' was open only to domestic bidders. Privatization of large industrial companies was organized through a combination of methods which consisted of traditional methods of privatization such as tenders and public offerings. However, also a unique method of coupon privatization was introduced. In this privatization method, citizens could purchase at a low price a book of vouchers that represent potential shares in any of the 1,664 state-owned joint-stock companies and to property worth CZK 350 billion. Individual coupon holders could also entrust their coupons to specially created investment privatization funds which gained the capacity to acquire majority or control stakes in privatized companies.[1] As a result, about 6 million investors have become shareholders of these large companies, and for a limited period of time, the Czech Republic was a country with a

1. On the privatization of Czech companies in the 1990s, *see*, e.g., Balasczyk, B. Privatization in Post-Communist Countries. Varšava: Center for Social and Economic Research, 1996, Dědek, O. Kupónová privatizace a rozvoj kapitálového trhu v Československu. Praha: Ekonomický ústav Československé akademie věd, 1992, Estrin, S., Nuti, D., Uvalic, M. The Impact of Investment Funds on Corporate Governance in Mass Privatization Schemes: Czech Republic, Poland and Slovenia. Londýn: London Business School, 2000, Holman, R. Transformace české ekonomiky: V komparaci s dalšími zeměmi střední Evropy. Praha: Centrum pro ekonomiku a politiku, 2000, Ježek, T. Privatizace české ekonomiky: její kořeny, metody a výsledky. Praha: Vysoká škola ekonomická, 2006, Ježek, T. Zrození ze zkumavky: svědectví o české privatizaci 1990–1997. Praha: Prostor, 2007, Kočenda, E., Lízal, L. Český podnik v české transformaci 1990–2000. Praha: Academia, 2003, Kopp, K.; Bartošík, M.; Minařík, J. Právní úprava malé privatizace. Ostrava: MONTANEX, 1991, Kuklík, J. Znárodněné Československo: Od znárodnění k privatizaci – státní zásahy do vlastnických a dalších majetkových práv v Československu a jinde v Evropě. Praha: Auditorium, 2010, Mejstřík, M. Czech investment funds as a part of financial sector and their role in privatization of the economy. Praha: Univerzita Karlova, 1994, Muroň, J. Malá privatizace. Praha: Panorama, 1991, Richter, T. Kuponová privatizace a její vlivy na správu a financování českých akciových společností. Praha: Univerzita Karlova, 2005, Švejnar, J. Česká republika a ekonomická transformace ve střední a východní Evropě. Praha: Academia, 1997, Tomšík, V. Proces ekonomické transformace v zemích střední a východní Evropy. Praha: Vysoká škola ekonomická, 1999 or Tříska, D. Kupónová privatizace: sborník textů. Praha: CEP Centrum pro ekonomiku a politiku, 2002.

corporate system based on dispersed ownership in Berle & Means terms.[2] Over time, however, the dispersed ownership has been transformed into concentrated ownership,[3] which is predominant in Czech corporations even today.

2. *See*, e.g., Berle, Adolf A., Means, Gardiner C. The Modern Corporation & Property. New Jersey: Transaction Publishers, 2009. Tenth Printing, p. 47, Milhaupt, Curtis J. Property Rights in Firms. In Mark J. Roe, Jeffrey N. Gordon. Convergence and Persistence in Corporate Governance. Cambridge: Cambridge University Press, 2004, p. 210 or Gilson, R.J., Whitehead, Ch.K. Deconstructing Equity: Public Ownership, Agency Costs, and Complete Capital Markets, Columbia Law Review, 2008, Vol. 108, pp. 231 et seq.
3. On the concentrated ownership theory, *see*, e.g., Gelter, M. Dark Side of Shareholder Influence: Managerial Autonomy and Stakeholder Orientation in Comparative Corporate Governance. 50 Harvard International Law Journal 129, 2009, pp. 179–181.

Part I. Commercial Law

Chapter 1. Concepts and Sources of Commercial Law

§1. Definition of Commercial Law

22. Czech Commercial law can be generally defined as the body of law that applies to the rights, relations, and conduct of persons and businesses engaged in intra-state and interstate commerce. Even though commercial law is generally considered to be a significant part of civil law, certain commercial law regulations could be classified as belonging to the area of public or administrative law (e.g., antitrust law or public subsidies law).

23. In the traditional Czech doctrine, commercial law is subdivided into (i) corporate law (regulation of the status of business companies, partnerships and cooperatives), (ii) competition law (including regulation of both antitrust and unfair competition), (iii) law of (business) obligations, and (iv) law of securities (including the regulation of capital markets). Intellectual property law is also generally considered to be a part of commercial law.

§2. Development of Commercial Law in the Czech Republic

24. On 28 October 1918, after the First World War, the Czechoslovak Republic declared its independence from the collapsing Austrian-Hungarian Empire. In order to prevent revolutionary chaos during the transitional days, the previously applicable Austrian-Hungarian laws and regulations were resumed by the Reception Act (No. 11/1918 Coll.). After the Second World War, the ambition to swiftly rebuild the country and restore the pre-war democracy was shortly thwarted by the communist 'putsch' of 25 February 1948. Massive collectivization and nationalization measures followed, and the remaining democratic institutions were promptly dismantled or significantly oppressed by the empowered communist regime. In law, many standard private law concepts dating back to Roman law were repealed, making way for the new Soviet-style (socialistic) legislation.

25. After the communist regime collapsed in Czechoslovakia in 1989, the newly elected leadership pursued massive economic and societal reforms towards democracy and a market economy, which were followed by liberal and market-oriented shifts in commercial law. The first private corporations and partnerships were incorporated back into Czech law as early as 1990, based on the rather hastily drawn up amendment to the Economic Code (which regulated so-called socialist organizations during the communist era[4]). As of 1 January 1992, however, this interim and rather rudimentary legislation was repealed by Act No. 513/1991 Coll., the Commercial Code, which truly enabled the establishment and incorporation of private corporations and partnerships.

26. When the Czech Republic was about to join the European Union (in 2004), the Commercial Code was harmonized with various European directives. Although the legal regime of corporations and partnerships eventually became somewhat stabilized, the Czech Government commissioned several private law specialists to work on the comprehensive recodification of private law. As a result, a new Civil Code (Act No. 89/2012 Coll., with '89' symbolically representing the year that communism fell) and new Corporations Act (Act No. 90/2012 Coll., with '90' symbolically representing the year private enterprises were reintroduced back into Czech law) were approved and became effective as of 1 January 2014.

§3. Principles of Commercial Law

27. Legal principles represent highly general rules of conduct that form the basis of a particular legal instrument, regulation or distinctive legal area, which form cornerstones of the legal order. Legal principles do not have to be (and quite often are not) codified in a written law; nevertheless, they are somewhat reflected in the legal order and guide the interpretation of Czech statutory provisions and/or contractual or tortious relationships.

28. Since commercial law represents an integral part of private law, traditional private law principles apply. The main principles underlying commercial law are, therefore, set out in section 3(2) of the Civil Code. These include the principle of protecting the weaker party[5] (including the prohibition of profiting from one's own inability), the principle of binding promise and that contracts are to be fulfilled (*pacta sunt servanda*),[6] or the (also constitutional) principle of protecting ownership. Private law also arises from other generally accepted principles of justice and

4. *See*, e.g., Pokorná, J. Vzpomínka na hospodářské právo. CPVP – Časopis pro právní vědu a praxi. 2019, Vol. 27, No. 100, pp. 107 et seq. or Plíva, S., Přibyl, Z. Socialistické organizace. 2. přeprac. vyd. Praha. Státní pedagogické nakladatelství, 1976.
5. On the principle of protecting the weaker party, *see*, e.g., Janoušek, M. Ochrana slabší smluvní strany v občanském zákoníku. Praha. C. H. Beck, 2018, Černá, S., ed. Obchodní korporace a ochrana slabší strany. Praha. Wolters Kluwer, 2017, Lavický, P. a kol Občanský zákoník I. Obecná část (§ 1-654). Komentář. 1. vydání, Praha. C. H. Beck, 2014. pp. 1651 et seq., Bejček, J. Soukromoprávní ochrana slabšího obchodního partnera. Bulletin advokacie. 2015, Vol. 2015, Nos 7–8, pp. 24 et seq. or Šlejharová, M. Vybrané projevy ochrany 'slabší strany' z pohledu civilního práva procesního. Bulletin advokacie. 2018, Vol. 2018, Nos 7–8, pp. 46 et seq.
6. Cf. Hulmák, M. a kol Občanský zákoník V. Závazkové právo. Obecná část (§ 1721–2054). Komentář. 1. vydání. Praha: C. H. Beck, 2014. pp. 189 et seq., Lavický, P. a kol Občanský zákoník I. Obecná část (§ 1-654). Komentář. 1. vydání, Praha: C. H. Beck, 2014. pp. 51 et seq., Dvořák, J.

law (section 3(3) of the Civil Code). These principles include the principle of uniformity of private law, the principle of the sovereignty of the law, the principle of equality of parties in commercial obligations, the principle of contractual freedom, the prohibition of abuse of rights, and others.

29. One traditional legal principle exclusive to commercial law is the principle of professionalism. The professionalism principle reflects, generally speaking, the fact that even though entrepreneurs are professionals in their respective fields of business and possess the expertise, the legislator finds no sound reasons to afford them a higher standard of protection than what is granted to non-professionals (especially to consumers). The professionalism principle is also closely linked with the standard of knowledge and care stated in section 5(1) of the Civil Code, which stipulates that a person who offers professional service or other performance as a member of an occupation or profession is required, generally speaking, to act with the knowledge and care associated with his/her occupation or profession. If such a person then fails to act with such professional care, he/she may be liable for failing to discharge such duty.

§4. Sources of Commercial Law

30. The main sources of law (including commercial law) in the Czech Republic are written legislative acts while regulation of commercial law in the Czech Republic is not codified in one comprehensive legislative act (as was, to some extent, true until 31 December 2013 when the former Commercial Code was applicable); rather the regulation is fragmented into many legislative acts which altogether form Czech Commercial law. The Czech Republic became a member of the European Union on 1 May 2004 and is, therefore, subject to European Union legislation.

I. Civil Code

31. The Civil Code is the fundamental source of private law in general and commercial law, in particular. In relation to commercial law, the Civil Code regulates, for instance, the legal status of entrepreneurs and forms of their representation, business names, business enterprises and branches, trade secrets, unfair competition law and commercial obligations arising from contracts or torts.

---

a Knidl, M., ed. Pocta Martě Knappové k 80. narozeninám. Praha: ASPI Publishing, 2005. pp. 45 et seq. or Steiner, M. Zásada 'pacta sunt servanda' jako součást ústavního pořádku. Soudní rozhledy. 2002, Vol. 8, No. 2, pp. 39 et seq.

II. Corporations Act

32. The Corporations Act is another major source of commercial law. It regulates mainly the legal status of commercial companies (unlimited partnerships, limited partnerships, limited liability companies, and joint-stock companies), cooperatives, and when applicable (European) companies (Societas Europaea or European Company, European economic interest grouping, and European cooperative societies).

33. The Corporations Act is a *lex specialis* in relation to the Civil Code. If a certain issue is regulated in the Corporations Act, the Civil Code provisions only complement the Corporations Act regulation when applicable. Only if a certain issue is not at all regulated in the Corporations Act will the general regulation of legal persons set out in the Civil Code then be applicable.

III. Trade Licensing Act

34. The Trade Licensing Act sets out conditions for conducting the entrepreneurial activities of natural and legal persons in a majority of business areas. Business activities which fall outside the scope of the Trade Licensing Act are, for example, the activities of doctors, veterinarians, pharmacists, lawyers, executors, notaries, experts, interpreters, auditors, banks, insurance companies, etc. Business in these activities is regulated by special laws (section 3 of the Trade Licensing Act).

35. The Trade Licensing Act mainly regulates the conditions for obtaining a trade licence (sections 6, 7 and 10 of the Trade Licensing Act), which is the authorization to engage in entrepreneurial activity. It also regulates bans on entrepreneurial activity (section 8 of the Trade Licensing Act) and the main conditions under which foreign persons can conduct business in the Czech Republic (section 5 of the Trade Licensing Act).

IV. Other Applicable Legislative Acts

36. Other significant (national) legislative acts in the field of commercial law include:

(a) Act No. 125/2008 Coll., on Transformation of Commercial Companies and Cooperatives, which supplements and modifies the general regulation of transformations of legal persons contained in the Civil Code with respect to business corporations.
(b) Act No. 104/2008 Coll., on Takeover Bids, which regulates certain issues connected with bids on company shares traded on a stock exchange which would result in the bidder taking over the company.
(c) Act No. 143/2001 Coll., on Protection of Competition, which regulates protection of competition against monopolies and abuse of a dominant position.

(d) Act No. 304/2013 Coll., on Public Registers of Legal and Natural Persons and on Records of Trusts, which regulates *inter alia* the registration of entrepreneurs into the Companies Register.
(e) Act No. 256/2004 Coll., on Capital Market Business, which regulates certain issues connected with conducting business on capital markets (e.g., Industrial Property Offices (IPOs), protection of investors, etc.).

V. Other Sources of Law

37. In the Czech Republic, case law is not a formal source of law. Nevertheless, judgments of supreme or higher courts guide the interpretation of legislative acts, whilst the Czech Supreme Court's constitutional role is *inter alia* to unite the decision-making process of the lower courts. From a practical point of view, even though the Czech Republic does not have a precedential legal system, lower courts, as a matter of principle, follow the case law of the higher courts for, if they did not, their decisions would likely be overturned before the higher courts.

In the commercial trade arena, Czech law also takes account of trade usages[7] or principles of conduct (either general or special to specific business areas) in the context of contract interpretation. Under section 558(2) of the Civil Code, the courts shall, when interpreting contracts amongst professional entrepreneurs, take into account such usages or business conduct principles if these are followed in general or in the given industry unless excluded by an agreement or by a statute.

38. On the other hand, soft law is not a formal source of law, and as such, the obligations imposed by these soft law sources are vastly unenforceable. Therefore, the term 'soft law' includes a variety of non-binding opinions, announcements, codices or declarations of public authorities (namely the ones given by the Competition Authority such as its leniency policy). From the standpoint of commercial law, the most important soft law sources include various corporate governance codices, which set out appropriate management and oversight systems in corporate governance corporate social responsibility programmes, and sustainable models of conducting business activities.

7. *See*, e.g., Lavický, P. a kol Občanský zákoník I. Obecná část (§ 1-654). Komentář. Praha: C. H. Beck, 2014. pp. 2001 et seq., Švestka, J., Dvořák J., Fiala, J. a kol Občanský zákoník (zák. č. 89/2012 Sb.). Komentář. Svazek I (obecná část). Praha: Wolters Kluwer ČR, 2020. pp. 1374 et seq. or Marek, K. a Žváčková L. Obchodní podmínky, obchodní zvyklosti a vykládací pravidla. Praha: ASPI-Wolters Kluwer, 2008.

§5. ENTREPRENEURIAL ACTIVITY & SUBJECTS ENGAGED THEREIN

I. Introductory Remarks

39. The Civil Code does not define the term 'entrepreneurial activity' ('podnikání'). Nevertheless, the term can be defined using the definition of an entrepreneur.[8] As such, 'entrepreneurial activity' can be defined as a systematic activity conducted independently in one's own name and on one's own account and responsibility for the purpose of generating profit. Thus, before an activity is considered to be entrepreneurial, several conditions have to be fulfilled. First, the activity has to be systematic. This does not mean, however, that the activity has to be done continuously (nonstop). It is sufficient if the entrepreneurial activity is performed with the intention to perform it on a permanent or repeated basis from the perspective of a longer period of time. Second, conducting activities independently on one's own account expresses the entrepreneur's independence from someone else and, therefore, the entrepreneurial activity cannot be seen as any subordinate relationship, as in that case, it would be dependent on employment and not independent entrepreneurship. The liability aspect, where the entrepreneur conducts the activity in his/her own name and his/her own responsibility, demonstrates the entrepreneur's individual liability for his/her own actions. In the case of an illegal action, it will be the entrepreneur himself/herself who will be held responsible. Lastly, the main purpose of entrepreneurial activity is to make a profit. Essentially, even in cases where one is unsuccessful (unprofitable), the mere intent to make a profit is sufficient to constitute an entrepreneurial activity under Czech law.

II. Natural Person: Entrepreneur

40. Natural persons residing in the Czech Republic are allowed to conduct any entrepreneurial activity under either a trade licence or other type of licence or authorization if the entrepreneurial activity in question is regulated by a specific act other than the Trade Licensing Act. Natural persons may opt to form a legal entity in order to legally separate their own personal estate from their entrepreneurial activity. However, if a natural person chooses not to form a separate legal entity, he/she is still permitted to start his/her own business once he/she obtains the appropriate trade licence (or, as the case may be, other types of licence or authorization). Depending on the specific activities of the self-employed individual, the process for obtaining a trade licence either may be very simple, or it may take longer if an additional concession is required. There are two types of entrepreneurial activities based on the prerequisites for obtaining a trade licence:

8. On the regulation of entrepreneurial activity under Czech law, *see*, e.g., Černá, S., Štenglová, I., Pelikánová, I. A Dědič J. Obchodní právo: podnikatel, podnikání, závazky s účastí podnikatele. Praha: Wolters Kluwer, 2016.

(a) notifiable entrepreneurial activities, which may be conducted once they have been notified to the respective trade authority, provided that the stated conditions are met; and
(b) concession, which may be conducted only after a licence has been granted.

41. Notifiable entrepreneurial activities are further subdivided based on the prerequisites for obtaining the trade licence. First, unqualified entrepreneurial activities are activities where no professional competence or experience is set as a condition for obtaining the trade licence and conducting the entrepreneurial activity. For conducting an unqualified entrepreneurial activity, the person has to meet only the general requirements for conducting an entrepreneurial activity (i.e., full legal capacity and integrity). Second, vocational entrepreneurial activities are activities where the condition for obtaining the trade licence and conducting the entrepreneurial activity is a professional qualification in a relevant apprenticeship (e.g., brewing, masonry, watchmaking). This professional qualification is evidenced by a certificate of completion (e.g., diploma) in the relevant apprenticeship. Last, professional, entrepreneurial activities are activities where the condition for obtaining the trade licence and conducting the entrepreneurial activity is some other professional qualification specifically prescribed in Annex No. 2 to the Trade Licensing Act.

42. Entrepreneurial activity can also be conducted on the basis of a licence or authorization other than a trade licence. This is the case when a certain entrepreneurial activity is governed comprehensively by a special regulation other than the Trade Licensing Act. These regulations lay down the conditions both for exercising a certain profession and for obtaining the required licence. Within this category, one can find attorneys, court executors, notaries and veterinarians, who are registered with the relevant competent authority.

III. Business Corporations

43. Business corporations registered in the Czech Companies Register also need to obtain a licence before they can conduct their entrepreneurial activities in the specific field. In the event that a professional qualification must be demonstrated, the company has to designate a natural person (responsible representative) who meets the professional qualifications in order to obtain the relevant trade licence.

44. The term 'business corporation' is an umbrella term that encompasses both commercial companies and cooperatives. Commercial companies are legal entities that are established primarily for the purpose of entrepreneurial activities. Cooperatives are legal entities that are established for the purpose of mutual support of their members or third parties or, where appropriate, for the purpose of entrepreneurial activities.

45. There are four domestic forms of commercial companies and one form of cooperative which may be established under the Czech law:

(a) Unlimited partnership (veřejná obchodní společnost)
(b) Limited partnership (komanditní společnost)
(c) Limited liability company (společnost s ručením omezeným)
(d) Joint-stock company (akciová společnost)
(e) Cooperative (družstvo).

46. In the Czech Republic, it is also possible to establish legal entities under the law of the European Union. These encompass two forms of commercial companies and one form of a cooperative:

(a) European Company (evropská společnost; Societas Europaea)
(b) European economic interest grouping (evropské hospodářské zájmové sdružení)
(c) European cooperative society (evropská družstevní společnost; Societas Cooperativa Europaea).

47. General regulation of business corporations is set out in the Civil Code through the regulation of legal entities. Special regulation of business corporations (and their forms) is provided in the Corporations Act. The provisions of the Corporations Act stipulate *inter alia* the extent to which the shareholders/partners are liable for the obligations of the company/partnership.

IV. Consumers

48. A consumer is defined in the Civil Code as any individual who, outside his/her trade, business or profession, enters into a contract or has other dealings with an entrepreneur. Therefore, three cumulative requirements have to be met for someone to be considered a consumer:

(a) he/she must be an individual (i.e., only a natural person can be a consumer);
(b) he/she must deal outside an individual's trade, business or profession; and
(c) he/she must deal with an entrepreneur.

49. Consumers are afforded greater protection in their dealings with entrepreneurs than is the standard in business-to-business contractual relations.[9] That is because they are considered to be the weaker party in the relationship, with the entrepreneur (i.e., a professional) being the stronger party. The obligations of entrepreneurs regarding direct dealings with consumers are mostly contained in Act No. 634/1992 Coll., the Consumer Protection Act, and in the Civil Code. Among the most important obligations are the obligation to be honest in trade (e.g., to indicate

9. On the protection of consumers, *see* generally Pokorná, J., Večerková E., Levická T. a Dudová J. Ochrana spotřebitele proti nekalým obchodním praktikám podnikatelů. Praha: Wolters Kluwer, 2017, Večeřa, J. Ochrana spotřebitele v České republice a Evropské unii. Praha: Leges, 2013, Balcarová, A. Nový zákon o spotřebitelském úvěru. Právní rozhledy. 2017, Vol. 25, No. 8, pp. 272 et seq. or Vymazal, L. Ochrana spotřebitele a její meze v obchodním závazkovém právu. Obchodněprávní revue. 2010, Vol. 2, No. 2, pp. 35 et seq.

the correct weight of goods), the obligation to properly inform the consumer about the good/service and his/her rights (e.g., warranty claims), the prohibition of unfair trade practices, and prohibition of discrimination in dealings with customers.

Chapter 2. Economic Operators

50. In an economic sense, an economic operator may be a natural person or legal entity (including entities that are without a legal personality or of a public law nature), or generally any person or entity engaged in economic activities (supplying and proving goods, works or services).

51. On the other hand, in a legal sense, an economic operator is a person (a natural person or a legal entity) who is considered an entrepreneur under applicable law. In the Czech legal landscape, the definition of an entrepreneur is provided for by the Civil Code. Thereunder, an entrepreneur is defined both materially and formally. The legal definition of an economic operator does not, however, distinguish between different types of persons, i.e., natural persons and legal entities (*see* sections 420 and 421 of the Civil Code), as the Civil Code's definition applies equally to both.

52. First, an entrepreneur is defined by the activity he/she/it pursues. Therefore, a person (whether it is a natural person or a legal entity) who, on its own account and responsibility, independently carries out a gainful activity in the form of a trade or in a similar manner with the intention to do so consistently for profit is considered, with regard to such activity, to be an entrepreneur (section 420(1) of the Civil Code). Moreover, for the purposes of consumer protection and for the purposes of section 1963 of the Civil Code, any person who enters into contracts related to his/her/its own commercial, production or similar activities, or within his/her/its trade, business or profession, or a person acting in the name or on account of an entrepreneur, is considered to be an entrepreneur (section 420(2) of the Civil Code).

53. Obviously, an entrepreneur is primarily defined by the activity which it is pursuing in a professional capacity (the material definition of an entrepreneur). Consequently, a natural person may be considered a consumer in some situations and an entrepreneur in others. Even associations, which under Czech law are legal entities created to implement the common interest of their members and are entitled to carry out business as a secondary economic activity, if the purpose thereof is to support the primary activity or for the economical use of the association's property, will be considered entrepreneurs in relation to the business activities which they are carrying out.

54. Second, an entrepreneur is defined in formal terms. Thus, a person registered in the Companies Register is considered to be an entrepreneur (section 421(1) of the Civil Code). Business corporations, which are mandatorily registered in the Czech Companies Register, are, therefore, always entrepreneurs. In addition, a person who is authorized to conduct his/her/its business activities on the basis of a trade or other licence under another statute is presumed to be an entrepreneur (section 421(2) of the Civil Code). This is a rebuttable legal presumption. Hence, a person who has a trade or other licence may rebut this presumption if he/she/it proves that he/she/it does not carry out (any) business.

§1. PERSONAL STATUS OF MERCHANTS

I. In General

55. Czech civil/commercial law distinguishes between two types of status (for both natural and legal persons): (i) legal personality (the capacity to have rights and obligations)[10] and (ii) legal capacity[11] (the capacity to assume rights and obligations).

56. The capacity of natural persons to have rights and obligations accrues at the moment of birth (section 23 of the Civil Code). Even an unborn child (nasciturus) has the legal capacity of a natural person if it is born alive (section 25 of the Civil Code). This legal capacity is conditional upon live birth. The concept of nasciturus was adopted from Roman law, and it represents one of many Roman law influences on Czech law.

57. Generally, full legal capacity (i.e., the capacity to assume rights and obligations) accrues by reaching adulthood, i.e., 18 years of age (section 30(1) of the Civil Code). However, even minors are presumed to have legal capacity, albeit only that which corresponds to their level of maturity (section 31 of the Civil Code). Hence, minors are able to exercise such rights and undertake such obligations that are adequate to their intellectual and mental capacity. Before that, a minor may acquire full legal capacity by entering into marriage, or by virtue of a court's decision (section 30(2) of the Civil Code). This 'acquired' legal capacity does not cease to exist if the marriage is dissolved or annulled before the minor reaches adulthood (section 30(2) of the Civil Code).

58. If a natural person is not able to exercise his/her full legal capacity (e.g., due to a mental disorder), the court shall temporarily limit his/her legal capacity for up to five years and specify the extent of his/her legal capacity (section 59(1) of the Civil Code); such a limitation may be imposed repeatedly (section 59(2) of the Civil Code) and can only be imposed by virtue of a court's decision (section 56(1) of the

10. To the legal personality concept under Czech law, *see*, e.g., Lavický, P. a kol Občanský zákoník I. Obecná část (§ 1-654). Komentář. Praha: C. H. Beck, 2014. pp. 129 et seq., Pelikán, R. Právní subjektivita. Praha: Wolters Kluwer ČR, 2012, Švestka, J., Dvořák J., Fiala, J. a kol Občanský zákoník (zák. č. 89/2012 Sb.). Komentář. Svazek I (obecná část). Praha: Wolters Kluwer ČR, 2020. pp. 71 et seq., Pilík, V. Pojetí a úprava ochrany právní osobnosti právnických osob v občanském právu. Právní rozhledy. 2016, Vol. 24, Nos 13–14, pp. 457 et seq. or Zibner, J. Akceptace právní osobnosti v případě umělé inteligence. Revue pro právo a technologie. 2018, Vol. 9, No. 17, pp. 19 et seq.
11. To the legal capacity concept under Czech law, *see*, e.g., Lavický, P. a kol Občanský zákoník I. Obecná část (§ 1-654). Komentář. Praha: C. H. Beck, 2014. pp. 129 et seq., Švestka, J., Dvořák J., Fiala, J. a kol Občanský zákoník (zák. č. 89/2012 Sb.). Komentář. Svazek I (obecná část). Praha: Wolters Kluwer ČR, 2020. pp. 71 et seq., Čech, P. Ke svéprávnosti právnické osoby a postavení člena statutárního orgánu při jednání za ni (nejen) v situaci zájmového střetu. Právní rozhledy. 2016, Vol. 24, Nos 23–24, pp. 835 et seq., Hexner, A. a Matas, M. Nabývání svéprávnosti nezletilými a nepříznivé důsledky současné právní úpravy (část I). Soukromé právo. 2018, Vol. 6, No. 5, pp. 9 et seq. or Hexner, A. a Matas, M. Nabývání svéprávnosti nezletilými a nepříznivé důsledky současné právní úpravy (část II). Soukromé právo. 2018, Vol. 6, No. 6, pp. 7 et seq.

Civil Code). If circumstances change, the court shall modify or revoke the limitation, even ex officio (section 60 of the Civil Code). The decision limiting the legal capacity does not deprive a natural person of his/her right to make legal acts in ordinary matters of everyday life (section 64 of the Civil Code). In its decision limiting the legal capacity of a natural person, the court shall appoint a guardian for that person (section 61 of the Civil Code). Limitation of a person's legal capacity, under Czech law, constitutes a necessary restriction, which may last only for as long as is strictly necessary, provided the reasons which led to the limitation remain.

II. Married Couples

59. Under Czech law, married couples can exercise commercial activities without any formal or informal requirements. Nonetheless, Czech family law, contained primarily in the Civil Code (Part II, sections 655–975 of the Civil Code), provides for certain rights of a spouse in relation to the commercial activities of the other spouse. Czech law distinguishes between three distinct regimes of community property[12] (i.e., property belonging to both spouses): statutory regime (applicable by default), contractual regime (assuming conclusion of an agreement between the spouses), and regime imposed by a court (imposed by a court's decision) (section 708 of the Civil Code).

60. Community property could be broadly defined as what belongs to spouses, has property value, and is not excluded from their legal relationship (section 708(1) of the Civil Code). In relation to the statutory regime, a married couple's community property is constituted by what was acquired by the spouses during the marriage by one of the spouses individually or both spouses jointly, profits from what belongs exclusively to one of the spouses, and a spouse's share in a company or cooperative if, during the marriage, a spouse becomes a shareholder in a company or a member of a cooperative (sections 709 et seq. of the Civil Code). What was acquired before the marriage does not form a part of their community property. However, their community property does not by virtue of law include what (section 709(1) of the Civil Code):

(a) serves the personal needs of one of the spouses;
(b) was acquired as a gift, inheritance or legacy by only one of the spouses, unless the donor or decedent expressed a different intention;
(c) was acquired by one of the spouses as compensation for non-pecuniary harm to his/her natural rights;

12. On the spouses' community property, *see*, e.g., Hrušáková, M., Králíčková, Z., Westphalová, L. a kol. Občanský zákoník II. Rodinné právo (§ 655-975). Komentář. Praha. C. H. Beck, 2014. pp. 155 et seq., Psutka, J. Společné jmění manželů. Praha: C. H. Beck, 2015, Klein, Š. Zákonný manželský majetkový režim z komparativního hlediska. Ad Notam. 2017, Vol. 23, No. 6, pp. 3 et seq., or Konečná, P. Vliv nového pojetí společného jmění manželů na exekuční řízení z pohledu manžela povinného. Komorní listy. 2015, Vol. 7, No. 2, pp. 10 et seq.

(d) was acquired by one of the spouses by a juridical act relating to his/her separate property; and
(e) was acquired by one of the spouses as compensation for damage, destruction or loss of his/her separate property.

61. The Civil Codes also defines which debts form a part of their community property (section 710 of the Civil Code). Community property includes debts assumed during the marriage, unless:

(a) they relate to the property that belongs exclusively to one spouse, to the extent which it exceeds the profits from such property; or
(b) they were assumed by only one spouse without the consent of the other, except for debts incurred to provide for everyday or usual needs of the family.

62. Under the statutory regime, both or one of the spouses use, take the fruits and revenues of, maintain, dispose of, manage and administer the community property as agreed between them (section 713(1) of the Civil Code). The rights and obligations pertaining to the community property are exercised by both spouses jointly and severally (section 713(2) of the Civil Code). Similarly, legal acts relating to community property or parts thereof oblige and entitle both spouses jointly and severally (section 713(3) of the Civil Code). However, in matters relating to community property and parts thereof which cannot be considered common, the spouses legally act jointly, or one of the spouses acts with the consent of the other (section 714(1) of the Civil Code). If one of the spouses refuses to give consent without a serious reason and contrary to the interests of the spouses, family or family household, or is unable to express his/her will, the other spouse may apply to a court to substitute the consent of his/her spouse (section 714(2) of the Civil Code).

63. Under the statutory regime, if a part of the community property is to be used for the business activities of one of the spouses and the property value of what is to be used exceeds the level appropriate to the spouse's property situation, the other spouse's consent is required upon the first such use; if the other spouse has been omitted, he/she may invoke invalidity of such act (section 715(1) of the Civil Code). Likewise, if a part of the community property is to be used to acquire a share in a company or cooperative, or if the acquisition of a share results in liability for the debts of that company or cooperative to the extent exceeding the level appropriate to the property situation of the spouses, the consent of the other spouse is also required with the first such acquisition (section 715(2) of the Civil Code).

64. Concerning the consent of the other spouse with the use of property from the spouses' community property for business activities, it is necessary to point out that the consent is required only with the first such use. Any and all subsequent uses of the community property for business activities are not subject to any consent, provided the consent of the other spouse was given with the first use. While the Civil Code remains silent on whether the consent should be general or specific, the author believes a general consent should be sufficient, especially in light of the principle of autonomy of will; hence; there is no need to individually specify the property to be used in the consent of the other spouse.[13] Similarly, the Civil Code remains silent on the matter of withdrawing one's consent. In light of the previous regulation, such withdrawal shall be possible but only if it prevented arbitrary conduct by the spouse and, at the same time, avoided serious harm to the rights of third parties acting in good faith.

65. Community property may be terminated (partly or completely) in several ways. Unsurprisingly, it can be terminated by divorce (since the community property follows the union of marriage). In this case, the community property as a whole ceases to exist as of the effective date of the judgment on divorce, and the property rights and obligations of the spouses are exercised in accordance with an agreement between the spouses; if no agreement is reached, a court may decide (section 765 of the Civil Code).

66. Furthermore, community property can be modified by an agreement concluded between the spouses (sections 716 et seq. of the Civil Code). This way, fiancées and spouses may agree on a different regime from the statutory regime. Such an agreement must be executed in the form of a public deed (a notarial deed) (section 716(2) of the Civil Code). Under the contractual regime, spouses typically provide for their rights and obligations relating to their already-existing community property. The contractual regime may consist in a separate property regime, a regime reserving the creation of community property as of the date the marriage terminates, as well as a regime constituting an extension or reduction of the scope of the statutory regime of community property (section 717(1) of the Civil Code). The contractual regime may be changed by an agreement of the spouses or a court decision (section 717(2) of the Civil Code).

67. Finally, the community property can be modified by a court's decision. The court shall, upon the application of a spouse, dissolve the community property or reduce its existing scope if there is a serious reason to take this course of action (section 724(1) of the Civil Code). In this regard, the fact that a spouse has started pursuing business activities or become a partner of a legal person with unlimited liability may also be considered to be a serious reason (section 724(2) of the Civil Code).

68. Under the regime of separate property, if spouses pursue business activities jointly or one of the spouses pursues business activities with the help of the other spouse, they divide the income from the business activities as agreed earlier in writing; otherwise, the income is divided equally (section 730 of the Civil Code). This regime may be established by a court's decision as well. This regime may be established both by an agreement between the fiancées or spouses or by a court's binding

13. There is no requirement as to the form of the other spouse's consent. Therefore, it can be concluded that the spouse's consent to use a part of the community property for business activities may be granted in any way and in any form. Hence, the consent may be even given orally or implicitly.

decision. The same approach will be observed in the case of the creation of community property as of the date the marriage terminates (contractual regime).

69. The contractual regime, as well as the regime imposed by a court both follow their own special rules, which are set forth in an agreement, concluded between the spouses or, respectively, in a court's binding decision.

III. Foreigners

A. In General

70. Under Czech law, all foreigners may carry out their business activities under the same conditions and to the same extent as Czech entities and persons, unless the law stipulates otherwise. This general principle stems primarily from Article 26(1) of the Charter of Fundamental Rights and Freedoms (Charter or CHRF), constitutional legislation according to which everybody (i.e., including foreigners) has the right to freely choose his/her profession and the training for such profession, as well as the right to engage in enterprise and other economic activity. On the other hand, as the Charter stipulates in its Article 26(4), different rules for foreign citizens may be set by law.

71. Pursuant to the Trade Licensing Act, any natural person and any legal entity may pursue business activities for which a trade licence is required, provided that person or entity satisfies certain conditions set forth by law (section 5(1) of the Trade Licensing Act). Furthermore, all foreigners may carry out a trade based on a respective trade licence on the territory of the Czech Republic under the same conditions and to the same extent as Czech nationals and entities, unless the law stipulates otherwise (section 5(2) of the Trade Licensing Act).

B. Foreigners: Natural Persons

72. Under the Trade Licenses Act, a foreigner is understood as a natural person who is not resident in the Czech Republic (section 5(2) of the Trade Licensing Act, *see also* section 3024(1) of the Civil Code). On the other hand, under the Act on International Private Law (AIPL), a foreigner is understood as a natural person who is not a citizen of the Czech Republic (section 26(1) AIPL). Foreigners have the same rights and obligations as Czech nationals, insofar as their personal and property rights are concerned, unless provided otherwise by virtue of the law (section 26(2) AIPL). A foreigner may, under the same conditions as Czech nationals, participate in establishing a legal entity, establish a legal entity himself/herself, or become a shareholder or a member of an existing legal entity.

73. The legal personality, as well as the legal capacity of a foreigner, is governed by the law of the place of his/her usual residence (section 29(1) AIPL). Therefore, in the case of legal personality and capacity, the AIPL does not use the criterion of nationality but that of usual residency, which is to be interpreted in accordance with the case law of the Court of Justice of the European Union (CJEU). However, in order to legally act, it is sufficient if a foreigner is entitled thereto under Czech law unless provided otherwise by the AIPL (section 29(2) AIPL).

74. On the Czech territory, all EU citizens benefit from the freedom of movement. In order to pursue a trade, nationals of a Member State of the European Union, another State of the European Economic Area, or the Swiss Confederation need not provide trade licence authorities with a visa or a long-term residency permit, whereas other natural persons are legally required to do so (section 5(5) of the Trade Licensing Act). Therefore, foreigners from outside the European Union (as well as those outside the European Economic Area and the Swiss Confederation) must satisfy stricter conditions under the Trade Licensing Act.

75. Moreover, a natural person under international protection and his/her family members may pursue a trade under the same conditions as Czech nationals (section 5(6) TLA).

C. Foreigners: Legal Entities

76. Under the Trade Licenses Act, a foreign legal entity is understood as a legal entity whose registered office is not located on the territory of the Czech Republic. The same rule is provided for by the AIPL (section 26(1) AIPL) and by the Civil Code (section 3024(2) of the Civil Code). Foreign legal entities have the same rights and obligations as Czech ones, insofar as their personal and property rights are concerned (unless provided otherwise by virtue of the law) (section 26(2) AIPL).

77. The legal personality, as well as the legal capacity of a foreign legal entity, is under Czech law governed by the law of the Member State under which it was established; this law also governs the trade name and internal circumstances of this person, the relationship between this person and its shareholders or members, and the mutual relations of the shareholders or members, the liability of the partners, shareholders or members for the obligations of this person, and its dissolution (section 30(1) AIPL). The same rule, albeit less elaborately, is provided for by the Civil Code (section 3024(2) of the Civil Code). Furthermore, in order to be legally bound in common affairs, it is sufficient if a foreign legal entity is entitled to legally act under Czech law (section 30(2) AIPL).

78. A legal entity with its registered office in the Czech Republic may be established only in accordance with Czech law; this is without prejudice to the possibility of transferring the registered office of a legal entity established under the law of a foreign country to the Czech Republic if permitted by an international treaty, directly applicable to the European Union legislation, or other legislation (section 30(3) AIPL). On the Czech territory, all EU-based companies (legal entities) benefit from the freedom of establishment. A foreign legal entity may also pursue business activities in the Czech Republic through a registered branch. In that connection, a foreign legal entity that has its registered office outside the European Union is always obliged to register its branch in the Companies Register if it conducts business (not only a trade) in the Czech Republic. This rule does not apply if a foreign legal entity has its registered office in a Member State of the European Union; however, if such a foreign entity establishes a branch in the Czech Republic, it is required to register the branch in the Czech Companies Register.

§2. Companies (Partnerships, Corporations & Cooperatives)

I. Historical Development

79. The first documented 'companies' to be regulated on the territory of what is today the Czech Republic were medieval artisan guilds called 'tovaryšstva', which were expressly sanctioned by a regulation of Emperor Charles VI from 1734. However, the first truly modern and comprehensive codification of corporations and partnerships in the Czech lands did not appear until 1863, when the General Commercial Code (Allgemeines Handelsgesetzbuch) was introduced in the Austrian Empire (Österreichisches Reichsgesetzblatt 1/1863).

80. On 28 October 1918, after the First World War, the Czechoslovak Republic declared its independence from the collapsing Austrian-Hungarian Empire. In order to secure a smooth transition (and to prevent revolutionary chaos), the previously valid Austrian-Hungarian laws and regulations were resumed by the Reception Act No. 11/1918 Coll. After the Second World War, the ambition to swiftly rebuild the country and restore the pre-war democracy was thwarted by the communist 'putsch' of 25 February 1948. Massive collectivization and nationalization measures were adopted, and the remaining democratic institutions were promptly dismantled or significantly oppressed. In law, many standard private law concepts dating back to Roman law were repealed, making way for the new Soviet-style (socialistic) legislation. This changed after 1989, i.e., after the so-called Velvet Revolution.

II. Different Forms of Business Corporations

81. Currently, the Corporations Act regulates business companies (in Czech: obchodní společnosti) and cooperatives (in Czech: družstva), which are, in section 1 of the Corporations Act, jointly referred to as 'business corporations' (in Czech: obchodní korporace). Given their registration in the Companies Register, all business corporations are, under section 421 of the Civil Code, deemed to be economic operators (entrepreneurs, in Czech: podnikatelé). Consequently, their business names (in Czech: obchodní firma) are protected as a matter of law, and they may grant per procuram (general) powers of attorney, etc. Within the general framework of legal persons' regulation, business corporations represent a subcategory of 'private corporations' (a general category provided by the Civil Code, not the Corporations Act), and as such, certain general principles applicable to private corporations pursuant to the Civil Code also apply to business corporations. For instance, section 212 of the Civil Code sets forth that 'a corporation may not unreasonably discriminate any of its members and must equally protect the rights and legitimate interests of its members' (equal treatment principle[14]). This prohibition is applicable also to business corporations. In addition, under section 213 of the Civil Code, a member of a private corporation may, under certain circumstances, seek reflective loss on its shareholding if such loss was incurred as a result of a board member's failure to act with due managerial care.

82. From a functional standpoint, the most distinctive division of business companies in the Czech Republic is that of so-called personal and capital companies. The category of personal companies and capital companies could somewhat be characterized as partnerships and corporations. As for limited partnerships and limited liability companies, they – to a various degree – combine the elements of both personal and capital companies.

83. The division described above between personal and capital companies does not fully apply to cooperatives (in Czech: družstva), which cannot be fully described and understood in terms of either of these categories. Unlike business companies, the purpose of a cooperative is mainly social and consists of supporting its members in accordance with the cooperative's statutes. Economical function (profit-making) comes second in a cooperative, which is based rather on the solidarity of their members. Moreover, in contrast to business companies, the number of members of a cooperative is not fixed by its statutes but varies over time (principle of openness). In a Czech context, housing cooperatives (in Czech: bytová družstva) are especially widespread as this legal 'vehicle' was predominantly used to privatize blocks of apartments after the fall of communism in 1989.

84. The Corporations Act currently makes a distinction between the following types of business corporations.

A. General Partnerships

85. A general partnership (in Czech: veřejná obchodní společnost) is defined as a 'company with at least two persons participating in its business activities or in the management of its assets who are jointly and severally liable for its debts'. General partnerships are based on the competence, knowledge and mutual trust of their partners, who are directly involved in the company's day-to-day business decisions and operations. A general partnership's shareholders (partners) are personally and jointly and severally liable for the company's debts under the rules of the Civil Code (sections 2018 et seq. of the Civil Code) and, thus, such liability is not limited to the amount of their contributions if any.

14. On the equal treatment principle, *see*, e.g., Špačková, M. Zásada rovného zacházení se všemi akcionáři. Obchodněprávní revue. 2016, Vol. 8, No. 1, pp. 1 et seq. or Hurychová, K. Zásada rovného zacházení se všemi akcionáři – k významu ustanovení § 244 odst. 2 ZOK. Obchodněprávní revue. 2015, Vol. 7, No. 10, pp. 285 et seq.

B. Limited Partnerships

86. A limited partnership (in Czech: komanditní společnost) is defined as a 'company where at least one member has limited liability (the "limited partner") and at least one member has unlimited liability (the "general partner") for the company's debts'. A limited partnership has two types of partners – limited partners, whose liability for the company's debts is limited in a similar way as the liability of shareholders in a limited liability (limited to the amount of the limited partner's unpaid contribution), and general partners, who are (just as partners of a general partnership) personally liable for the company's debts without any limitation. Although a limited partnership is often described as a personal company, it is rather obvious that it more constitutes a sort of 'combined' company, which includes elements of both personal and capital companies.

C. Limited Liability Companies

87. A limited liability company (in Czech: společnost s ručením omezeným) is a 'company whose members are jointly and severally liable for the company's debts up to the amount of their unfulfilled contribution obligation, pursuant to the record in the Companies Register at the time when fulfilment was demanded by a creditor' (section 132 of the Corporations Act). Although the limited liability company is historically the newest corporate form, it is currently the most widespread legal form of a business corporation in the Czech Republic due to its flexibility, the limited liability of its shareholders and rather insignificant incorporation costs (e.g., there is no minimum registered capital requirement, only a minimum contribution requirement of CZK 1). A limited liability company can be described as a capital company with elements inherent to personal companies.

D. Joint-Stock Companies

88. Section 243 of the Corporations Act defines a joint-stock company (in Czech: akciová společnost) rather tersely as a 'company whose registered capital is apportioned among a certain number of shares'. Joint-stock companies are mostly used by medium or large enterprises as the required corporate governance structure is more complex and rather substantive capital requirements are set out (the minimum registered capital of a Czech joint-stock company is CZK 2,000,000 or EUR 80,000).

E. Cooperatives

89. A cooperative (in Czech: družstvo) is a business corporation forming a 'community of an indefinite number of persons, established for the purpose of the mutual support of its members or third parties or, where appropriate, for the purpose of doing business' (section 552 of the Corporations Act). In contrast to the business companies listed above, profit-making is typically only an auxiliary purpose of cooperatives as they focus primarily on supporting their members. In the Czech Republic, the two most common forms of cooperatives are housing cooperatives and social cooperatives.

F. Other

90. Recently, new Act No. 240/2013 Coll., on Management Companies and Investment Funds, provided for two new subtypes of corporations, namely a Limited partnership with investment certificates and a joint-stock company with variable registered capital (inspired by Société d'Investissement en Capital à Risque (SICAR) and Societe d'Investissement A Capital Variable (SICAV) from Luxembourg law), which can operate on financial markets. Apart from these national legal forms of corporations and partnerships regulated by the Corporations Act, Czech law also recognizes all supranational legal forms set forth by European Union Law, namely European Economic Interest Grouping, Societas Cooperativa Europaea and Societas Europaea.

III. General Remarks

91. Business corporations are established by executing articles of association (or, in the case of a cooperative, at the first members' meeting). While the capital companies (i.e., limited liability companies and joint-stock companies) can be established by a single shareholder (being either an individual or another legal entity), a general partnership and a limited partnership both require at least two shareholders. Cooperatives can be established by at least three members. The requirements for the articles of association are set forth by the Civil Code and the Corporations Act. Pursuant to the Civil Code, any legal entity's (including any business corporation's) foundation document, which governs the internal circumstances of that entity, has to contain at least the name of the entity, its registered office and scope of activity, and the person who is entitled to represent it. More detailed rules are set by the Corporations Act for general partnerships, limited partnerships, limited liability companies, joint-stock companies, and cooperatives.

92. All the business corporations regulated by the Corporations Act come into existence on the day when they are registered in the Companies Register (incorporated in the Companies Register). However, legal acts on behalf of a business corporation may even be performed prior to its incorporation. A person who performs such acts is the only person entitled and obliged under these acts; where the acts are performed by several persons, these persons are entitled and obliged jointly and severally. As per section 127 of the Civil Code, a business corporation may assume the effects of these acts within three months from its incorporation. In this case, it is presumed that the business corporation is entitled to and obliged under these acts from the beginning (ex tunc).

93. A business corporation ceases to exist on the date when it is deleted from the Companies Register unless the law provides for otherwise. Before a business corporation is deleted from the Companies Register, it has to be dissolved with or without liquidation (if its assets are being transferred to its legal successor or the law so stipulates). Liquidation represents a process aimed at settling a wound-up legal entity's assets (liquidation estate), paying the debts to creditors, and disposing of any net property balance resulting from the liquidation (liquidation balance) amongst the shareholders in accordance with the law (section 187(1) of the Corporations Act). The general rules for liquidating a legal entity are embodied in the Civil Code (sections 187–209 of the Civil Code).

94. A legal entity enters into liquidation when it is wound up or declared invalid (section 187(2) of the Civil Code). Only a court can declare a legal entity invalid after the entity has been incorporated. On the date the legal entity is declared invalid, it enters into liquidation. When a business corporation enters into liquidation, the liquidator shall, as the initial task, without undue delay, file an application to register that corporation's entry into liquidation in the Companies Register. During the liquidation process, the business corporation shall affix the words 'v likvidaci' (in liquidation) to its business name.

95. In certain situations, liquidation is not required; for example, if a business corporation's bankruptcy was cancelled by the insolvency court because the corporation's assets were completely insufficient to satisfy creditors in the insolvency proceedings.

IV. Partnerships

A. Unlimited Partnerships

96. An unlimited partnership (in Czech: veřejná obchodní společnost) is regulated in sections 95–117 of the Corporations Act and represents the basic form of a business company. It is established by a membership agreement with notarized signatures of at least two persons, which can be either legal entities or natural persons or a combination of both. To perfect its incorporation, the unlimited partnership must be registered in the Companies Register. Unlimited partnerships are required to draft annual financial accounts and to publish them in the Collection of Deeds.

97. An unlimited partnership is a separate legal entity which is able to own its own assets, have its own employees and act as an employer. It is also primarily liable for its debts and acts on its own behalf.

98. As it is a legal person, an unlimited partnership must have its own business name attached with 'v.o.s.', 'veř. obch. spol.' or 'veřejná obchodní společnost' (section 96 of the Corporations Act). Besides its business name, its scope of business, registered office and name of all members must also be stated in the membership agreement. All such information is publicly accessible as the company must be registered in the Companies Register, and the membership agreement must be deposited in the Collection of Deeds. As the simplest form of a business company, it does not have to create any mandatory corporate bodies, such as a general meeting or supervisory board.

99. All members are liable as guarantors for the unlimited partnership's debts by all of their property. Therefore, the financial condition of the individual member's matters and, as a matter of law, a person cannot be a member of an unlimited partnership if bankruptcy was declared against his/her assets in the past three years, or if the insolvency proceedings were closed due to 'absolutely insufficient assets' (section 95(3) of the Corporations Act).

100. The Corporations Act sets forth that every member of an unlimited partnership bears the loss generated by the unlimited partnership, which cannot be contracted away. If a new member co-joins the unlimited partnership, he/she shall also be liable vis-à-vis third parties for the debts incurred prior to joining. However, such a member may request that the other members fully compensate him/her for any payment he/she made as a guarantor for the debts which the partnership incurred prior to the date on which he/she became a member of the partnership. A member who has left an unlimited partnership shall only be liable for the debts incurred before his/her participation is terminated.

101. Although no contribution duty exists, the membership agreement can stipulate one. The member may agree to make his/her contribution in cash or in another way. The subject matter of the contribution can be a thing (e.g., a house), right to use a thing (e.g., a licence), right to use and enjoy a thing (e.g., renting real estate) or even activity (work).

102. Profits and losses shall be distributed among the members equally unless otherwise agreed in the membership agreement. If a member has made a voluntary contribution, he/she has a preferential right to a profit share of up to 25% of the amount of his/her contribution before the other members who did not make a contribution. For example, if only one of four members contributed EUR 100 and the partnership gains a profit of EUR 120, the member who made the contribution has a preferential right to 25% of EUR 120, i.e., EUR 30. The rest of the profit (EUR 90) is distributed among all members equally, i.e., every other member (including the one who made the contribution) shall receive EUR 22.5.

103. Decisions in all matters of the unlimited partnership require the consent of all members unless otherwise stated in the partnership agreement. Each member shall have one vote unless otherwise agreed. The statutory body, i.e., the main body responsible for business management, shall consist of all members (section 106(1) of the Corporations Act) who are of full legal capacity and impeccable character (section 46 of the Corporations Act). However, the membership agreement may also provide that only some members hold the position of the statutory body. In any case, all members enjoy supervisory rights; by operation of law, they are entitled to review all company documents and check the information contained therein (section 107 of the Corporations Act).

104. Partnership interests are not transferable; however, a new member can join the company, and a current member can withdraw from it via an amendment to the membership agreement; the membership agreement can only be amended by an agreement among all members. Partnership interests cannot be inherited.

B. Limited Partnerships

105. A limited partnership (in Czech: komanditní společnost) is regulated in sections 118–131 of the Corporations Act. A limited partnership has a separate legal personality and must have at least two members, who can be legal entities, natural persons or a combination of both. The basic characteristic of a limited partnership is that at least one member has limited liability, the so-called limited partner, and at least one member has unlimited liability, the so-called general partner, for the company's debts. As the general partner's liability is unlimited, the law excludes persons from the possibility of becoming a general partner if bankruptcy was declared against his/her assets in the past three years, or if insolvency proceedings against him/her were closed due to 'absolutely insufficient assets' (section 95(3) of the Corporations Act).

106. A limited partnership is established by a membership agreement with the notarized signatures of the members, and to perfect its establishment and become incorporated, it must be registered in the public Companies Register.

107. As it is a legal person, a limited partnership must have its own business name attached with 'k.s.', 'kom. spol.' or 'komaditní společnost' (section 118(2) of the Corporations Act). Besides the business name, the membership agreement must state which of the members is a general partner and which is a limited partner, and include the amount of each limited partner's contribution.

108. The limited partnership is required to draft annual financial accounts and publish them in the Collection of Deeds.

109. A limited partnership is a separate legal entity which is able to own its own assets, have its own employees and act as an employer. It is also primarily liable for its debts and acts on its own behalf.

110. The general partner's liability is unlimited; i.e., he/she is liable as guarantor for the company's debts with his/her entire property. The extent of the limited partner's liability depends on whether or not the limited partner undertakes to bear liability for the company's debts up to a certain amount (so-called commandite amount). If there is no commandite amount, a limited partner is jointly and severally liable as a guarantor for the company's debts only up to the amount of his/her unpaid contribution, pursuant to the record in the Companies Register, unless a different share is agreed. If a limited partner agrees to be liable up to the commandite amount, which must be stated in the membership agreement and also entered in the Companies Register, he/she, together with the other members, is jointly and severally liable for the company's debts up to the amount of his/her commandite amount registered in the Companies Register at the time when fulfilment is demanded by a creditor (section 129(2)(c) of the Corporations Act). The creditor must require the partnership's debt to be fulfilled by the particular limited partner. The commandite amount is reduced to the extent to which the contribution obligation was fulfilled by the limited partner (section 130 of the Corporations Act).

111. The Corporations Act provides one exception to the limited partner's limited liability: if his/her name is included in the company's business name, he/she is liable for the company's debts as a general partner (section 118(2) of the Corporations Act).

112. General partners have no statutory contribution duty; however, the general partner is allowed to undertake to make a contribution if he/she so prefers. In such a case, he/she has a preferential right to a profit share up to 25% of the amount of the contribution before general partners who did not make a contribution.

113. Limited partners are required to make a contribution, although no minimum amount is prescribed by law. However, their shareholding in the company is determined pursuant to the proportion of the limited partner's contributions. The subject matter of the contribution can be a thing (e.g., a house), right to use a thing (e.g., a licence), right to use and enjoy a thing (e.g., renting real estate), or even activity (work).

114. The Corporations Act sets forth that profits and losses are distributed among the company and the general partners equally. The amount of the profit and loss belonging to the general partners is distributed among the general partners equally. The amount of profit belonging to the company is taxed and then distributed among the limited partners according to the proportion of their shares. If the limited partner agreed to provide a commandite amount, the part of the profits allocated to the company shall be, after taxes, distributed among the limited partners according to the proportion of their commandite amounts (section 129(2)(a) of the Corporations Act).

115. Losses shall not be borne by the limited partners (section 126(3) of the Corporations Act) unless the limited partner agreed to be liable up to the commandite amount. In such a case, losses shall be covered by the limited partner, together with the general partners (who are, as a matter of law, required to cover the partnership's loss without limitation in proportion to their shares), in accordance with his/her share, but only up to the amount of his/her commandite amount; thus, his/her obligation to cover the partnership's loss is limited (section 129(2)(c) of the Corporations Act).

116. The statutory body, i.e., the main body responsible for business management, includes all general partners, but this rule can be modified in the partnership agreement (i.e., that only some partners are members of the statutory body). All members enjoy supervisory rights as they are entitled to review all company documents and check the information contained therein.

117. Any matters not falling under the competence of the statutory body are to be decided by all members by majority vote (per capita), with the general partners and the limited partners voting separately unless the membership agreement provides otherwise (section 125(2) of the Corporations Act).

118. The general partner's share is not transferable; thus, the same applies here as in the case of a general partnership. As regards a limited partner's share, it can be transferred to another member and also to a third party, but the transfer may be subject to the approval of all members (in the case of a transfer to another member if the membership agreement so provides, or in the case of a transfer to a third party where approval is required, unless the membership agreement provides otherwise).

V. Companies

A. Limited Liability Companies

119. The youngest corporate form in the Czech Republic is the limited liability company (in Czech: 'společnost s ručením omezeným'). It differs in many ways from a joint-stock company, which is also considered to be a part of the family of 'capital' companies. A limited liability company is a company whose members are jointly and severally liable for the company's debts up to the amount of the unpaid portions of their investment contributions according to the entry in the Companies Register at the time when fulfilment is demanded by a creditor (limited liability). A limited liability company must have its own business name attached with 'spol. s r.o.', or 's.r.o.' (section 132(2) of the Corporations Act).

120. A limited liability company can be founded by one or more natural persons or legal entities (prospective members). In that regard, a limited liability company has no restrictions on the minimum or a maximum number of its members (in contrast to the previous regulation set forth in the Commercial Code, effective until 31 December 2013, which prescribed the maximum number of members to be fifty). In the event the limited liability company is established by a single person, the founding document is a foundation deed, not articles of association (section 8(2) of the Corporations Act).

121. The limited liability company is, in terms of the Corporations Act, increasingly understood as a private company and, thus, the public is not fundamentally privy to its internal relations. Adjusting the internal conditions/regulations of a limited liability company is for that reason largely voluntary, and members can decide to waive a whole range of their rights or choose a legal regime which completely diverges from the Corporations Act.

122. For a limited liability company, the minimum share capital has been abolished. The Corporations Act sets forth only a minimum capital contribution, which amounts to CZK 1 (i.e., in the case of, e.g., three founders, the minimum registered capital of the limited liability company equals CZK 3) (section 142(1) of the Corporations Act). Generally, each member holds an interest in the company in the amount that, by default, corresponds to the amount of capital contribution it represents in proportion to the company's registered capital (section 133 of the Corporations Act).

123. The articles of association can establish an additional payment obligation; however, members can provide optional payments voluntarily. A member's premium can be refunded to the member who provided it, whereas in a joint-stock company, it is not possible to return a premium payment. In respect of financial assistance, limited liability companies have less stringent rules than joint-stock companies; in particular, it is not necessary to create a special reserve fund.

124. Registered capital in limited liability companies can be increased both as a result of receiving new deposit obligations and by the company's own resources (including a combination of both) (sections 216 et seq. of the Corporations Act). On the other hand, a capital reduction can occur to the benefit of the members and for other purposes (sections 233 et seq. of the Corporations Act). Protecting creditors in connection with a share capital reduction in both forms of capital companies is, in principle, governed in the same manner.

125. In a limited liability company, the only mandatory statutory body for corporate governance is one or more executives (section 194(1) of the Corporations Act). The articles of association may specify that more executives can form a collective body. In this case, the decision-making of the executives is subject to the rules for the decision-making of collective bodies. The executives' terms of office can be set for a limited or unlimited duration. The supervisory board is only a voluntary company body and must be established in the articles of association (section 201(1) of the Corporations Act).

126. The limited liability company's supreme body is the general meeting (sections 167 et seq. of the Corporations Act). The general meeting consists of members who oversee the company's fundamental issues and attend the general meeting regardless of whether they do so in person or via a representative.

127. As regards the rights and obligations of members, a limited liability company has a flexible legal framework allowing for its articles of association to set forth obligations not regulated by law. Regarding the rights relating to the participation of members in the business management of a limited liability company, such rights can also be exercised outside the general meeting.

128. Interests in a limited liability company, like shares in a joint-stock company, represent participation in the company. However, unlike shares, interests are not considered securities by law. They predominantly take the form of immaterial interest recorded in the Companies Register (there is an exception to this in the event that the limited liability company issues common certificates – in Czech 'kmenový list'). These certificates shall meet statutory requirements for securities. Nevertheless, both forms of participation may be associated with different rights and obligations (shares of different classes/interest of a different kind). Generally speaking, interests have fewer formal requirements (and are thus less regulated) and are somewhat more difficult to transfer, as compared to shares in a joint-stock company. Moreover, in a limited liability company, the inheritance of interest can be restricted or prohibited.

129. Regarding a limited liability company, ownership interests are freely transferable between members (section 207(1) of the Corporations Act); however, the articles of association may subject the transfer to the approval of any company body. Unjustified refusal or inactivity of the company bodies grants the right of a member to withdraw from the company if this right is not excluded by the articles of association. An ownership interest is transferable to a third party only with the consent of the general meeting, but the articles of association may specify that a member's ownership interest is freely transferable also to a third party. If the ownership interest in a limited liability company is freely transferable, the articles of association may specify that in respect of such ownership interest a security certificate will be issued, which is transferable by endorsement (i.e., common certificate). However, the obligation to evidence the member in the list of shareholders and enter them in the Companies Register remains.

130. Furthermore, it is possible to withdraw from a limited liability company, and a member is entitled to seek to terminate its interests in that company in court, both in cases stipulated by law (sections 202(1) and 205(1) of the Corporations Act). The articles of association can, however, exclude the right of members to withdraw from a limited liability company, but it cannot eliminate the right of a member to have its participation in a company cancelled by the court if it would be unfair to demand that the member remains in the company.

131. It is always possible to expel a member from a limited liability company in the event of a delay in the payment of contribution obligations, or if the member is in default with fulfilling an additional payment obligation (sections 151 and 165 of the Corporations Act). It is also possible to exclude a member from a limited liability company by a decision of the court if the member seriously violates his/her responsibilities (section 204 of the Corporations Act).

132. When a member of a limited liability company is declared insolvent, this does not terminate the ownership interest in the limited liability company. In any case, the ownership interest becomes part of the insolvency estate (assets). The participation of a member of a limited liability company, however, ceases to exist upon the cancellation of bankruptcy for the reason that the assets of the member are totally inadequate to satisfy creditors, or upon the expiry of six months from the date of the declaration of bankruptcy if it is not possible to sell the ownership interest.

133. A limited liability company may be dissolved either by an agreement of its members or a court's decision; the agreement of members must be notarized (section 241(1) of the Corporations Act). A member may also file a request with a court to dissolve the limited liability company under the terms and conditions set forth in the articles of association (section 241(2) of the Corporations Act). The Corporations Act includes only a few rules for liquidating a joint-stock company.

B. Joint-Stock Companies

134. A joint-stock company (in Czech 'akciová společnost') is a common form of a capital company which is required to have its registered capital in the prescribed statutory amount. Shareholders are not engaged in managing the company as administrative matters are delegated to a professional management body (the board of directors or the management board). Shareholders exercise their powers at general meetings via holding securities (shares), which authorize them to exercise shareholder rights. A joint-stock company must have its own business name attached with 'akc. spol.', or 'a.s.' (section 243(2) of the Corporations Act).

135. What is typical for joint-stock companies is that shareholders cannot be held liable for the company's debts. The company is the party which primarily bears and benefits from profit and losses. Creditors do not have the right to demand the shareholders to pay the company's debts (e.g., on the grounds of a guarantee) if the company is unable to pay them itself. However, this principle is not without exceptions since former shareholders are held liable for the company's debts up to their share of the liquidation balance after the company is dissolved (*see* section 39 of the Corporations Act). Shareholders may also be held liable for the debts of a business group as influential, controlling or managing parties.

136. A joint-stock company can be founded by one or more natural persons or legal entities. The Corporations Act does not set a maximum number of subscribers. In the event the joint-stock company is established by a single person, the founding document is a foundation deed, not statutes. The initial share capital must be subscribed by the founders in full. Shares cannot be subscribed by the joint-stock company itself or by a person acting in its own name but on account of the joint-stock company. In the event of such subscription, the Corporations Act makes the founders, as a matter of law, statutory subscribers of such shares and, therefore, they are required to pay their subscription price. Until the subscription price of such subscribed shares is paid up, their owner (i.e., a founder) cannot exercise the rights attached to the shares.

137. Every joint-stock company is required to register in the Companies Register (it is not actually incorporated until it is registered) regardless of whether it is designed to be engaged in doing business or not. Unlike personal companies, joint-stock companies may even be established for a purpose other than doing business (there is a minor exemption for personal companies engaged in managing their own assets).

138. Given the prevailing business nature of joint-stock companies, some special laws set forth that certain types of business operations cannot be carried out under any company form other than a joint-stock company. For example, banks are required to be joint-stock companies (*see* section 1(1) of the Banking Act).

139. A joint-stock company's registered capital must amount to at least CZK 2 million (or EUR 80,000), in line with EU law requirements, although the Corporations Act does not perceive joint-stock companies' registered capital as a primary category designed to protect creditors. A joint-stock company's registered capital is the sum of its contributions both in cash and in kind. If the contribution to the company is made in kind, the price is determined by an expert in an expert report. The required expert report is designed to prevent companies from creating fictitious registered capital.

140. A joint-stock company's registered capital is divided into a certain number of shares or book-entry shares of a specific par value which are publicly tradable. A share may be a registered security or a bearer security; the same shall apply *mutatis mutandis* to book-entry shares. Whereas materialized shares can be issued as registered shares only, book-entry shares can also be issued as bearer shares. Where so provided in the company's statutes, a joint-stock company may also issue no-par value shares. The share in the registered capital of the no-par values share is then determined by the number of shares.

141. The Corporations Act outlines methods for increasing and reducing a joint-stock company's registered capital. The rules are fairly complicated, and they are primarily purely technical standards. However, generally speaking, there are two basic principles present in the rules: protection of existing shareholders; and protection of creditors. Registered capital in joint-stock companies can be increased as a result of the subscription of new shares or from the company's own resources. A joint-stock company may not reduce its registered capital below the minimum capital requirement; there are no exceptions. A joint-stock company may acquire its own shares if certain conditions provided for in the Corporations Act are met (*see* section 298(2) of the Corporations Act).

142. Joint-stock companies have internal bodies prescribed by law which govern the company. The power to manage the company is vested in professional management. As of 1 January 2014, Czech joint-stock companies can choose to have a one or two-tier management structure. Two-tier companies are managed by a board of directors, while a one-tier structure is managed by the management board. The other statute-required body (in addition to the company's supreme body) is the supervisory board. In addition to the system of statute-required bodies, joint-stock companies may set optional bodies (such as advisory ones).

143. The executive body of a joint-stock company can either be collective (several directors on the board of directors) or individual (a sole director – board member). A joint-stock company's executive body may represent the joint-stock company in all matters and is in charge of managing the company's business.

144. Two types of internal set-up are distinguished: one- and two-tier internal management systems. The two-tier system requires the joint-stock company to have a board of directors and a supervisory board. One-tier joint-stock companies' obligatory body is the management board. The company's statutes set forth whether the company is a one- or two-tier company.

145. The general meeting is a joint-stock company's supreme body. The general meeting consists of company shareholders who attend the general meeting regardless of whether they do so in person or via a representative. Also, one person designated by the shareholder may be present at the general meeting with the shareholder, unless provided otherwise in the statutes. The general meeting is in charge of the company's vital and fundamental issues or, as the case may be, audit mechanisms are concentrated at the level of the general meeting. The invitation to the general meeting must be posted on the joint-stock company's website until the date of the general meeting. Under section 412 of the Corporations Act, the general meeting has a quorum if the present shareholders hold shares the par value or the number of which exceeds 30% of the registered capital unless provided otherwise in the statutes (therefore, a quorum can either be higher or lower or none at all). If the general meeting does not have a quorum, the board of directors shall convene a substitute general meeting (which by default, i.e., unless the statutes provide otherwise, does not have a quorum). A substitute general meeting can only be held with the same agenda as an ordinary general meeting (unless all shareholders, i.e., not only those present, agree otherwise).

146. By default, the general meeting adopts decisions by a (simple) majority of votes of the present shareholders unless a different majority is required by law or by its statutes. Under section 416 of the Corporations Act, a majority of at least two-thirds of the votes of the present shareholders is required to adopt certain decisions (e.g., to amend the statutes). Moreover, as per section 417 of the Corporations Act, certain other decisions require a majority of at least three-fourths of the votes of the present shareholders holding the respective shares (e.g., to change the type or form of shares).

147. If the joint-stock company has only one shareholder, the general meeting is not held, and the sole shareholder exercises all rights and makes all decisions within the powers of the general meeting (section 12(1) of the Corporations Act).

148. Moreover, the Corporations Act allows for the establishment of optional bodies in addition to the obligatory ones; the powers of such bodies (or how they make their decisions) are defined by the company's statutes and must not overlap with the mandatory powers of the joint-stock company's obligatory body.

149. The shares via which shareholders exercise their shareholder rights are transferable. In general, shares could be transferred by operation of law (inheritance, mergers, spin-offs, enterprise transfers, etc.) or by a contract.

150. Shares can be issued as a security (share certificates) or as book-entered (dematerialized) securities. Share certificates can only be issued as registered shares (i.e., with the owner's name indicated on the certificate and transferable only by endorsement). A bearer share may be fully transferable without endorsement or other restriction. The Corporations Act allows a joint-stock company to issue several classes of shares. Shares with identical rights and obligations constitute one class. The only explicit restriction pursuant to the Corporations Act is that shares to which the right to a certain interest regardless of the company's economic results is attached are prohibited.

151. There is an obligation on joint-stock companies with more than 500 employees to have one-third of the members of the supervisory board elected by the employees. The company's statutes may provide a higher proportion; however, the number of members elected by employees should not exceed the number of members elected by the general meeting. Details on the election and removal process should be determined in the statutes and in the internal voting 'act', which shall be drafted and executed by the joint-stock company's board of directors. The articles of association may grant a right attached to the share to appoint one or more members of the supervisory board and to remove a member so appointed. The total number of members so appointed shall not exceed the number of members of the supervisory board elected by the general meeting.

152. The Corporations Act only includes a handful of specific rules for liquidating a joint-stock company, such as the shareholder's right to participate in the distribution of the liquidation balance, etc.

C. Cooperatives

153. A cooperative (in Czech: *družstvo*) is defined as a 'community of an indefinite number of persons, established for the purpose of mutual support of its members or third parties or, where appropriate, for the purpose of doing business' (section 132 of the Corporations Act). Obviously, the primary purpose of a cooperative is usually not to conduct business activities. In fact, the two most common forms of cooperatives in the Czech Republic are housing and social cooperatives, which do not (primarily) pursue business activities; these two subtypes of cooperative are expressly regulated by the Corporations Act. In that connection, a housing cooperative may only be established for the purpose of securing the housing needs of its members and may manage buildings with apartments and non-residential premises owned by other persons (section 727 of the Corporations Act). Other activities may be carried out only provided that, by doing so, the cooperative does not jeopardize the housing needs of its members, and that such activities are only of an ancillary nature in relation to the aforementioned housing activities. A social cooperative, on the other hand, is a cooperative which continuously carries out activities for the public benefit and is aimed at supporting social cohesion in order to ensure labour and social integration of disadvantaged groups into society, preferably by meeting the needs and using the resources local to the registered office and sphere of activities of the social cooperative, particularly in the areas of job creation, social services and health care, education, housing and sustainable development (section 758 of the Corporations Act). A social cooperative also may not transform into another cooperative, that is to say into a cooperative with a different primary purpose, and may not alter its purpose in violation of the law. It can be said that social cooperatives are engaged in social welfare on a local level.

154. A different type of cooperative altogether is a credit union pursuant to Act. 87/1995 Coll.; these entities are entitled to accept contributions from their members and, on the other hand, to provide them with loans.

155. A cooperative must have its own business name attached with 'družstvo' (section 552(3) of the Corporations Act) and at least three members (section 552(2) of the Corporations Act). Members of a cooperative cannot be held liable for the cooperative's debts.

156. A cooperative is founded at the first members' meeting (section 555 of the Corporations Act), where the cooperative's statutes are agreed upon and concluded. The agenda of the first members' meeting and a decision adopting the cooperative's statutes must be notarized (section 560 of the Corporations Act). The Corporations Act does not set a maximum number of members. Nonetheless, a cooperative comes into existence on the date of its incorporation in the Companies Register.

157. Founders of a cooperative are the persons who filed their application for membership in the cooperative (by the time of the first members' meeting), whose application was approved by the first members' meeting, and who fulfilled the requirements for membership, save for the members' deposit obligation (section 559(1) of the Corporations Act). Founders of a cooperative are obliged to fulfil their members' deposit obligation within fifteen days after the first members' meeting took place.

158. Membership in a cooperative arises on the basis of a voluntary commitment of a member to participate in the registered capital of the cooperative in accordance with the cooperative's statutes. Therefore, each member of the cooperative contributes to its registered capital with an initial members' deposit; if so provided for by the statutes, members contribute to the registered capital also via an additional members' deposit (section 563 of the Corporations Act). In order to become a member of a cooperative, a person is obliged to issue a written declaration on the acceptance of the initial members' deposit obligation and to fulfil the initial members' deposit obligation and, if so stipulated by the Corporations Act, to establish an employment relationship with the cooperative in question (section 564(1) of the Corporations Act). The amount of the initial members' deposit is the same for all members, whereas the amount of an additional members' deposit may be different for different members (sections 563 and 564 of the Corporations Act).

159. The registered capital of a cooperative is comprised of members' deposits (initial and additional deposits). If the statutes so allow, the member's meeting can decide to increase the initial members' deposit, albeit only once in three years and up to three times the current amount of the initial members' deposit. The decision to amend the articles of association to allow an increase in the initial member's deposit by a member's additional deposit and the decision to increase the initial member's deposit require the consent of three quarters of all members of the cooperative. Furthermore, the amount of the initial members' deposit may be decreased. The Corporations Act sets forth no minimum registered capital requirement. The registered capital of a cooperative is not entered in the Companies Register. The initial members' deposit obligation may be provided either in cash or in kind.

160. A member's participation in a cooperative is represented by a cooperative interest, which in turn represents that member's rights and obligations arising out of his/her membership in the cooperative. Each member of the cooperative may hold one cooperative interest. The transferability of cooperative interests is restricted by the Corporations Act (*See* sections 599 et seq. of the Corporations Act). Members exercise their powers at members' meetings via holding cooperative interests, which authorize them to exercise their members' rights.

161. For a cooperative, the Corporations Act prescribes three mandatory bodies (section 629 of the Corporations Act):

(a) members' meeting;
(b) board of directors; and
(c) audit committee.

162. Only a member of a cooperative may be a member of the cooperative's body (section 630 of the Corporations Act) and only for a definite term (the maximum of which is five years). Each member has one vote when voting in a cooperative's body unless the cooperative's statutes provide otherwise in cases where this is allowed by the Corporations Act.

163. The power to manage a cooperative is vested in the board of directors, which is the cooperative's statutory body. In a small cooperative (one with fewer than fifty members in total), the board of directors may be replaced with the chairman of the cooperative if the cooperative's statutes so allow.

164. On the other hand, the audit committee checks all of the cooperative's activities, handles complaints of members, and may request any information and documents on the cooperative's management; the audit committee is independent of the cooperative's other corporate governance bodies. In a small cooperative, an audit committee is not established unless its statutes provide otherwise.

165. The cooperative's supreme body is the members' meeting, which consists of the cooperative's members who attend the members meeting regardless whether they do so in person or via a representative. The members' meeting is in charge of the cooperative's fundamental issues (such as, for example, amending the cooperative's statutes). The invitation to the members' meeting must be posted on the cooperative information board, and at the same time it must be sent to the members at the address given in the list of members.

166. The members' meeting has a quorum of a majority of all members which have a majority of all votes are present at the members' meeting unless the Corporations Act or the cooperative's statutes require the participation of members which have a higher number of votes. Cooperatives are required to convene a substitute members' meeting if the members' meeting did not have a quorum. Sometimes, a higher quorum of two-thirds of all members is required (e.g., to adopt a decision to dissolve the cooperative).

167. In addition, the statutes of a cooperative may stipulate that the powers of the members' meeting shall be exercised (in part, or in full) by an assembly of delegates (sections 669 et seq. of the Corporations Act). This is especially practical if a cooperative has a high number of members, which makes convening and holding a members' meeting rather difficult, if not impossible. Each delegate of a cooperative then represents a particular constituency of that cooperative.

168. Moreover, the Corporations Act allows for the establishment of optional bodies in addition to the obligatory ones; the powers of such bodies (or how they make their decisions) are defined by the cooperative's statutes, and no optional body may reserve the powers of an obligatory one.

169. A member of a cooperative may withdraw from that cooperative (e.g., in the case of disagreement with an amendment to the cooperative's statutes) or may even be expelled if he/she has seriously or repeatedly breached his/her membership obligations, has ceased to fulfil the conditions for membership, or for other serious reasons provided for in the statutes.

170. A cooperative may be dissolved by either a decision of the members' meeting or a court's decision; the decision of the members' meeting to that effect must be notarized (section 659(2) of the Corporations Act). The Corporations Act includes only a few rules for dissolving and liquidating a cooperative and only in relation to a housing cooperative (section 757 of the Corporations Act) and social cooperatives (section 773 of the Corporations Act).

Chapter 3. Economic Institutions

§1. Professional Organizations

I. Freedom of Trade and Profession

171. The CHRF of the Czech Republic stipulates in its Article 26, subsection 1 that 'everybody has the right to freely choose a profession and the training for that profession, as well as the right to engage in work and to pursue other economic activities'. In principle, engaging in an economic activity is not subject to membership in a professional organization. However, a few professions, such as medical professions, lawyers, pharmacists, auditors and others, are exceptions to the general rule. A list of professional organizations (usually called chambers) in which membership is mandatory is available on the website of the Czech Supreme Administrative Court.[15] The law sets out certain requirements with regard to education, experience and liability insurance for engaging in certain professions. Most professions require obtaining a business licence to be performed legally, and the preconditions for obtaining a licence vary depending on the economic activity.

II. Trade Associations

172. Most branches of trade and industry have an association ('*spolek*') whose aim is to defend the interests of the branch as a whole and the members. The legal status, establishment and termination of these associations are regulated by sections 214 et seq. of the Civil Code. An association is a self-governing and voluntary group of members established to satisfy and protect the interests it was formed to implement. An association may be formed by its founders if they agree on the contents of its articles of association or by a resolution of the constituting meeting of the association being formed. The primary activity of an association may not involve business or other gainful activities. Nevertheless, an association may also pursue a secondary economic activity consisting in business or other gainful activities if the purpose thereof is to support the primary activity or is for the economical use of the association's property. All associations must be incorporated in the relevant public register maintained by the Ministry of Justice. Based on the articles of association, a subsidiary association may be formed as an organizational unit of the association, or the articles may determine how the subsidiary association is formed and which body decides on forming, dissolving or transforming the subsidiary association (*sections 214 et seq. of the Civil Code*).

173. Associations which defend the interests of a particular branch of industry sometimes further coalesce into larger bodies. The key organization involving employers at a national and international level is the Federation of Industry ('*Svaz průmyslu a dopravy*'). This non-governmental organization focuses on promoting

15. The website of the Supreme Administrative Court: http://www.nssoud.cz/Profesni-komory/art/575?menu=274.

the conditions in which businesses of all sizes and sectors in the Czech Republic and brings together more than thirty associations. The Federation also supports international trade, which includes organizing trade missions with the highest political representatives of the Czech Republic and receiving foreign business delegations, organizing various seminars and trade promotion meetings, and providing related information.[16] The majority of small- and medium-sized enterprises (SMEs) are represented by the Association of SMEs and Crafts of the Czech Republic ('*Asociace malých a středních podniků a živnostníků ČR*'), which was founded in 2001 and provides an open, apolitical platform for SMEs, self-employed persons and their organizations across the Czech Republic. Primarily, the Association provides its members with information services focused on the segment of SMEs – i.e., news regarding subsidy offers, banking products, education, support of exports, research, development and innovation, information regarding the EU, statistics, legislation, etc. In cooperation with important companies and partners, it also offers discounted bundles of products and services to its members.[17]

§2. CHAMBERS OF COMMERCE

I. The Chamber of Commerce and the Agrarian Chamber of the Czech Republic

174. Under Act No. 301/1992 Coll., the Chamber of Commerce of the Czech Republic and the Agrarian Chamber of the Czech Republic were established as the only legal collective bodies to defend and protect the interests of entrepreneurs and agriculturists, respectively.

175. According to the aforementioned Act, the Chamber of Commerce of the Czech Republic ('*Hospodářská komora České republiky*') protects the interests of Czech entrepreneurs from all regions and from all sectors except agriculture, food and forestry (which is performed by the Agrarian Chamber). The Chamber of Commerce is the largest and most representative business association in the Czech Republic. It has more than 16,000 members organized into 60 regional chambers and 129 branch associations. The Chamber of Commerce refers to the historical legacy of medieval guilds, whose roots date back to the fourteenth century, and even earlier.

176. The Chamber of Commerce participates in the legislative process as it is a mandatory point of reference for materials concerning the legal regulation of business. The statutory head of the Chamber of Commerce is the President, who is elected by the Assembly. The working body is the praesidium, which is made up of the President and Vice Presidents, each of which is entrusted with a particular responsibility. The managing authority of the Czech Chamber of Commerce is the

16. The website of the Federation of Industry: https://www.spcr.cz/en/about-us.
17. The website of the Association of Small and Medium-Sized Enterprises and Crafts of the Czech Republic: http://amsp.cz/about-us/?lang=en.

board of directors. The supervisory board is established as a control body, while the Conciliation Commission's main task is to resolve any disputes between members. The Office of the Czech Chamber of Commerce is the executive body of the Chamber. The Secretary General, who is appointed and dismissed by the board of directors, is responsible for the Chamber of Commerce's activities. Through its individual departments, the office ensures the fulfilment of tasks arising from the competence of the Chamber according to the law and current priorities and tasks that have been approved by the board of directors or by the Assembly.[18]

177. The Agrarian Chamber of the Czech Republic (*'Agrární komora České republiky'*) represents and defends the interests of agriculture and related sectors. The Agrarian Chamber is an association comprising most entrepreneurs in agriculture, forestry and food processing industry. It provides advisory, consultation and legal services for its members. The Agrarian Chamber represents the interests of more than 100,000 farmers, foresters, food processors, beekeepers and many more. The Agrarian Chamber partners with Czech municipalities and other public authorities concerned with rural space and its development.[19] Like the Chamber of Commerce, the Agrarian Chamber acts through its bodies, which are the President, the Vice Presidents, the Assembly, the board of directors and the supervisory board. The President represents the Chamber externally and acts on its behalf, while the managing authority is the board of directors, and the supervisory board controls the Agrarian Chamber's activities and management.[20]

II. Other Chambers of Commerce

178. Apart from the Czech Chamber of Commerce and the Agrarian Chamber, there are a number of foreign chambers of commerce. Foreign chambers of commerce are usually established by a foreign country on a long-term basis. They have the legal status of a chamber (*'komora'*), and since 2014 they may also be incorporated as associations (*see* above). The legal status and designation of a chamber come from the previous legal regulation of the act on economic contacts with foreign partners, which was cancelled by the Civil Code as of 1 January 2014. Currently, there is no special regulation on foreign chambers as legal entities, although chambers existing before 2014 may keep the old designation. Under the act on economic contacts with foreign partners, consent from the Ministry of Industry and Trade was needed to establish a foreign chamber. According to the current legal regulation, no such consent is required, and the Ministry plays no role in the establishment of a foreign chamber of commerce. In fact, no contact with the Ministry is necessary at all. There is one global chamber of commerce – the International

18. The website of the Chamber of Commerce of the Czech Republic: https://www.komora.cz/en/about-us/.
19. The website of the Agrarian Chamber of the Czech Republic: http://www.akcr.cz/.
20. The Statute of the Agrarian Chamber: http://www.akcr.cz/txt/statut-ak.

Chamber of Commerce Czech Republic, and more than 150 other chambers of commerce with different scopes and levels of services.[21]

§3. Other Important Bodies

179. There are four key bodies established to promote trade in the Czech Republic: the Czech Trade Promotion Agency CzechTrade, the Investment and Business Development Agency CzechInvest, the Export Guarantee and Insurance Corporation, and Czech Export Bank.

180. The Investment and Business Development Agency CzechInvest (‘*Agentura pro podporu podnikání a investic CzechInvest*’) is a state contributory organization which is subordinate to the Czech Ministry of Industry and Trade. The agency arranges both domestic and foreign investments in the areas of manufacturing, business support services and technology centres. It also supports small, medium-sized and innovative start-up companies, the country's business infrastructure, innovation, and Czech firms that are interested in becoming involved in the supply chains of multinational companies.[22] The Czech Trade Promotion Agency CzechTrade (‘*Česká agentura na podporu obchodu CzechTrade*’) is a government trade promotion agency whose main objective is to develop international trade and cooperation between Czech and foreign entities.[23]

181. Czech Export Bank (‘*Česká exportní banka*’) provides export-related financial services. The bank's aim is to support Czech exports and the renown of the Czech Republic as a well-established international exporter, and thus to promote the overall competitiveness of Czech products throughout the world. In addition to financing exports of goods and services, the Czech Export Bank recently decided to finance construction work, especially infrastructure projects abroad as well. Furthermore, the bank offers a range of structured and project financing models. Czech investors are provided with favourable financing options to support them in building new production capacities abroad or for their plans to invest capital into foreign companies. Czech Export Bank has also significantly expanded its services of financing the export-related activities of SMEs.[24]

182. The Export Guarantee and Insurance Corporation (EGAP, ‘*Exportní garanční a pojišťovací společnost*’), a state-owned joint-stock company, is a credit insurance corporation insuring credit connected with exports of goods and services from the Czech Republic against political and commercial risks uninsurable by commercial insurance. In particular, EGAP insures bank loans due in over two years which are intended to finance the export of energy, machinery and technological

21. The website Businessinfo.cz, maintained by the Czech Ministry of Industry and Trade: https://www.businessinfo.cz/navody/prehled-zahranicnich-obchodnich-komor/.
22. The website of the CzechInvest: https://www.czechinvest.org/en/About-CzechInvest/About-Us.
23. The website of the CzechTrade: https://www.czechtradeoffices.com/en/about-us.
24. The website of Czech Export Bank: https://www.ceb.cz/en/about-us/our-profile/.

systems, investment projects, transport structures and investments, usually to countries where the political, economic and legal environment increases the risk of default. It complements the range of commercial credit insurance products and fills the gap on the market, acting as a standard export credit insurance company in the role of a government tool to promote exports. The corporation provides insurance services to all exporters of Czech goods, services and investments, irrespective of their size, legal form and volume of insured exports.[25]

183. The Czech-Moravian Guarantee and Development Bank (*'Českomoravská záruční a rozvojová banka'*) fulfils a similar role as Czech Export Bank although not related to exports. This state-owned joint-stock company focuses on providing assistance to SMEs with the aim to provide them easier access to financial capital, share their business risk, and reduce their project costs through different types of support tools, such as bank guarantees, preferential loans and financial subsidies.[26]

§4. COMMERCIAL COURTS AND COMMERCIAL ARBITRATION

184. Besides dispute resolution by courts, which are governed primarily by the Code of Civil Procedure (*Act No. 99/1963 Coll.*), or alternative dispute resolution,[27] parties may decide to resolve a dispute by means of arbitration. However, in general, only property-related disputes can be subject to arbitration.

I. Applicable Law

185. Arbitration in the Czech Republic is governed by the Arbitration Act. The Arbitration Act came into force as of 1 January 1995, and as a result, international as well as domestic trade disputes can now be resolved in arbitration. Currently, the provisions of the Arbitration Act apply to both domestic and international arbitration proceedings provided that the arbitration takes place in the Czech Republic.

186. The Arbitration Act has been amended several times, with the most significant amendments being as follows. As of 1 April 2012, certain requirements related to the arbitrators were added: they have to be at least 18 years of age, have the legal capacity and have a clean criminal record. The amendment (*Act No. 19/2012 Coll.*) also stipulated stricter requirements for arbitrators deciding on disputes arising from consumer contracts and some other conditions to be met in such contracts and possible disputes arising therefrom. On 1 January 2014, requirements for proceedings held before the arbitration commissions of an industry association took effect (*Act No. 303/2013 Coll.*). Some Czech associations have established such commissions,

25. The website of the Export Guarantee and Insurance Corporation: https://www.egap.cz/en/profile.
26. The website of the Czech-Moravian Guarantee and Development Bank: https://www.cmzrb.cz/en/.
27. Some consider arbitration to be a special type of alternative dispute resolution, however.

particularly in the domain of sport. Finally, as of 1 December 2016 (*Act No. 258/ 2016 Coll.*), disputes arising out of consumer contracts may no longer be subject to arbitration.

187. As regards the rules governing the arbitration process, the Arbitration Act stipulates in its section 30 that unless stated otherwise '*the arbitral proceedings shall be reasonably governed by the provisions of the Code of Civil Procedure*'. The Supreme Court of the Czech Republic brought more light to the issue, however, stating that the Czech rules of Civil Procedure apply only in the absence of specific rules of arbitration proceedings.[28] Should the dispute contain an international element, the relevant provisions of the Act on Private International Law (PIL) (*Act No. 91/2012 Coll., as amended*) shall be applicable as well.

188. Regarding multilateral conventions, the Czech Republic is a party to the New York Arbitration Convention from 1958, the ICSID (International Centre for Settlement of Investment Disputes) Convention from 1966, the Seoul Convention on Multilateral Investment Guarantee Agency from 1985 and the Energy Charter Treaty. The Czech Republic has also signed and ratified a large number of investment protection treaties, which are used by investors to invoke the dispute resolution clause therein against the Czech Republic. Finally, the Arbitration Act is significantly influenced by the UNCITRAL (the United Nations Commission on International Trade Law) Model Law on International Commercial Arbitration.[29]

II. Arbitration Agreement

189. Pursuant to section 2 paragraph 1 of the Arbitration Act, parties are free to agree that their property disputes (with the exception of disputes arising from consumer contracts and those arising from the enforcement of decisions and incidental disputes), which would otherwise fall within the jurisdiction of the courts, or which are subject to arbitration under special laws, shall be decided by one or more arbitrators or by a permanent arbitral institution (*section 1 paragraph 2 of the Arbitration Act*).[30] Arbitration agreements must be executed in writing; otherwise, it is invalid (*section 3 paragraph 1 of the Arbitration Act*). An arbitration agreement can be concluded as an arbitration clause in a contract or as a separate agreement. The agreement shall also determine the specific arbitrator or arbitrators, or at least the

28. Decision of the Supreme Court of the Czech Republic File No. 32 Odo 1528/2005, dated 25 Apr. 2007.
29. Bělohlávek, A.J.: Arbitration in the Czech Republic, in Arbitration Journal, 7 Feb. 2019: https://journal.arbitration.ru/analytics/arbitration-in-the-czech-republic/.
30. Generally, to the arbitration agreement under Czech law, *see*, e.g., Makarius, V. Rozhodčí smlouvy v mezinárodním obchodě: prevence, plánování a řízení sporu v mezinárodním obchodě. Praha. C. H. Beck, 2015, Zákon o rozhodčím řízení a o výkonu rozhodčích nálezů. Komentář. Praha. C. H. Beck, 2012. pp. 103 et seq., Kindl, M. Na co nezapomínat při sjednávání rozhodčí smlouvy. Bulletin advokacie. 2018, Vol. 2018, No. 9, pp. 29 et seq., David, M. K povaze rozhodčí smlouvy podruhé a jinak. Bulletin advokacie. 2011, Vol. 2011, No. 10, pp. 27 et seq., or Pospíšil, P. Kdo může uzavírat rozhodčí smlouvu?. Bulletin advokacie. 2010, Vol. 2010, No. 12, pp. 34 et seq.

manner of appointment, or a specific arbitral tribunal, the place of arbitration, the procedure rules and the substantive law governing the dispute.

190. As regards an arbitration agreement's validity and enforceability, the general provisions on contracts under Czech law apply. An arbitration agreement is binding on legal successors, and the separability principle, as well as the *Kompetenz-Kompetenz* doctrine, are recognized. Thus, the arbitration agreement is valid even if the main contract is not. The arbitration agreement is then used to resolve disputes between the parties concerning entitlements under the invalid contract.[31]

III. Arbitral Tribunal

191. Arbitrators must have full legal capacity under the law of their nationality. However, an arbitrator may not be a Czech judge, a Czech public prosecutor, or a judge of the Constitutional Court. An arbitrator may be a foreigner or a Czech citizen (*section 4 paragraph 1 of the Arbitration Act in connection with section 118 of the Act on PIL*).

192. The arbitral tribunal must always be composed of an odd number of arbitrators. Disputes are resolved by three arbitrators unless agreed otherwise. If the parties fail to agree on the appointment of the arbitrators, each party appoints one arbitrator and, subsequently, these arbitrators appoint the chairman (in the case of three arbitrators). The parties may also agree on an appointing authority. Should any of the parties fail to appoint an arbitrator, or if the arbitrators appointed by the parties do not agree on the chairman, or if a dispute is to be settled (by express agreement of the parties contained in the arbitration agreement) by a sole arbitrator and the parties cannot agree on this arbitrator, and the parties have not made an agreement on an appointing authority, the arbitrator is appointed by the court.[32]

193. An arbitrator is disqualified from hearing and resolving the case if his/her connection to the case, the parties, or their representatives gives rise to doubts of a lack of bias. The candidate who is to be or was the selected or appointed arbitrator must notify the parties or the court without delay of any and all circumstances which could give rise to legitimate doubts regarding the candidate's lack of bias and which would disqualify the candidate as an arbitrator (*section 8 paragraphs 1 and 2 of the Arbitration Act*).

194. In the Czech Republic, there are three permanent Arbitration Courts: the Arbitration Court attached to the Chamber of Commerce of the Czech Republic and

31. Bělohlávek, A.J.: Arbitration in the Czech Republic, in Arbitration Journal, 7 Feb. 2019: https://journal.arbitration.ru/analytics/arbitration-in-the-czech-republic/ or the Decision of the Supreme Court of the Czech Republic File No. 29 Odo 1222/2005, dated 19 Dec. 2007.
32. Bělohlávek, A.J.: Arbitration in the Czech Republic, in Arbitration Journal, 7 Feb. 2019: https://journal.arbitration.ru/analytics/arbitration-in-the-czech-republic/.

the Agrarian Chamber of the Czech Republic,[33] the International Arbitration Court of the Czech Commodity Exchange,[34] and the Exchange Court of Arbitration attached to the Prague Stock Exchange.[35]

IV. Procedure

195. In accordance with the Arbitration Act, parties are free to agree on the procedure to be followed by the arbitrators in conducting the proceedings. Matters regarding the conduct of the proceedings may be resolved by the chairman provided he/she was authorized to do so by the parties or by all arbitrators. If no such agreement is reached by the parties or no procedure is determined by the chairman, the arbitrators shall conduct the proceedings in such a manner as they consider appropriate and which enables the facts of the case necessary for resolving the dispute to be sufficiently ascertained, while giving all parties equal opportunity to plead their case (*section 19 paragraphs 1 and 2 of the Arbitration Act*).

196. Unless the parties agree otherwise, the arbitration proceedings shall be oral, and the public is always excluded from the proceedings (*section 19 paragraph 3 of the Arbitration Act*).

V. Award

197. The arbitral award must be adopted by a majority of the arbitrators, made in writing, and signed by at least a majority of the arbitrators. The operative part of the arbitral award must be clear and unambiguous. The award must contain reasoning unless the parties have agreed otherwise (*section 25 paragraphs 1 and 2 of the Arbitration Act*).[36]

198. Pursuant to section 27 of the Arbitration Act, parties may agree in the arbitration agreement that the arbitral award may be subject to review by other arbitrators at the request of either party or both parties.

199. The written arbitral award must be served to the parties and, after having been duly served, stamped with a confirmation of the award's legal force and effect.

---

33. The website of the Arbitration Court attached to the Chamber of Commerce of the Czech Republic and the Agrarian Chamber of the Czech Republic: https://en.soud.cz/arbitration-court.
34. The website of the Czech-Moravian Commodity Exchange Kladno: https://www.cmkbk.cz/en/legislatureregulations/arbitration-court/.
35. The website of the Prague Stock Exchange: https://www.pse.cz/en/exchange-court-of-arbitration.
36. Generally to the arbitration award under Czech law, *see*, e.g., Bělohlávek, A. J. Zákon o rozhodčím řízení a o výkonu rozhodčích nálezů. Komentář. Praha. C. H. Beck, 2012. pp. 915 et seq., Řezníček, D. Vykonatelnost a výkon rozhodčích nálezů. Bulletin advokacie. 2018, Vol. 2018, No. 9, pp. 43 et seq., Sadecký, L. Odmítnutí podpisu rozhodčího nálezu rozhodcem s vazbou na jeho odlišné stanovisko. Obchodní právo. 2020, Vol. 29, No. 2, pp. 16 et seq. or Vlachová, B. Rozhodčí nález jako exekuční titul. Komorní listy. 2017, Vol. 9, No. 3, pp. 20 et seq.

If the arbitral award cannot be subject to review as described above or if the time limit for filing a motion has expired without a motion having been lodged, the award has the effects of a final and conclusive court judgment and is enforceable by courts upon receipt (*section 28 of the Arbitration Act*).

VI. Role of the Courts

200. The courts may order interim measures if subsequent enforcement could be endangered or in the case of a risk of serious injury. The Czech courts are in this matter rather restrictive; however, arbitrators do not have any authority to order interim measures.[37] Moreover, arbitral awards may be subject to review and subsequent annulment by the courts.[38] The motion to annul an arbitral award must be lodged with the court within three months following the receipt of the arbitral award by the requesting party. The motion per se does not suspend the enforceability of the arbitral award. This may happen only upon request of an obligor provided that immediate enforcement of the arbitral award could cause serious harm or if the motion to annul the arbitral award justifies the conclusion that the motion is legitimate *(section 32 paragraphs 1 and 2 of the Arbitration Act*).

37. Bělohlávek, A.J.: Arbitration in the Czech Republic, in Arbitration Journal, 7 Feb. 2019: https://journal.arbitration.ru/analytics/arbitration-in-the-czech-republic/.
38. Cf. Bělohlávek, A. J. Zákon o rozhodčím řízení a o výkonu rozhodčích nálezů. Komentář. Praha. C. H. Beck, 2012. pp. 1059 et seq. or Doleček, M. Pravomoc soudů ve vztahu k rozhodčímu řízení. Bulletin advokacie. 2018, Vol. 2018, No. 9, pp. 40 et seq.

Chapter 4. Bankruptcy and Related Institutions

§1. General Overview

201. The Czech law governing insolvent commercial entities (or those who are at risk of being insolvent) has gone through a turbulent evolution in the past thirty years. Following the fall of communism in former Czechoslovakia, the newly established free-market economy was without any insolvency law. After all, socialist commercial entities were dissolved due to insolvency only when the socialist state so decided. The absence of a national insolvency law was resolved by the adoption of the Bankruptcy Act (No. 328/1991), which came into force on 1 October 1991.

202. The aim of the Bankruptcy Act was to arrange the financial relationship of insolvent debtors, both natural persons and entrepreneurs. For that purpose, the Bankruptcy Act provided for two different proceedings: (i) bankruptcy proceedings; and (ii) settlement proceedings. In bankruptcy proceedings, the goal was to simply liquidate (realize) any and all of the debtor's assets and to redistribute the returns among creditors in a just and proportional way. Generally, bankruptcy proceedings served as a platform where unsuccessful commercial entities could exit the market. As a rule, bankruptcy proceedings resulted in a commercial entity being deleted from the Companies Register and, therefore, in the definite cessation of that entity's commercial activities. On the other hand, in settlement proceedings, the goal was to reach a consensus between the debtor and its creditors on restructuring the debts (which then had to be approved by a court) and allowing the debtor to further operate on the market. As is obvious, the primary goal of settlement proceedings was to rescue the debtor (to allow a commercial entity to further carry on with its entrepreneurial activities). Both types of proceedings, however, rested upon the same keystone: the principle of *par conditio creditorum*, i.e., equal treatment of creditors in equal (or comparable) positions.

203. The Bankruptcy Act was not without its flaws; consequently, it was amended on twenty-seven occasions by virtue of more than thirty different legal regulations. While some of the changes were rather cosmetic, some were conceptually significant.[39] Nevertheless, the Bankruptcy Act was widely criticized for not being suitable for a modern-day market economy and for neglecting modern trends in insolvency law (such as, e.g., providing more ways for a debtor to be rescued, having its own version of reorganization, etc.). The provisions on settlement proceedings (aimed at debtor rescue) were considered de facto obsolete, as their impact was practically non-existent.[40] Also, many proceedings were conducted unprofessionally since judges lacked any formal economic education.[41]

39. Smrčka, L., Plaček, J., Schönfeld, J., Louda, L. Insolvenční řízení (očekávání, realita a budoucnost insolvenčního zákona). 1. vydání. Praha: Kamil Mařík – Professional Publishing, 2016, p. 18.
40. Kislingerová, E., Richter, T., Smrčka, L. et al. Insolvenční praxe v České republice v období 2008–2013. 1. vydání. Praha: C. H. Beck, 2013, p. 4.
41. Smrčka, L., Plaček, J., Schönfeld, J., Louda, L. Insolvenční řízení (očekávání, realita a budoucnost insolvenčního zákona). 1. vydání. Praha: Kamil Mařík – Professional Publishing, 2016, p. 54.

204. In 2006, the Insolvency Act (No. 182/2006 Coll.) was adopted. It came into force on 1 January 2008 while repealing the Bankruptcy Act and became the second major recodification on the Czech territory since the fall of communism (the first being the new Labour Code of 2006).[42] From the start, the Insolvency Act was built on different conceptual foundations than the Bankruptcy Act; it substituted the concept of different proceedings (bankruptcy and settlement proceedings) with the principle of one single type of proceedings (insolvency proceedings) that differentiate depending on the mode of resolving the debtor's insolvency.[43] Moreover, the Insolvency Act substantially widened the array of legal instruments available under Czech insolvency law as well as introduced new ways to resolve a debtor's insolvency (which, on the other hand, cannot be considered anything new, at least from a global perspective). Nevertheless, some aspects of Czech insolvency law remained unchanged, such as the principle of *par conditio creditorum* (sections 1 and 5 of the Insolvency Act).

205. The goal of insolvency proceedings is to first assess whether a particular debtor is indeed insolvent and, provided it is, to decide on how to resolve its insolvency (to decide on one of the modes of resolving insolvency).[44] Of course, the final overarching goal is to carry out the mode selected or, in other words, to satisfy the debtor's creditors.[45] Consequently, the insolvency proceedings are uniform until a particular mode of resolving insolvency is selected (decided by the insolvency court), and, following that, differentiate depending on the mode selected.[46] Hence, all insolvency proceedings are governed by the same provisions until the mode is designated.

206. The first stage of insolvency proceedings ends when the insolvency court issues a decision on the debtor's insolvency. During this phase, the insolvency court is called upon to assess the debtor's insolvency. The goal of the following stage is to decide on the particular mode; however, it is also possible that a court's decision on insolvency also designates the mode of resolution.[47] In that case, this stage is skipped altogether. The aim of the third and final stage is to carry out the selected mode and, finally, to satisfy creditors in a just and proportional way in accordance

42. Richter, T.: Insolvenční zákon: od vládního návrhu k vyhlášenému znění. In: Právní rozhledy 21/2006, p. 765.
43. Hásová, J. Moravec, T. Insolvenční řízení. Vydání druhé. Praha: C. H. Beck, 2018, p. 3.
44. Sprinz, P., Jirmásek, T., Řeháček, O., Vrba, M., Zoubek, H. et al. Insolvenční zákon. Komentář. 1. vydání. Praha: C. H. Beck, 2019, p. 1.
45. This statement is, however, not entirely correct. In the case of debt discharge, the goal of insolvency proceedings is not to satisfy creditors but to allow the debtor (a natural person or a legal entity non-entrepreneur) to return to an active economic life. *See* s. 1 of the Insolvency Act á contrario. *See*, e.g., Sprinz, P., Jirmásek, T., Řeháček, O., Vrba, M., Zoubek, H. et al. Insolvenční zákon. Komentář. 1. vydání. Praha: C. H. Beck, 2019, p. 1.
46. This fact is reflected by the Insolvency Act and its division into its parts, whereas the first (general) part applies to all insolvency proceedings and the second (special) part contains provisions on different modes of resolving insolvency.
47. This is the case when there is only one mode of resolving insolvency available with respect to a particular debtor (i.e., bankruptcy). *See* s. 148(1) IA.

with the Insolvency Act. However, phases of insolvency proceedings may overlap, and the borders between them are blurry.

207. According to the Insolvency Act, the insolvency of a commercial entity can be resolved either by:

(a) bankruptcy; or
(b) reorganization.

208. In addition, the Insolvency Act recognizes debt discharge as the mode of resolving the insolvency of natural persons, both non-entrepreneurs and entrepreneurs (entrepreneurs must, however, satisfy certain special conditions in order to be eligible for debt discharge (section 389(2) of the Insolvency Act)). Sometimes, the insolvency of financial institutions (e.g., banks) is also mentioned as a separate mode of resolving insolvency (even by the Insolvency Act itself (section 4(1) of the Insolvency Act)); such a designation is, however, incorrect as the insolvency of financial institutions is rather a modified version of bankruptcy (intended for special categories of debtors) with special rules to protect creditors.[48]

209. It is also possible to resolve a debtor's insolvency outside the regulatory framework of the Insolvency Act, although it is more than likely that the individual actors in such an unformal arrangement will act under the influence of the Insolvency Act (with regard to their position in eventual insolvency proceedings).[49] Needless to say, this approach presupposes a consensus between the debtor and its creditors, which might be impossible to achieve in some situations.

210. To date, the Insolvency Act has been amended on more than thirty occasions; the last amendment came into force on 1 January 2022. A rather high number of amendments can be partially explained by the fact that the Insolvency Act also regulates the insolvency of non-commercial persons and entities; in other words, there is a social aspect to the Insolvency Act.[50]

211. The Insolvency Act is in compliance with Regulation (EU) 2015/848 of the European Parliament and of the Council of 20 May 2015 on insolvency proceedings. While there are some discrepancies in terms of the terminology between the Insolvency Act and the Regulation (such as, e.g., the difference between proceedings and modes of resolving insolvency), these will likely cause no problems in

48. Winterová, A., Macková, A. et al. Civilní právo procesní. Část druhá: Řízení vykonávací, řízení insolvenční. 1. vydání. Praha: Leges, 2015, p. 286.
49. Sprinz, P., Jirmásek, T., Řeháček, O., Vrba, M., Zoubek, H. et al. Insolvenční zákon. Komentář. 1. vydání. Praha: C. H. Beck, 2019, p. 2.
50. Winterová, A., Macková, A. et al. Civilní právo procesní. Část druhá: Řízení vykonávací, řízení insolvenční. 1. vydání. Praha: Leges, 2015, p. 296.

practice. It must be stressed, however, that European insolvency law does not intrude into national insolvency procedures; any opinion to the contrary must be rejected as a distortion of reality.[51]

§2. Insolvency Proceedings

I. General Description

212. Insolvency proceedings are collective court proceedings[52] and, as such, are administered by a court with insolvency jurisdiction (so-called insolvency court (section 9(a) of the Insolvency Act)). Insolvency proceedings are conducted by the debtor's general regional court (typically the regional court where the debtor has its registered office) (sections 7a and 7b of the Insolvency Act). The insolvency court is not a special court body; it is a regional court (that is generally Courts of Second Instance in Czech Civil Procedure) that is equipped with judges educated in insolvency law. Insolvency proceedings represent a major exception in Czech Civil Procedure as they combine elements of both normal and execution (enforcement) proceedings into one consolidated procedure.[53] Once the proceedings are commenced, the court must first decide whether the debtor in question is truly insolvent and, if it is, it must decide upon the mode of resolving its insolvency. Hence, insolvency proceedings always begin the same and differentiate later, namely when a particular mode of resolving insolvency is decided upon by the insolvency court. Following that, the selected mode is carried out, and after the debtor's creditors are satisfied, the insolvency proceedings are terminated. In other words, the ultimate goal of insolvency proceedings is to rearrange the debtor's proprietary relations.[54]

213. The actors who participate in insolvency proceedings are the insolvency court, the debtor and its creditors (who are jointly called the participants in or parties to the proceedings), an insolvency administrator, the state prosecution (if it has entered the proceedings), and the debtor's liquidator if any (section 9 of the Insolvency Act).

214. A typical feature of insolvency proceedings is the creditors' bodies. These include the creditors' meeting and the creditors' committee, or, alternatively, the creditors' representative (section 46 of the Insolvency Act). The creditors' meeting

---

51. Smrčka, L., Plaček, J., Schönfeld, J., Louda, L. Insolvenční řízení (očekávání, realita a budoucnost insolvenčního zákona). 1. vydání. Praha: Kamil Mařík – Professional Publishing, 2016, p. 59.
52. Hásová, J. Moravec, T. Insolvenční řízení. Vydání druhé. Praha: C. H. Beck, 2018, p. 2; Sprinz, P., Jirmásek, T., Řeháček, O., Vrba, M., Zoubek, H. et al. Insolvenční zákon. Komentář. 1. vydání, Praha: C. H. Beck, 2019, pp. 1 and 133.
53. Smrčka, L., Plaček, J., Schönfeld, J., Louda, L. Insolvenční řízení (očekávání, realita a budoucnost insolvenčního zákona). 1. vydání. Praha: Kamil Mařík – Professional Publishing, 2016, pp. 40–41. Generally, a combination of proceeding on merits with execution (enforcement) proceedings is forbidden under Art. 36(1) of the Charter of Fundamental Rights and Liberties.
54. Sprinz, P., Jirmásek, T., Řeháček, O., Vrba, M., Zoubek, H. et al. Insolvenční zákon. Komentář. 1. vydání, Praha: C. H. Beck, 2019, p. 1.

is summoned and organized by the insolvency court (section 47(1) of the Insolvency Act), and it is the highest body of creditors, which may reserve for itself anything that falls within the scope of creditors' bodies (section 46(2) of the Insolvency Act). Most importantly, it elects and dismisses the members of the creditors' committee and their substitutes (or the creditors' representative) and decides upon the mode of resolving insolvency (assuming there is more than one mode available in relation to a particular debtor) (section 46(2) of the Insolvency Act). The creditors' committee, on the other hand, exercises the powers of the creditors' bodies, with the exception of matters falling within the scope of the creditors' meeting or which the creditors' meeting has reserved (section 46(3) of the Insolvency Act). The creditors' committee protects the creditors' mutual interest and, in cooperation with the insolvency administrator, safeguards and contributes to the purpose of the insolvency proceedings (section 58(1) of the Insolvency Act). If there are more than 50 registered creditors, the election of a creditors' committee (by the creditors' meeting) is obligatory (section 58(1) of the Insolvency Act). If the election of the creditors' committee is not mandatory, the creditors' meeting may elect the creditors' representative and a substitute representative instead; the creditors' representative then exercises the rights and obligations of the creditors' committee (section 68 of the Insolvency Act). If neither the creditors' committee nor creditors' representative has been elected, the rights and obligations of the creditors' committee are exercised by the creditors' meeting 0 (section 46(2) of the Insolvency Act) or, if so expressly provided by the Insolvency Act, by the insolvency court.[55]

215. With some exceptions, any person (whether natural or legal) may be subject to insolvency proceedings pursuant to the Insolvency Act. These exceptions include entities such as the Czech state, Czech National Bank (CNB), public colleges, etc. (section 6 of the Insolvency Act).

216. Any and all insolvency proceedings must abide by the principles of insolvency proceedings set forth by the Insolvency Act (in addition to the principles of Czech Civil Procedure). These principles include the already mentioned principle of *par conditio creditorum*, the prohibition of favourable arbitral treatment of some creditors, the protection of creditors' rights acquired in good faith prior to the commencement of the insolvency proceedings, the conduction of insolvency proceedings so as to prevent unjust harm or favourable treatment, and other principles (section 5 of the Insolvency Act). These 'special' principles reflect the very nature of insolvency proceedings. They mainly serve as guidance when interpreting provisions of the Insolvency Act.[56]

217. One of the major features of the Insolvency Act is the establishment of the Insolvency Register; with it, insolvency proceedings became a public affair. Each

---

55. For example, if the creditors' meeting, summoned for that purpose, does not elect a creditors' committee, the powers of the creditors' committee are exercised by the insolvency court (s. 61(2) IA).

56. Sprinz, P., Jirmásek, T., Řeháček, O., Vrba, M., Zoubek, H. et al. Insolvenční zákon. Komentář. 1. vydání, Praha: C. H. Beck, 2019, p. 21.

insolvency court decision, virtually every motion, and other major information are published in the Insolvency Register (section 71(1) of the Insolvency Act), which is accessible to the public online. Not only does the Insolvency Register serve as an information portal for the public but it is also used as a method of judicial delivery to participants in insolvency proceedings[57] (i.e., once the document in question is published in the register, it is considered delivered (sections 71 et seq. of the Insolvency Act)). However, certain decisions and documents are still delivered through traditional means of delivery.

II. Definition of Insolvency

218. Unsurprisingly, it is the Insolvency Act that defines when a debtor is insolvent. However, contrary to a common misconception, an insolvent debtor is not a precondition for insolvency proceedings (i.e., it is not a precondition for filing an insolvency petition); whether a debtor is actually insolvent is assessed during the proceedings by the insolvency court. Therefore, a creditor who is in good faith that a debtor is insolvent may file an insolvency petition and initiate insolvency proceedings.

219. The Insolvency Act recognizes two forms of insolvency:

(a) payment insolvency (section 3(1)(2)(3) of the Insolvency Act); and
(b) excessive indebtedness (section 3(4) of the Insolvency Act).

220. First, a debtor is insolvent (payment insolvency) provided certain conditions are cumulatively satisfied: a debtor has at least two creditors (plurality of creditors), has (at least two) pecuniary obligations that are overdue for more than thirty days and is unable to satisfy these obligations. Whether a debtor is unable to satisfy its pecuniary obligations is assessed through a system of rebuttable presumptions (*praesumptio iuris tantum*). For example, a debtor is unable to satisfy its pecuniary obligations if it has suspended payments of a substantial part of its pecuniary obligations. Once all three of these conditions are satisfied, the insolvency court shall decide that a debtor is insolvent.

221. Second, a debtor is considered insolvent if it is excessively indebted. This form of insolvency is applicable only to entrepreneurs (regardless of whether they are natural persons or legal entities). Excessive indebtedness is a situation where the total value of a debtor's liabilities (including those that are not yet due) surpasses a total value of its assets while the debtor has at least two creditors. Naturally, such a situation is recognized from the debtor's accounting and financial statements; however, the insolvency court takes into account the future administration of the debtor's assets and future operation of the debtor's enterprise (especially future

57. Hásová, J. Moravec, T. Insolvenční řízení. Vydání druhé. Praha: C. H. Beck, 2018, pp. 11–12.

returns), provided it is reasonable to assume that the debtor will continue to administer its assets or enterprise. Thus, there is no room for automatically applying excessive indebtedness once the value of liabilities surpasses the value of assets.[58] In practice, from the creditors' standpoint, it is rather difficult to argue that a debtor has excessive indebtedness as many debtors point to the future administration and returns and courts are usually hesitant to proclaim a debtor insolvent. Consequently, debtors may legally engage in risky business operations even when they are excessively indebted in terms of the Insolvency Act.[59]

222. The common denominator of both types of insolvency is the plurality of creditors. Unlike some other insolvency law systems, the insolvency court in the Czech Republic may not decide that a debtor is insolvent if it has only one creditor, regardless of how dire the debtor's financial situation is. This requirement stems from the fact that insolvency proceedings are collective proceedings, the goal of which is to organize the mutual relationships between a larger number of participants; the technical minimum of insolvency proceedings is three participants (a debtor and two creditors).[60]

III. Course of Insolvency Proceedings

223. Insolvency proceedings are formally commenced on the day when an insolvency petition is delivered to the insolvency court (section 97(1) of the Insolvency Act). As of this moment, the opening (first) phase of the proceedings has begun, and creditors may file their lodgements of receivable(s) with the insolvency court.

224. An insolvency petition may be filed by either a debtor or its creditor (section 97(7) of the Insolvency Act). Once an insolvency petition is made public in the Insolvency Register, the legal effects associated with the commencement of insolvency proceedings start to apply (section 109(4) of the Insolvency Act); sometimes, these effects are referred to as the automatic or statutory moratorium.[61] The principal effect is that the creditors' ability to individually recover claims against the debtor through 'traditional' legal instruments and remedies is limited. The purpose here is to prevent any eventual destruction of the debtor's assets as a whole and to support the *par conditio creditorum* principle (in other words, creditors' claims are satisfied in a collective insolvency procedure). Automatic moratorium persists until the end of the insolvency proceedings, or if a debtor's insolvency is being resolved by reorganization until the reorganization plan comes into effect (section 109(5) IA). It is rather appropriate to note that it is necessary to distinguish automatic moratorium from judicial moratorium, i.e., a legal instrument that serves to overcome a debtor's transitional economic crisis (where the debtor is an entrepreneur) by

58. Sprinz, P., Jirmásek, T., Řeháček, O., Vrba, M., Zoubek, H. et al. Insolvenční zákon. Komentář. 1. vydání, Praha: C. H. Beck, 2019, pp. 16–17.
59. Hásová, J., Moravec, T. a kol. Insolvenční zákon, 3. vydání. Praha: C. H. Beck, 2018, pp. 35–36.
60. Smrčka, L., Plaček, J., Schönfeld, J., Louda, L. Insolvenční řízení (očekávání, realita a budoucnost insolvenčního zákona). 1. vydání. Praha: Kamil Mařík – Professional Publishing, 2016, p. 41.
61. Richter, T. Insolvenční právo. 2. vydání. Praha: Wolters Kluwer ČR, 2017, p. 263.

restricting creditors in their ability to individually recover claims against the debtor.[62] In addition, there are effects associated with the commencement of insolvency proceedings that affect the debtor itself, who is thus limited in disposing of its property where substantial changes to the property are concerned (section 111 IA of the Insolvency Act). Besides that, the insolvency court may further restrict the debtor by virtue of an interim measure and, at the same time, appoint a provisional insolvency administrator (section 112 of the Insolvency Act).

225. Generally, all insolvency petitions are published in the Insolvency Register. However, if an insolvency petition is filed by a creditor, the insolvency court will always first make a preliminary assessment of whether the petition is justified (section 100a of the Insolvency Act). If the court has doubts, it shall decide that such petition will not be published in the Insolvency Register (to protect the alleged debtor). The preliminary assessment of the creditors' petition must be done by the end of the following business day of the insolvency court as of the delivery of the petition to the court. As a rule, insolvency courts announce the commencement of insolvency proceedings in the Insolvency Register within two hours of receiving a debtor's petition, or once the preliminary assessment is completed; however, in some cases, the insolvency court will announce the commencement of insolvency proceedings within the first two opening hours of its next business day (section 101(1) of the Insolvency Act).

226. If insolvency proceedings are commenced upon a creditor's petition, that creditor is obliged to make a deposit (to cover the costs of the insolvency proceedings) in the amount of either CZK 50,000 (approx. EUR 1,950) or CZK 10,000 (approx. EUR 390) (section 108 of the Insolvency Act). The insolvency court shall reject a creditor petition if the deposit is not made. In the case of a debtor's petition, the insolvency court may require a deposit up to CZK 50,000 (approx. EUR 1,950); if such a deposit is not made, the insolvency may either reject the petition or enforce the obligation to make a deposit. In any case, it is the petitioner who has an obligation to make the deposit.

227. Once an insolvency petition is published in the Insolvency Register, insolvency proceedings progress to the stage where the insolvency court must assess whether the insolvency petition contains all the necessary information, essentials, and schedules. Creditors must provide the insolvency court with different information and schedules than debtors.[63] Most importantly, the Insolvency Act requires a creditor's insolvency petition to be supplemented with that creditor's lodgement of receivable(s) (section 105(1) IA of the Insolvency Act).

---

62. Judicial moratorium is legislated for in ss 115–127 IA.
63. Generally, a debtor is obliged to supplement his or her insolvency petition with defined lists, which a creditor would, in principle, not be able to provide; these lists are: list of assets and receivables, list of obligations, and list of employees (s. 104 IA).

228. If the insolvency court concludes that an insolvency petition is incomplete, incomprehensible, or unclear, it will dismiss the petition (provided that the petition's deficiencies preclude the continuation of the insolvency proceedings) (section 128(1) of the Insolvency Act). The court will do so without undue delay, within seven days at the latest from when the insolvency petition was filed. If an insolvency petition does not contain all the required schedules and their particulars, the insolvency court will set a time limit for the petitioner to complete the insolvency petition; if the petition is not completed within the set time limit, the insolvency court will dismiss the petition (section 128(2) of the Insolvency Act). On the other hand, if an insolvency petition is complete, clear, and comprehensible, insolvency proceedings progress to the phase where the insolvency court decides upon the debtor's insolvency.

229. If the insolvency court concludes that the debtor is actually insolvent, it shall issue a court decision, whereby the debtor is declared insolvent (decision on insolvency). Such a decision may be, in certain situations, accompanied by the insolvency court's decision on the mode of resolving the insolvency (section 148(1) of the Insolvency Act). If this is not the case, the insolvency court shall decide how to resolve the insolvency by a separate decision within three months of the decision on insolvency (section 149(1) of the Insolvency Act).

230. Moreover, the insolvency court may reject an insolvency petition if it considers the petition unsubstantiated; the insolvency court shall always take this course of action if it deems that the insolvency petition follows an unjust interest (e.g., unfair competition practice)[64] (section 128a(1)(2) of the Insolvency Act in connection with section 142(a) of the Insolvency Act).

231. In the decision on insolvency, the insolvency court appoints an insolvency administrator. Once the decision on insolvency is issued, the debtor's creditors, if they have not already done so, may file their lodgements of receivable(s) within two months. This period is procedural and preclusive;[65] therefore, creditors who do not lodge their receivable(s) within that period lose their right to be satisfied in insolvency proceedings and their receivables may cease to exist (section 173(1) of the Insolvency Act).

232. It should be noted that most types of receivables (both secured and unsecured) have to be lodged in insolvency proceedings; otherwise, their creditors lose their right to be satisfied in the proceedings. Besides that, however, there are certain other types of receivables that follow special rules. First and foremost, there are receivables against assets and receivables equal to those against assets, which are expressly and exhaustively enumerated in the Insolvency Act (sections 168 and 169

64. In this regard it should be noted that every creditor's insolvency petition is being reviewed by the court in order to assess whether such a petition is substantiated; such a review is to be carried out within seven days as of the submission of the petition at the latest.
65. Sprinz, P., Jirmásek, T., Řeháček, O., Vrba, M., Zoubek, H. et al. Insolvenční zákon. Komentář. 1. vydání, Praha: C. H. Beck, 2019, p. 477.

of the Insolvency Act). These receivables are satisfied at any time during the insolvency proceedings after the decision on insolvency is made (within their due dates) if possible (considering the state of the assets). They include, for example, the insolvency administrator's expenses, and receivables of debtor's employees arising from their employment. There is also a category of receivables which are not satisfied in insolvency proceedings at all (section 170 of the Insolvency Act); as the name suggests, these cannot be lodged or satisfied in insolvency proceedings and include, *inter alia*, contractual penalties, the right to which accrued following the decision on insolvency. Finally, there are some other types of receivables which follow their own special rules, which include, *inter alia*, receivables for the payment of damages caused by a criminal offence.[66]

233. Furthermore, the Insolvency Act associates certain legal effects with the decision on insolvency; however, these do not differ substantially from those associated with the commencement of insolvency proceedings.[67]

234. An insolvency administrator is a person authorized to perform the activities of an insolvency administrator by virtue of a permit or a special permit issued by the Czech Ministry of Justice.[68]

235. In particular, the insolvency administrator examines lodged receivables, draws up a list thereof, and ascertains the extent of the debtor's assets. Assets represent the debtor's property from which the debtor's creditors are to be satisfied. The role of the insolvency administrator is largely dependent on the specific circumstances of the insolvency proceedings and the way in which the insolvency is settled. In any case, as the Czech Constitutional Court has ruled, the insolvency administrator represents a public interest in insolvency proceedings and is obliged to always exercise due diligence and professional care while making every effort to be fairly required to satisfy creditors to the fullest extent;[69] in the performance of his or her duties, the insolvency administrator is considered a public body sui generis. [70] Only an insolvency administrator holding a special permit can perform the role of insolvency administrator in reorganization (section 3(2) IAdm).

236. Furthermore, the insolvency administrator is empowered to challenge certain legal acts of the debtor which were executed in the period directly preceding the commencement of the insolvency proceedings or during the proceedings and takes part in incidental proceedings before the insolvency court. The right of the insolvency administrator to challenge the debtor's legal acts which were executed

66. Maršíková, J. et al. Insolvenční zákon s poznámkami, judikaturou, nařízením Evropského parlamentu a Rady (EU) č. 2015/848 a prováděcími předpisy. 3. aktualizované vydání. Praha: Leges, 2018, pp. 351–352.
67. Hásová, J., Moravec, T. a kol. Insolvenční zákon, 3. vydání. Praha: C. H. Beck, 2018, p. 503.
68. The position and rights and obligations of an insolvency administrator are regulated by Act No. 312/2006 Coll., on insolvency administrators, as amended (the 'IAdm'), besides the Insolvency Act.
69. Decision of the Czech Constitutional Court dated 13 Jul. 2010, File No. Pl. ÚS 14/10.
70. Decision of the Czech Constitutional Court dated 12 Mar. 2012, File No. IV. ÚS 3089/11; decision of the Czech Constitutional Court dated 24 Sep. 2009, File No. III. ÚS 2101/09.

prior to the insolvency proceedings relates to those acts by which the debtor reduces the possibility of satisfying creditors or favours some creditors to the detriment of others. In this way, the Insolvency Act aims to combat debtors who, prior to the commencement of the insolvency proceedings, transfer or otherwise dispose of their property so that creditors may not be satisfied therefrom. The insolvency administrator is thus entitled to challenge the debtor's acts (sections 235–243 of the Insolvency Act):

(a) for which the debtor has not received equivalent counter-performance (e.g., transferring assets without adequate consideration);
(b) by which the debtor favours some creditors to the detriment of others (e.g., satisfying a creditor's receivable prior to its maturity); and
(c) by which the debtor intentionally reduces the possibility of satisfying creditors (e.g., intentional transfers of assets to related persons).

237. The lodged receivables are examined during a review session held before the insolvency court. The purpose thereof is to review the lodged receivables so as to determine whether and in what form these creditors' (lodged) receivables shall be satisfied. Lodged receivables are first pre-reviewed by the insolvency administrator, but the final review takes place at the review session ordered and held by the insolvency court. There, the insolvency administrator, the debtor and the creditors may deny any lodged receivable as to its existence, amount and/or order. Generally, the insolvency administrator determines lodged receivables; if the debtor or creditors do not agree, they are entitled to launch an action. The insolvency court then has the final word as only it is empowered to decide upon such an action and, consequently, to ultimately determine the contested receivable. In any case, the court will decide, albeit in the first instance, during the review session.[71] Lodged receivables are only satisfied in the determined amount and in the established order.

238. It should be pointed out that, at the creditors' meeting immediately following the review session, creditors may recall the insolvency administrator appointed by the court and appoint another one of their own choosing (section 29 of the Insolvency Act).

239. After the decision of the insolvency court on the method of resolving the insolvency is made, the insolvency proceedings differentiate according to the chosen method. The Insolvency Act regulates the following modes of resolving insolvency (in the order of legal regulation) (section 4(1) of the Insolvency Act):

(a) bankruptcy;
(b) reorganization;
(c) debt discharge; and
(d) special methods of liquidating financial institutions.

---

71. Hásová, J. Moravec, T. Insolvenční řízení. Vydání druhé. Praha: C.H. Beck, 2018, pp. 121–144.

240. The order is not random; the legislator's intention was for bankruptcy and reorganization to become the basic methods of resolving insolvency[72] (which, in fact, can be said about bankruptcy, but certainly not about reorganization). Interestingly, special methods of liquidating financial institutions represent a rather special kind of bankruptcy (a modified bankruptcy) than a stand-alone mode of resolving insolvency, designed to take into account the specificities of certain types of bankruptcies and debtors (e.g., banks).[73] Finally, debt discharge is a special arrangement designated to resolve insolvency of consumers and non-entrepreneurs. It should be pointed out, as was first ruled by Czech courts[74] and later legislated, that entrepreneurs may also utilize debt discharge, but only provided that the consent of each creditor of a receivable arising out of business relations is given in advance (section 389(2) of the Insolvency Act). In comparison to the previous legislation, the Insolvency Act expanded the portfolio of ways to resolve insolvency.

241. Each mode of resolving bankruptcy is substantially different from the others. In light of the focus of this publication, the most time and effort will be dedicated to bankruptcy and reorganization. Debt discharge will only be briefly described since it is not primarily aimed at entrepreneurs but at consumers.

242. Generally, modes of resolving insolvency are divided into two separate categories: (1) liquidation modes; and (2) rescue modes. This is an international trend and, consequently, this division is observed all around the world despite the fact that it is mostly built upon an insufficient understanding of insolvency law and its goals.

243. From a macroeconomic perspective, insolvency law acts as a platform for helping economically unsuccessful entities exit from the market.[75] The ultimate goal of the liquidation modes (represented mainly by bankruptcy[76]) is to liquidate and redistribute the debtor's assets. The underlying intention is to transfer assets from an unsuccessful commercial entity to another, a more successful one so that the assets can be utilized in an effective manner on the market.[77] Sometimes, the goal is also to liquidate the debtor itself; as a general rule, the bankruptcy of a commercial entity results in the dissolution of that entity (the entity ceases to exist immediately after the insolvency proceedings end) (section 173(2) of the Civil Code). Of course, this cannot naturally be the case of insolvency of natural persons. On the

72. Explanatory memorandum to the Insolvency Act, p. 146.
73. Winterová, A., Macková, A. et al. Civilní právo procesní. Část druhá: Řízení vykonávací, řízení insolvenční. 1. vydání. Praha: Leges, 2015, p. 286. The Insolvency Act's legislation on insolvency of financial institutions is a result of transposition of Directive 2001/24/EC of the European Parliament and of the Council. Maršíková, J. et al. Insolvenční zákon s poznámkami, judikaturou, nařízením Evropského parlamentu a Rady (EU) č. 2015/848 a prováděcími předpisy. 3. aktualizované vydání. Praha: Leges, 2018, pp. 796–797.
74. Decision of the Czech Supreme Court dated 21 Apr. 2009, File No. 29 NSČR 3/2009; decision of the Czech Supreme Court dated 21 Apr. 2009, File No. 29 NSČR 3/2009; and the decision of the High Court in Prague dated 14 Jun. 2012, File No. 2 VSPH 755/2012-A-18.
75. Richter, T. Insolvenční právo. 2. vydání. Praha: Wolters Kluwer ČR, 2017, p. 93.
76. Winterová, A., Macková, A. et al. Civilní právo procesní. Část druhá: Řízení vykonávací, řízení insolvenční. 1. vydání. Praha: Leges, 2015, p. 270.
77. Richter, T. Insolvenční právo. 2. vydání. Praha: Wolters Kluwer ČR, 2017, p. 93.

other hand, the second category was invented (artificially for that matter) to encompass all the modes of resolving insolvency that lead or may lead to rescuing the company (or entrepreneur rescue) in an economic sense. Reorganization is typically named as one of these modes (certainly in the Czech landscape[78]). However, this definition is incorrect and misleading for various different reasons. First, in most (if not all) insolvency law systems, there are no modes of resolving insolvency that inevitably lead to rescuing an entrepreneur; there certainly are many modes that may, *inter alia*, lead to such a rescue but probably none that always will. This is the case of Czech reorganization: it may lead to a rescue, but it may also serve as a liquidation mode with a different set of rules with different rights for the creditors.[79]

244. Once the mode of resolving insolvency is decided upon by the insolvency court (sections 148 and 149 of the Insolvency Act), it is carried out by or under the supervision of the insolvency administrator. After the creditors are satisfied (and some closing tasks are performed), the insolvency proceedings are terminated.

245. During the proceedings, certain related disputes may arise, which are known as incidental disputes. These are disputes caused by or arising out of insolvency proceedings and are discussed during the insolvency proceedings at the insolvency court.[80] Disputes that can be considered incidental are listed exhaustively in the Insolvency Act (section 159 of the Insolvency Act). These disputes include, *inter alia*, disputes about the authenticity, amount or order of the lodged receivables.

§3. Bankruptcy

246. Bankruptcy is a basic mode of resolving insolvency (a basic liquidation method[81]) which is available to both entrepreneurs (including commercial entities) and non-entrepreneurs (including consumers). Bankruptcy presupposes that the debtor's assets are ascertained (by the insolvency administrator) and subsequently realized (monetized) and that the returns gained are redistributed among the debtor's creditors in accordance with the equal treatment of creditors principle.[82] In bankruptcy, the role of the insolvency administrator is rather strong. Consequently, the outcome of bankruptcy is heavily dependent on the insolvency administrator's activity during bankruptcy. Generally, the creditor's receivables do not cease to exist after the insolvency proceedings are terminated (unless the Insolvency Act stipulates otherwise) (section 244 of the Insolvency Act).

---

78. Kislingerová, E., Richter, T., Smrčka, L. et al. Insolvenční praxe v České republice v období 2008–2013. 1. vydání. Praha: C. H. Beck, 2013, p. 9.
79. Hásová et al. 2018, pp. 1200–1212. Kislingerová, E., Richter, T., Smrčka, L. et al. Insolvenční praxe v České republice v období 2008–2013. 1. vydání. Praha: C. H. Beck, 2013, footnote No. 4.
80. Hásová, J. Moravec, T. Insolvenční řízení. Vydání druhé. Praha: C. H. Beck, 2018, p. 105.
81. Winterová, A., Macková, A. et al. Civilní právo procesní. Část druhá: Řízení vykonávací, řízení insolvenční. 1. vydání. Praha: Leges, 2015, p. 289.
82. Hásová, J. Moravec, T. Insolvenční řízení. Vydání druhé. Praha: C. H. Beck, 2018, p. 169.

247. The main goal of bankruptcy is, therefore, to realize the debtor's assets and to redistribute the returns among the creditors.

248. The insolvency court's decision proclaiming bankruptcy on the debtor (declaration of bankruptcy) may be issued together with the insolvency decision provided that the debtor's insolvency cannot be resolved in any other way (e.g., by way of reorganization) (section 148(1) of the Insolvency Act). In other cases, the bankruptcy decision is issued within three months of the insolvency decision (section 149 of the Insolvency Act). Also, both reorganization and debt discharge may be transformed into bankruptcy in certain situations (sections 363 and 418 of the Insolvency Act). These situations generally include the debtor's inability to satisfy its debts in the estimated amount, or the debtor acting in an unlawful or illegal manner. It can be said that when other modes of resolving insolvency fail or when the debtor acted unfairly or illegally in connection with the insolvency proceedings, the insolvency court shall declare bankruptcy. The debtor may appeal the insolvency court's decision on bankruptcy.[83]

249. The insolvency court's declaration of bankruptcy is made publicly available in the Insolvency Register. Once the declaration of bankruptcy is published, certain legal effects associated therewith start to apply (section 245 of the Insolvency Act). First and foremost, the insolvency administrator acquires any and all rights to the debtor's assets and exercises any and all obligations connected to those assets (if they would be exercised by the debtor under normal circumstances) (section 246 of the Insolvency Act). This does not imply that the debtor is not legally allowed to act; however, his/her acts are ineffective towards creditors by virtue of law.[84] Furthermore, the insolvency administrator acts as an employer vis-à-vis the debtor's employees, exercises rights connected to the debtor's shares, controls the operation of the debtor's enterprise, and fulfils tax obligations on behalf of the debtor (section 246(1) of the Insolvency Act). There are various other legal effects associated with the declaration of bankruptcy, such as unilateral acts of the debtor (affecting assets) cease to apply; creditors may claim their rights only in accordance with the Insolvency Act; immature receivables become mature (unless the Insolvency Act stipulates otherwise); servitudes cease to be effective; certain types of contracts (concluded by the debtor) may be terminated or their performance rejected (by the counterparty or the insolvency administrator, as the case may be) (sections 248–260 of the Insolvency Act). Further legal effects are provided for in various other legal acts (section 262 of the Insolvency Act).[85]

250. Once bankruptcy is declared, the insolvency administrator focuses his/her activities on ascertaining, securing and listing the debtor's assets, completing the list of lodged receivables, and preparing the review meeting and the creditors' meeting

83. Decision of the Czech Supreme Court dated 23 Mar. 2011, File No. 29 NSCR 12/2011.
84. This rule constitutes a significant exception to the Insolvency Act's general rule, according to which the ineffectiveness of debtor's legal acts is can only be ascertained on the basis of an insolvency administrator's action.
85. For example, the Trade License Act (Act No. 455/1991 Coll.) sets forth in its s. 8(1) that a person cannot conduct trade if it has been declared bankrupt.

(section 277(2) of the Insolvency Act). These activities are a necessary precondition for a lawful and fair realization of assets and redistribution of returns among creditors. The insolvency administrator also executes financial statements if the debtor keeps accounting (section 277(3) of the Insolvency Act), and reports on the economic situation of the debtor (section 281 of the Insolvency Act).

251. The crucial part of bankruptcy, at least from a creditor's perspective, is the realization of assets. In bankruptcy, all the debtor's assets must be converted into cash (realized).[86] It is the insolvency administrator who carries out the realization of the debtor's assets and redistributes the proceeds therefrom among creditors in accordance with the equal treatment of creditors principle (and in accordance with the insolvency court's decisions). The list of assets entitles the insolvency administrator to realize the assets provided that the list was properly publicized in the Insolvency Register.[87]

252. The realization itself is carried out in one of the ways set forth by the Insolvency Act. Generally, assets may be realized once the declaration of bankruptcy is in force, and the first meeting of creditors takes place. There are, of course, exceptions to that rule. For example, assets immediately threatened by destruction may be realized earlier (section 283(1) of the Insolvency Act).

253. The debtor's assets may be realized in one of the following ways (section 286(1) of the Insolvency Act):

(a) sale in a public auction;
(b) sale of movable and/or immovable property pursuant to the provisions of the Civil Procedure Code on the enforcement of a decision;
(c) sale outside a public auction; and
(d) sale in an auction carried out by an executor.

254. The decision on the realization method is made by the insolvency administrator with the consent of the creditors' committee (section 286(2) of the Insolvency Act). In extreme cases, where no consent of the creditors' committee can be achieved, the insolvency court shall decide upon the realization method.[88] This decision by the insolvency court cannot be appealed.[89]

255. The first option is to realize assets in a public auction carried out pursuant to Act No. 26/2000 Coll., on public auctions, as amended (sections 286(1)(a) and 287(1) of the Insolvency Act). Before proceeding with the auction, the insolvency

86. Hásová, J., Moravec, T. a kol. Insolvenční zákon, 3. vydání. Praha: C. H. Beck, 2018, pp. 1083–1088.
87. Maršíková, J. et al. Insolvenční zákon s poznámkami, judikaturou, nařízením Evropského parlamentu a Rady (EU) č. 2015/848 a prováděcími předpisy. 3. aktualizované vydání. Praha: Leges, 2018, p. 608.
88. Hásová, J., Moravec, T. a kol. Insolvenční zákon, 3. vydání. Praha: C. H. Beck, 2018, pp. 1099–1101.
89. Decision of the High Court in Prague dated 12 Dec. 2010, File No. 1 VSPH 1036/2010-B-148.

administrator must acquire the creditors' committee's consent with the contract on the performance of auction. Until consent is given, the contract does not become effective (section 287(2) of the Insolvency Act); therefore, the contract may be negotiated and concluded first and presented for approval afterwards. Following approval, the contract becomes effective, and the auction is carried out by an auctioneer upon the proposal of the insolvency administrator. The insolvency court's consent is not required.[90] Because of its transparent nature, sale in a public auction can be described as a preferred way of realization in bankruptcy.[91]

256. The second option is to utilize the provisions of the Civil Procedure Code on the performance of a decision by means of a sale of movable and/or immovable property (sections 286(1)(b) and 288 of the Insolvency Act). The insolvency administrator proposes the sale of assets to the relevant regional court with jurisdiction. This way of realization is used in exceptional cases only as it is considered slower and less effective than a public auction.[92]

257. Third, assets may be sold outside a public auction (sections 286(1)(c) and 289 of the Insolvency Act). This is by far the most flexible way of realization among those provided for by the Insolvency Act, where the insolvency administrator concludes a sale agreement with a prospective buyer. It is also quite common in practice.[93] On the other hand, both the insolvency court and the creditors' committee must approve the sale agreement; otherwise, it will not become effective (section 289(1) of the Insolvency Act). Generally, insolvency administrators request these consents in advance; however, *ex ante* consents are also an option. Furthermore, the insolvency court may set conditions of the sale that must be observed (such as, e.g., minimum price).[94]

258. The last way of realization is a sale carried out by an executor, who is a public body (sections 286(1)(d) and 289a of the Insolvency Act). For that purpose, the insolvency administrator concludes a contract with an executor, which must be approved by the creditors' committee in order to become effective (section 289a(2) of the Insolvency Act). Once the contract becomes effective, the executor will carry out the sale upon the proposal of the insolvency administrator. The sale itself is carried out pursuant to Act No. 120/2001 Coll., Execution Code, as amended, with the subsidiary application of the Civil Procedure Code.[95]

---

90. Hásová, J. Moravec, T. Insolvenční řízení. Vydání druhé. Praha: C. H. Beck, 2018, pp. 179–181.
91. Maršíková, J. et al. Insolvenční zákon s poznámkami, judikaturou, nařízením Evropského parlamentu a Rady (EU) č. 2015/848 a prováděcími předpisy. 3. aktualizované vydání. Praha: Leges, 2018, p. 617.
92. *Ibid.*, p. 619.
93. Hásová, J., Moravec, T. a kol. Insolvenční zákon, 3. vydání. Praha: C. H. Beck, 2018, pp. 1107–1111.
94. Maršíková, J. et al. Insolvenční zákon s poznámkami, judikaturou, nařízením Evropského parlamentu a Rady (EU) č. 2015/848 a prováděcími předpisy. 3. aktualizované vydání. Praha: Leges, 2018, p. 622.
95. Hásová, J., Moravec, T. a kol. Insolvenční zákon, 3. vydání. Praha: C. H. Beck, 2018, pp. 1112–1113.

259. In addition to the four ways of realization described above, the Insolvency Act also allows for the debtor's business enterprise to be realized by a single contract of sale (section 290 of the Insolvency Act). Such a contract must be approved by both the insolvency court and the creditors' committee; otherwise, it will not become effective.[96] As in the case of a sale outside a public auction, the insolvency court may set conditions of the sale (such as, e.g., minimum price). Once the contract becomes effective, the buyer of the debtor's enterprise acquires all the rights and obligations pertaining to the sale, with the exception of those rights and obligations that arose before the effectiveness of the sale contract (section 291(1) IA).

260. Also, the realization of secured assets follows its own special rules (section 293 IA). The insolvency administrator is obliged to follow the instructions of a secured creditor as to the realization of assets secured in favour of that creditor. However, the insolvency administrator may reject such instructions if he/she believes the secured assets can be realized in a more effective manner; in that case, the insolvency administrator shall request the insolvency court to review the instructions. If certain assets are secured in favour of more than one creditor, the secured creditor whose security precedes the securities of others is the one who gives the instructions, and the others give their consent therewith; if consent is not given, the insolvency court will ultimately decide upon those instructions (whether they are to be observed or not).[97]

261. There are certain legal effects associated with the realization of assets as well. Crucially, realized assets cease to be affected by execution (enforcement) proceedings (and legal effects arising out of those proceedings), legal defects (such as, e.g., lien, prohibition to alienate, etc.) and by servitudes that are *ex lege* ineffective during bankruptcy (these servitudes also cease to exist and include such servitudes that were created under obviously disadvantageous conditions after the legal effects associated with the commencement of insolvency proceedings started to apply) (section 285 of the Insolvency Act); other servitudes remain in existence.[98]

262. To motivate insolvency administrators to realize assets in the most effective manner possible, their remuneration is calculated from the proceeds gained from the realization. Generally, insolvency administrators receive a certain fixed amount along with a percentage of the proceeds (section 1 of Decree No. 313/2007 Coll).

263. During realization, the insolvency administrator provides the insolvency court and the creditors' committee with interim reports on realization (section 300 of the Insolvency Act). At the conclusion of realization, the insolvency administrator draws up a final report and provides it to the insolvency court, which subsequently publishes the final report in the Insolvency Register (section 302 of the

96. *Ibid.*, pp. 1114–1116.
97. *Ibid.*, pp. 1121–1124.
98. Generally, servitudes under Czech law include legal instruments such as, e.g., right to access, right of passage, right to proceeds, etc.

Insolvency Act). There is no statutory period for drawing up the final report.[99] Participants in insolvency proceedings (i.e., the debtor and creditors) may then file their objections against the final report. The final report is a crucial document since it states the amount to be redistributed among creditors. For that reason, the final report is scrutinized at the insolvency court's hearing, which is ordered for that purpose (section 304 of the Insolvency Act). During this hearing, the court will deal with the objections raised and the final report itself; it may approve the final report, order its supplementation, or reject it. If the report is rejected, the insolvency court shall order the insolvency administrator to draw up a new final report within a set period of time. Along with the final report, the insolvency administrator provides the insolvency court with the billing of his/her remuneration and expenses (section 303 of the Insolvency Act). Once the final report is approved, it serves as a basis for redistributing the proceeds from the realization among creditors[100] (in accordance with the equal treatment of creditors principle).

264. After the decision of the insolvency court approving the final report comes into force, the insolvency administrator provides the insolvency court with a draft schedule decision (section 306(1) of the Insolvency Act). The insolvency court shall then review whether the draft decision is materially correct; following this review, the insolvency court shall issue its schedule decision, which states how much should be paid on each receivable that is listed in the modified list of lodged receivables (section 306(2) of the Insolvency Act). Under certain conditions, the insolvency court may also issue an interim schedule decision. In order to do so, the insolvency administrator must first propose interim redistribution to the insolvency court and the creditors' committee must give its consent to such a proposal; subsequently, the insolvency court must authorize the proposal, which it will do if certain stipulated conditions are met (such as, e.g., if the redistribution after the final report is not endangered by an interim redistribution) (section 301 of the Insolvency Act). Both the interim schedule decision and schedule decision, once issued, are delivered to the insolvency administrator, the debtor, and the creditors, all of whom may appeal the (interim) schedule decision (section 307 of the Insolvency Act). Once the schedule decision becomes effective, the returns from the realization are redistributed.

265. The redistribution itself is carried out by the insolvency administrator. The lodged and reviewed receivables of creditors are satisfied in the amount and within the period set forth by the schedule decision along with other receivables, which are considered lodged *ex lege*. All of these receivables are satisfied only after the receivables against assets and receivables equal to those against assets are satisfied (section 305 of the Insolvency Act). The time period for redistribution to be carried out cannot be longer than two months (section 307(2) of the Insolvency Act). The schedule decision shall always respect the equal treatment of creditors principle (*par conditio creditorum*).

---

99. Hásová, J., Moravec, T. a kol. Insolvenční zákon, 3. vydání. Praha: C. H. Beck, 2018, pp. 1151–1155.
100. Hásová, J. Moravec, T. Insolvenční řízení. Vydání druhé. Praha: C. H. Beck, 2018, p. 182.

266. The secured receivables are satisfied from the proceeds of realization of secured assets at any time during the insolvency proceedings provided the insolvency court's consent is given; however, the secured receivables must be satisfied before the schedule decision is made (as is the case with receivables against assets and receivables equal to those against assets).[101] If a receivable of a secured creditor is not satisfied in full, the remaining part shall be deemed to be lodged and shall be settled in the same manner as the other unsecured lodged and reviewed receivables, in accordance with the schedule decision.[102]

267. Subordinated receivables and receivables of the debtor's shareholders and members (which constitute a subgroup of subordinated receivables) and satisfaction thereof follow special rules set forth by the Insolvency Act (section 172 of the Insolvency Act). Most notably, all of these subordinated claims are satisfied only after all the other receivables (that are being satisfied in insolvency proceedings) are satisfied in full.[103]

268. Bankruptcy may be cancelled in certain specified situations and, when the court's decision on cancellation of bankruptcy comes into force, insolvency proceedings are terminated (section 309 of the Insolvency Act). The insolvency court shall cancel the bankruptcy (section 308 of the Insolvency Act):

(a) if the court finds out that the debtor's insolvency has not been certified (this does not apply if a substantial part of the assets has been realized);
(b) if there is no registered creditor and all the receivables against assets and receivables equal to those against assets are satisfied;
(c) after the insolvency administrator's report on the fulfilment of the schedule resolution is received;
(d) if it ascertains that the debtor's assets are totally inadequate to satisfy creditors;
(e) upon the debtor's petition if the debtor has attached to this petition a document on which all creditors and the insolvency administrator have consented to the cancellation of bankruptcy.

269. The insolvency court may decide on the cancellation of bankruptcy ex officio.

270. If the bankruptcy is cancelled because the assets are completely insufficient to satisfy the creditors, the cancellation of the bankruptcy is a ground for removing the debtor from the Companies Register (upon removal, the debtor ceases to exist) (section 312(3) of the Insolvency Act). If the bankruptcy is cancelled after the schedule decision is met or due to complete insufficiency of assets, the unsatisfied portion of the creditors' receivables ceases to exist (section 311 of the Insolvency Act). The cancellation of bankruptcy does not automatically entail termination of

101. *Ibid.*, pp. 184–187.
102. Hásová, J., Moravec, T. a kol. Insolvenční zákon, 3. vydání. Praha: C. H. Beck, 2018, pp. 1135–1146.
103. Hásová, J. Moravec, T. Insolvenční řízení. Vydání druhé. Praha: C. H. Beck, 2018, pp. 184–187.

the insolvency administrator's position; he/she will carry out certain tasks connected with the cancellation of bankruptcy (e.g., tax and accounting obligations – section 313 of the Insolvency Act).[104] After these tasks are fulfilled, the insolvency court shall relieve the insolvency administrator of his/her function (section 313(3) of the Insolvency Act).

271. The Insolvency Act also provides for so-called minor bankruptcy. Minor bankruptcy is not another mode of resolving insolvency, but a special subcategory of bankruptcy.[105] It represents a simplified and, therefore, less costly procedure for insolvency proceedings, where the debtor's assets situation is clear, and the number of creditors is limited. It is always up to the insolvency court to decide whether the provisions on minor bankruptcy will be applied. It shall do so of its own motion either in connection with or after the declaration of bankruptcy (section 314(2) of the Insolvency Act). The prerequisite for minor bankruptcy is that either the debtor is a non-entrepreneur or the quantitative conditions are met, which include a total turnover of up to CZK 2,000,000 in the last accounting period prior to the decision on bankruptcy and the fact that the debtor does not have more than fifty creditors (section 314(1) of the Insolvency Act). The purpose of minor bankruptcy is that since it follows a simplified procedure, insolvency proceedings are less costly and more expeditious.[106]

§4. Reorganization

272. Reorganization is a relatively new mode of resolving insolvency. The very concept of reorganization is based on the American Bankruptcy Law of the 1970s.[107] The term 'reorganization' has become part of the Czech insolvency dictionary only after the adoption of the Insolvency Act, whose authors were inspired by the federal insolvency law of the USA and by certain European legislation (mainly German and Austrian).[108] Although the Czech legislation is not a mere transcription of US law, a number of provisions of the Insolvency Act have been directly transcribed from it.[109] When drafting the provisions on reorganization, the Czech legislators' intention was to create, in addition to bankruptcy, another basic mode of resolving insolvency, designed for entrepreneurs and based on the company-rescue principle, which would simultaneously enable and support the active role of creditors (by strengthening their rights).[110]

104. *Ibid.*, p. 190.
105. Hásová, J., Moravec, T. a kol. Insolvenční zákon, 3. vydání. Praha: C. H. Beck, 2018, pp. 1194–1196.
106. Said simplified procedure is provided for in s. 315 IA.
107. Winterová, A., Macková, A. et al. Civilní právo procesní. Část druhá: Řízení vykonávací, řízení insolvenční. 1. vydání. Praha: Leges, 2015, p. 291.
108. Explanatory memorandum to the Insolvency Act, p. 216.
109. Richter, T. Insolvenční právo. 2. vydání. Praha: Wolters Kluwer ČR, 2017, p. 460.
110. Explanatory memorandum to the Insolvency Act, p. 146.

273. The main goal of reorganization is to rescue the debtor (in an economic sense) by means of special measures which result in the debtor subsequently being able to continue its business unless a different effect of reorganization is envisaged (such as, e.g., gradual sale of the debtor's assets) (section 316 of the Insolvency Act).

274. Based on the processes that underline the reorganization, we can divide reorganizations into Sale Reorganization and Equity Reorganization. As part of a Sale Reorganization, the debtor's business is sold or otherwise taken over, and the creditors are satisfied by the proceeds of such transfer to a new investor (or one of the creditors).[111] The purpose of a Sale Reorganization is to save the debtor's business (under the new owner), not the debtor itself. Equity Reorganization assumes the entry of new capital, usually at the expense of the original owners in the business corporation losing their positions.[112] The purpose of Equity Reorganization is to save the debtor itself (not only its business) under a new capital structure. We can also distinguish Combined Reorganization; as the name suggests, it combines elements of both a Sale and Equity Reorganization.

275. Reorganization is generally understood to mean the gradual satisfaction of creditors' receivables while maintaining the operation of the debtor's business, which is secured by measures to rescue the debtor's business according to a reorganization plan approved by the insolvency court (section 316(1) IA). Since reorganization is primarily intended to enable creditors to decide upon the best way to resolve the debtor's insolvency,[113] creditors are expected to be more actively involved (as opposed to bankruptcy and debt discharge) as they are responsible for negotiating the reorganization plan and its outcome. An unwritten prerequisite for reorganization is the economic viability of the debtor's business, which makes reorganization an exceptional rather than a dominant (or, in the words of the legislators, basic) mode of resolving insolvency.[114]

276. Reorganization is only available to debtors who are entrepreneurs and concerns a business enterprise (section 316(2) of the Insolvency Act). There are some types of entrepreneurs, however, who are by virtue of law ineligible for reorganization (e.g., stockbrokers) (sections 6 and 316(3) IA). The Insolvency Act also prohibits reorganization of financial institutions whose insolvency is being resolved separately under special rules.[115]

---

111. Maršíková, J. et al. Insolvenční zákon s poznámkami, judikaturou, nařízením Evropského parlamentu a Rady (EU) č. 2015/848 a prováděcími předpisy. 3. aktualizované vydání. Praha: Leges, 2018, p. 676.
112. Kozák J., Brož, J. Dadam A., Stanislav A., Strnad Z., Zrůst L., Žižlavský M. Insolvenční zákon. Komentář. 5. vydání. Praha: Wolters Kluwer ČR, 2019, pp. 1163–1164.
113. Richter, T. Insolvenční právo. 2. vydání. Praha: Wolters Kluwer ČR, 2017, pp. 459–460.
114. Maršíková, J. et al. Insolvenční zákon s poznámkami, judikaturou, nařízením Evropského parlamentu a Rady (EU) č. 2015/848 a prováděcími předpisy. 3. aktualizované vydání. Praha: Leges, 2018, p. 675.
115. *Ibid.*, p. 677.

277. A basic condition for proposing reorganization (its permissibility) is the size of the debtor's business (quantitative test or quantitative gateway of the reorganization). Reorganization is generally available to debtors whose total annual net turnover in the last financial year preceding the insolvency petition amounted to at least CZK 50,000,000, or (alternatively) who employ at least fifty employees. It is sufficient if the debtor meets one of the criteria (section 316(4) of the Insolvency Act). The quantitative test is applied in relation to each debtor individually; concern groups are not taken into account in any way.[116] It should be pointed out that compliance with at least one of the conditions of the quantitative test does not in itself guarantee that the insolvency court will authorize (approve) the reorganization; it merely gives the debtor the right to propose reorganization. If the debtor meets the quantitative test (alternatively at least one criterion), the insolvency court shall decide on the debtor's insolvency and leave the decision on how to resolve it up to the first creditors' meeting following the insolvency decision (section 149 of the Insolvency Act).

278. However, the Insolvency Act regulates the conditions under which the quantitative test is not applied. Reorganization is permissible if the debtor submits, together with the insolvency petition or, by the time the insolvency decision is issued, a reorganization plan which has been accepted by at least half of the secured and half of the unsecured creditors calculated according to the amount of their receivables (section 316(5) of the Insolvency Act). Debtors who do not meet the criteria of the quantitative test are thus offered the opportunity to pre-negotiate reorganization with creditors. Hence, this type of reorganization is called pre-negotiated reorganization.[117] Debtors may also request the prolongment of this period for up to thirty days after the insolvency decision is issued, provided the insolvency petition was filed by a creditor (section 316(6) of the Insolvency Act). For debtors who fail the quantitative test, the adopted reorganization plan is an obligatory precondition for permitting the reorganization.

279. A petition for reorganization may be filed by the debtor until the insolvency decision is issued (or until the prolonged period) or by the creditor up to ten days before the first creditors' meeting following the insolvency decision (section 317 of the Insolvency Act). Where reorganization is possible, the insolvency decision cannot at the same time declare bankruptcy on the debtor because, as explained, the creditor may also file a petition for reorganization. There is a simple general rule: if another mode of resolving insolvency is available, the insolvency court shall not decide upon the mode of resolving insolvency until the first creditors' meeting following the insolvency decision. The creditor's petition for reorganization must be approved by the creditors' meeting; it may do so only after the insolvency administrator's report on the debtor's economic situation (section 323 of the Insolvency Act).

---

116. Richter, T. Insolvenční právo. 2. vydání. Praha: Wolters Kluwer ČR, 2017, p. 471.
117. Decision of the High Court in Prague, File No. 1 VSPH 837/2010-B-16.

280. When filing a petition for reorganization, the petition must always include the general requirements of filing provided for in the Civil Procedure Code (section 42(4) of Act. No. 99/1964 Coll., the Civil Procedure Code, as amended) and the special requirements of the Insolvency Act (section 319 of the Insolvency Act). The petition must always identify the debtor, identify the persons authorized to act on behalf of the debtor, and contain details of the proposed reorganization. If a debtor files an application, he/she must also provide the insolvency court with known information on its capital structure and assets of the persons controlling the debtor or forming a group with the debtor, including whether any insolvency proceedings in respect of these persons are in progress (or, as the case may be, that there are no such persons). Furthermore, the debtor must submit a list of assets, a list of liabilities and, where appropriate, a statement of changes to the data contained in the lists already submitted. The creditor may also provide this information if known to him/her, but this is not his/her obligation.

281. From the moment the petition for reorganization is submitted, certain restrictions start to apply. The persons authorized to dispose of the assets (i.e., in principle, the debtor) are obliged to refrain from legal acts that could endanger or thwart the proposed reorganization (section 324(1) of the Insolvency Act). Typically, this may be the termination of the debtor's contractual relations.[118] Such conduct may only take place with the prior consent of the insolvency court.[119]

282. As regards the petition for reorganization, the insolvency court may decide to dismiss the petition (a procedural decision due to, for example, missing requirements), or reject the petition, take note of the petition withdrawal, or allow the reorganization (a decision on merits). If, at the same time, the debtor submits as the insolvency petition a reorganization plan approved by at least half of the unsecured and secured creditors (pre-negotiated reorganization), the insolvency court shall issue an insolvency decision (declaring insolvency) and a decision on the mode of resolving the insolvency (allowing reorganization), provided the debtor is a person eligible for reorganization (section 148(2) IA). If there is no dismissal, refusal or withdrawal of the petition for reorganization, the insolvency court shall allow the reorganization (there is no room for judicial discretion) (section 328 of the Insolvency Act).

283. If the petition is rejected or dismissed by a decision of the insolvency court, the petitioner may appeal (section 320(3) IA and section 326(3) of the Insolvency Act). On the other hand, if the decision of the insolvency court allows reorganization, an appeal is not admissible (section 328 of the Insolvency Act).

284. A prerequisite for allowing reorganization is that the petition for reorganization must have an honest intention. The insolvency court is obliged to reject the

---

118. Hásová, J., Moravec, T. a kol. Insolvenční zákon, 3. vydání. Praha: C. H. Beck, 2018, pp. 1228–1230.
119. Kozák J., Brož, J. Dadam A., Stanislav A., Strnad Z., Zrůst L., Žižlavský M. Insolvenční zákon. Komentář. 5. vydání. Praha: Wolters Kluwer ČR, 2019, p. 1201.

petition for reorganization if it can reasonably be assumed that the petition pursues a dishonest intention (such as, e.g., favouring some of the creditors). This condition reflects the legal principle of *nemo turpitudinem suam allegare potest* (i.e., no one may benefit from his/her dishonest act).[120]

285. The legal effects of the reorganization start to apply when the decision allowing the reorganization is published in the Insolvency Register (section 89(1) of the Insolvency Act). Once such a decision comes into force, any restrictions on the debtor's rights to assets (whether by virtue of law or decision of the insolvency court) automatically expire (section 330(1) of the Insolvency Act). The purpose of restoring the debtor's right to its assets is to bring the debtor's situation closer to how it was prior to insolvency.[121] However, nothing prevents the insolvency court from issuing an interim measure whereby it restricts the debtor in disposing of its assets.[122] Even if the debtor has rights over its assets after the reorganization has been allowed, it can still make legal acts of fundamental importance (in terms of assets) only with the prior approval of the creditors' committee; breaching this obligation activates the debtor's liability for damage or other harm (and the members of the debtor's statutory body are liable jointly and severally for such damage or harm) (section 330(2) IA). Furthermore, there are some other restrictions that start to apply, which are connected to certain types of contracts. For the duration of reorganization, the debtor exercises certain rights that the insolvency administrator would have exercised in bankruptcy only with the prior consent of the creditors' committee (section 330a of the Insolvency Act).

286. After the reorganization has been allowed by the insolvency court, the insolvency administrator supervises the debtor's activities, supervises the identification and inventory of assets, and compiles and complements the list of creditors and reports to the creditors' committee (section 331 IA). In addition, he/she also performs other tasks and activities assigned to him/her by the insolvency court or by the Insolvency Act. In that connection, the insolvency administrator performs the function of the debtor's general meeting (section 333(1) of the Insolvency Act). Nevertheless, the insolvency administrator is not entitled to appoint or elect and recall members of the debtor's statutory body and the debtor's supervisory board. This right remains with the shareholders; however, the approval of the creditors' committee is required (section 333(2) of the Insolvency Act).

287. The debtor, if it is a natural person or the statutory body of the debtor, if the debtor is a legal person, has the obligations and responsibilities of the insolvency administrator once the reorganization is allowed (if the debtor is an insolvency petitioner, then from the moment of filing the insolvency petition) (section

120. Decision of the Czech Supreme Court dated 13 Jun. 2018, File No. 29 NSČR 92/2016; Decision of the Czech Constitutional Court dated 28 Nov. 2017, File No. III. ÚS 2849/17.

121. Maršíková, J. et al. Insolvenční zákon s poznámkami, judikaturou, nařízením Evropského parlamentu a Rady (EU) č. 2015/848 a prováděcími předpisy. 3. aktualizované vydání. Praha: Leges, 2018, p. 710.

122. Kozák J., Brož, J. Dadam A., Stanislav A., Strnad Z., Zrůst L., Žižlavský M. Insolvenční zákon. Komentář. 5. vydání. Praha: Wolters Kluwer ČR, 2019, p. 1219.

229(5) of the Insolvency Act in connection with sections 36 and 37 IA). At this stage, the debtor becomes bound by the fiduciary obligations towards creditors (instead of its shareholders).[123]

288. In the case of reorganization, the Insolvency Act modifies the general rights of creditors as participants in insolvency proceedings. Therefore, only registered creditors, as well as creditors of receivables against assets and creditors of receivables equal to those against assets, are involved in the reorganization (section 334 of the Insolvency Act). The debtor's shareholders and members are also considered to be the debtor's creditors, and their receivables include the rights arising from their participation in the debtor (section 335(1) of the Insolvency Act).

289. For the purposes of determining the extent of satisfaction of receivables and of the creditors' vote on a reorganization plan, creditors are divided into groups in such a way that the creditors in each group have substantially the same legal status and economic interests (section 337 of the Insolvency Act). How the creditors will be divided into individual groups, including the criteria according to which the division is made, is included in the reorganization plan. The proposer of the reorganization plan divides the creditors into groups. Each secured creditor, the shareholders and members of the debtor, and the creditors whose claims are not affected by the reorganization plan must constitute a separate group.[124] This does not preclude the formation of additional groups. If a debtor's creditor has more than one receivable, he/she may be a member of more than one group, while he/she can vote in each group only in relation to the claim giving rise to his/her group membership.[125]

290. Each individual secured creditor forms a separate group (with some exceptions[126]), with the secured creditor's receivable being included in the value of the collateral (section 167(3) of the Insolvency Act). There is a simple equation: how many are secured creditors, as many are groups of secured creditors.

291. Upon the proposal of the creditor identified in the reorganization plan or the proposer, the insolvency court may test the creditors' division into groups in order to assess its appropriateness.[127] On the basis of such a proposal, the insolvency court is entitled to assign creditors to another group (section 330(6) of the Insolvency Act) or to create a new group of creditors altogether.[128]

---

123. Richter, T. Insolvenční právo. 2. vydání. Praha: Wolters Kluwer ČR, 2017, p. 482.
124. Hásová, J. Moravec, T. Insolvenční řízení. Vydání druhé. Praha: C. H. Beck, 2018, pp. 204–205.
125. Maršíková, J. et al. Insolvenční zákon s poznámkami, judikaturou, nařízením Evropského parlamentu a Rady (EU) č. 2015/848 a prováděcími předpisy. 3. aktualizované vydání. Praha: Leges, 2018, p. 724.
126. Some Czech scholars argue that secured creditors whose security has the same seniority order (e.g., based on an agreement), such secured creditors should be assigned to the same group. *See* Richter, T. Insolvenční právo. 2. vydání. Praha: Wolters Kluwer ČR, 2017, p. 500.
127. Kozák J., Brož, J. Dadam A., Stanislav A., Strnad Z., Zrůst L., Žižlavský M. Insolvenční zákon. Komentář. 5. vydání. Praha: Wolters Kluwer ČR, 2019, p. 1246.
128. Decision of the High Court in Olomouc dated 12 Nov. 2012, File No. 36 INS 4962/2010.

292. The reorganization agreement, referred to by the Insolvency Act as the reorganization plan, is an essential component of every reorganization, as it regulates the status of the persons affected by the reorganization, based on measures to rescue the debtor's business (if any) and to arrange the relationships between the creditors and debtor (section 338(1) of the Insolvency Act). These measures are listed in the Insolvency Act only by demonstration (sections 316 and 347 of the Insolvency Act). Thus, other measures may be proposed. The reorganization plan defines not only the manner of implementation and rules of reorganization but also the extent to which the creditors are satisfied, the constraints and role of the debtor's statutory body and supervisory body (if any), and the relationship between the debtor and its shareholders.[129] The reorganization plan should be thorough and accurate, and it should include relevant, clearly formulated, and objectively controllable compliance conditions. It can be said that the reorganization plan is a contract sui generis.[130]

293. The reorganization plan is submitted to the insolvency court. Once the reorganization plan is submitted, no person shall engage in any activity aiming to accept or reject the reorganization plan, and the petitioner must refrain from activities that conflict with or affect its fulfilment (section 338(2) of the Insolvency Act).

294. In the pre-negotiated reorganization, the reorganization plan is always submitted by the debtor. In all other cases, the debtor has the priority right to submit the reorganization plan within 120 days of the authorization of the reorganization, even if the creditor filed the insolvency petition (this period can be prolonged up to 360 days) (section 339 of the Insolvency Act). However, the debtor loses its priority right to submit the reorganization plan if the creditors' meeting so decides by a simple majority of the creditors present (according to the amount of their receivables) or the debtor waives its priority right. The creditors' meeting may also designate a person who has the right to submit the reorganization plan. Furthermore, the insolvency court may, on application or ex officio, decide to shorten or terminate the period for submitting the reorganization plan.

295. The reorganization plan is a comprehensive document by which the reorganization is run. It is, therefore, imperative that all the information contained therein accurately reflects the debtor's legal and economic reality (section 340(3) of the Insolvency Act). A fundamental element of the reorganization plan is the way the reorganization is carried out. The Insolvency Act demonstratively sets out seven

129. Maršíková, J. et al. Insolvenční zákon s poznámkami, judikaturou, nařízením Evropského parlamentu a Rady (EU) č. 2015/848 a prováděcími předpisy. 3. aktualizované vydání. Praha: Leges, 2018, p. 727.
130. Kozák J., Brož, J. Dadam A., Stanislav A., Strnad Z., Zrůst L., Žižlavský M. Insolvenční zákon. Komentář. 5. vydání. Praha: Wolters Kluwer ČR, 2019, p. 1260.

methods to reorganize; the reorganization plan may, however, resort to a combination of the methods listed in the Insolvency Act or use a different method altogether. In practice, there is almost always a need for a combination of several different methods.[131] Here, the Insolvency Act acts as an inspiration rather than a mandatory guideline.[132]

296. The methods of carrying out the reorganization listed in the Insolvency Act include (section 341(1) of the Insolvency Act):

(a) restructuring the creditors' receivables;
(b) sale of all or part of the assets or sale of the debtor's business as a whole;
(c) transfer of the debtor's assets to the creditor or a newly incorporated legal entity in which the creditors participate;
(d) merger of a debtor or transfer of assets to a shareholder;
(e) issuance of shares or other securities;
(f) ensuring the financing of the operation of the business enterprise or part thereof; and
(g) amendment to the foundation deed, articles of association, or other document regulating the debtor's internal circumstances.

297. Although the Insolvency Act assumes that rescue measures are included in the reorganization plan, in practice, there are frequent cases where the debtor's business is sold according to the conditions set out in the reorganization plan (Sale Reorganization).[133] Simply, the reorganization plan is a set of economic measures designed to ensure the highest and essentially proportional satisfaction of creditors. Without exaggeration, the reorganization plan can be described as a reorganization project.[134]

298. Along with the reorganization plan, its proposer is also obliged to submit a report containing sufficient information on the draft reorganization plan, including the plan itself or a summary thereof, as well as an assessment of its impact on creditors (section 343 of the Insolvency Act).

299. The particular requirements that the reorganization plan and the aforementioned report must fulfil are further provided for in Decree No. 191/2017 Coll.

300. The creditors discuss and ultimately vote on the reorganization plan at the creditors' meeting that is convened for this purpose only, voting by group as divided in the reorganization plan (section 344(1) of the Insolvency Act). If the reorganization plan is adopted by voting outside the creditors' meeting (and provided that

---

131. Hásová, J., Moravec, T. a kol. Insolvenční zákon, 3. vydání. Praha: C. H. Beck, 2018, p. 1260.
132. Maršíková, J. et al. Insolvenční zákon s poznámkami, judikaturou, nařízením Evropského parlamentu a Rady (EU) č. 2015/848 a prováděcími předpisy. 3. aktualizované vydání. Praha: Leges, 2018, p. 736.
133. *Ibid.*, p. 727.
134. Kozák J., Brož, J. Dadam A., Stanislav A., Strnad Z., Zrůst L., Žižlavský M. Insolvenční zákon. Komentář. 5. vydání. Praha: Wolters Kluwer ČR, 2019, p. 1249.

each group of creditors has voted), the insolvency court may not convene the creditors' meeting or cancel an already convened meeting; however, this procedure is only possible once the circle of creditors is known, that is to say, after the expiry of the period for lodging receivables.[135]

301. When voting to adopt a reorganization plan, a group of creditors is deemed to have voted in favour of the plan if the majority of creditors in the group whose receivables constitute at least half of the total nominal value of all voting creditors within that group have voted so (section 347(1) of the Insolvency Act).[136] A quorum is, therefore, constituted by only those creditors who actively participate in voting.[137] A group of creditors whose claims are not affected by the reorganization plan shall be regarded as having voted in favour of the reorganization plan (section 347(2) of the Insolvency Act).

302. The reorganization plan should, in theory, be adopted by each group of creditors (or there should be an acceptance fiction). If this does not happen, the next step depends on the proposer: he/she can either propose an amendment to the reorganization plan or propose to the insolvency court to approve the plan anyway.[138] After the creditors' vote, the fate of the reorganization plan lies in the hands of the insolvency court. The insolvency court shall approve the proposed reorganization plan provided that (section 348(1) of the Insolvency Act):

(a) it complies with the Insolvency Act and other legal regulations;
(b) it does not pursue a dishonest intention with regard to all circumstances;
(c) it has been accepted by each creditors group;
(d) each creditor will receive satisfaction which, on the effective date of the plan, is at least equal to or greater than the value he/she would likely receive under bankruptcy unless the creditor agrees to lower satisfaction (so-called best interest test[139]); and
(e) the receivables against assets and receivable equal to those against assets were paid or are due to be settled immediately after the plan becomes effective unless otherwise agreed between the debtor and the creditors.

---

135. Hásová, J. Moravec, T. Insolvenční řízení. Vydání druhé. Praha: C. H. Beck, 2018, pp. 206–218.
136. However, a group of creditors constituted by the debtor's members or shareholders have voted in favour of the reorganization plan only if a majority of such creditors voted so; if the debtor has a registered capital, the group has voted in favour of the reorganization plan if the majority of creditors represent at least two-thirds of the debtor's registered capital. *See* s. 347(2) IA.
137. Maršíková, J. et al. Insolvenční zákon s poznámkami, judikaturou, nařízením Evropského parlamentu a Rady (EU) č. 2015/848 a prováděcími předpisy. 3. aktualizované vydání. Praha: Leges, 2018, p. 749.
138. Richter, T. Insolvenční právo. 2. vydání. Praha: Wolters Kluwer ČR, 2017, p. 510.
139. The best interest test lies upon the foundation that reorganization should, in principle, provide to creditors at least the same position (satisfaction) as in bankruptcy. Richter, T. Insolvenční právo. 2. vydání. Praha: Wolters Kluwer ČR, 2017, pp. 508–509; Decision of the High Court in Prague dated 7 Oct. 2011, File No. MSPH 94 INS 7917/2009 3 VSPH 835/2011-B-269.

303. It is imperative to point out that the insolvency court may also approve a reorganization plan that has not been approved by each group of creditors but otherwise fulfils other conditions (including the best interest test) if the reorganization plan (section 348(2) of the Insolvency Act):

(a) was adopted by at least one group of creditors other than the debtor's shareholders;
(b) ensures equal treatment of each receivable within each group of creditors that has not adopted it;
(c) is fair to any and all groups that have not adopted it; and
(d) will not lead to another insolvency of the debtor or its liquidation, unless liquidation is foreseen by the reorganization plan.

304. The Insolvency Act does not leave the term 'fair' to the discretion of the judge but defines it in relation to individual groups of creditors who have not accepted the plan. In principle, the measure of fairness is the value of future satisfaction of creditors, which is, however, a subjective and estimation-based measure.[140]

305. If the conditions above are met, the insolvency court shall approve the reorganization plan, and if not, the court shall reject it (section 351 of the Insolvency Act). A person whose plan has been rejected may resubmit the plan if the submission deadline has not expired. In justified cases, the deadline may be extended in a decision rejecting the reorganization plan (section 351(3) of the Insolvency Act). If the reorganization plan is approved, only those creditors who have voted against it may appeal. If the insolvency court rejects the plan, only the debtor, the plan proposer, or the creditor who voted in favour of the plan may appeal (section 351(2) of the Insolvency Act).

306. The reorganization plan becomes effective once the decision approving it comes into force unless the approved plan or the insolvency court sets a later effective date (section 352(1) of the Insolvency Act). The decision approving the reorganization plan is binding on all participants in the insolvency proceedings and on other persons whose rights and obligations are affected by the reorganization plan (section 352(2) of the Insolvency Act).

307. From the effective date of the reorganization plan, the debtor regains rights to assets unless it is restricted by the plan to the benefit of other persons, and at the same time, all other restrictions imposed on the debtor are cancelled (section 353(1)

---

140. Hásová, J., Moravec, T. a kol. Insolvenční zákon, 3. vydání. Praha: C. H. Beck, 2018, pp. 1273–1274.

of the Insolvency Act). Furthermore, all of the debtor's economic activities are carried out according to an approved reorganization plan. Any limitation on the debtor's rights may be imposed only by the reorganization plan.[141] This scheme is valid until the reorganization ends (in any way). Again, an effort to normalize the debtor's economic life is rather obvious. However, at this stage of the insolvency proceedings, the debtor's statutory body should act in the interest of the creditors.[142] Also, the function of the general meeting or the member's meeting of the debtor is renewed, and the reorganization plan shall determine the conditions of voting in these bodies (section 353(2) of the Insolvency Act). If the reorganization plan changes the foundation deed, articles of association, or other documents regulating the internal circumstances of the debtor, these changes come into effect when the plan becomes effective. The reorganization plan serves as a basis for entering changes in the Companies Register (section 353(3) of the Insolvency Act).

308. Most importantly, the effectiveness of the plan results in the remediation (rescue) effect of reorganization: the receivables of the creditors cease to exist, and the persons specified in the reorganization plan are deemed to be the creditors of the debtor under the conditions specified therein, including the extent of their rights (section 356(1) of the Insolvency Act). The existing creditors' rights are, therefore, replaced by the rights under the approved plan. The rights of creditors that have not been lodged in the insolvency proceedings or are not identified by the plan also expire. For this reason, the accuracy of the reorganization plan is essential, and it also should identify the preferred and intact receivables.[143] Similarly, receivables that are not settled in the insolvency proceedings (with the exception of non-contractual sanctions) shall also cease to exist unless the plan provides otherwise (section 359 of the Insolvency Act). This rule allows the proposer of the plan to include creditors who are not satisfied in the insolvency proceedings, for example, in exchange for a vote for the plan at the creditors' meeting.[144] Moreover, the rights of third parties to assets cease to exist, and the rights of third parties arise to the extent described in the reorganization plan, which also affects the assets to be attributed to a person other than the debtor (section 356(2) of the Insolvency Act).[145] The reorganization plan is, therefore, a legal title for the creation, modification or termination of rights of third parties. The approval of the reorganization plan also changes the credit financing regime of the debtor, which follows its own special

141. Maršíková, J. et al. Insolvenční zákon s poznámkami, judikaturou, nařízením Evropského parlamentu a Rady (EU) č. 2015/848 a prováděcími předpisy. 3. aktualizované vydání. Praha: Leges, 2018, p. 766.
142. Richter, T. Insolvenční právo. 2. vydání. Praha: Wolters Kluwer ČR, 2017, p. 522.
143. *Ibid.*, pp. 516–517.
144. Maršíková, J. et al. Insolvenční zákon s poznámkami, judikaturou, nařízením Evropského parlamentu a Rady (EU) č. 2015/848 a prováděcími předpisy. 3. aktualizované vydání. Praha: Leges, 2018, p. 774.
145. It is questionable whether all the rights of third parties to assets cease to exist since, as some Czech scholars argue, such an interpretation of s. 356 IA is likely unconstitutional. *See* Hásová, J. Moravec, T. Insolvenční řízení. Vydání druhé. Praha: C. H. Beck, 2018, pp. 206–2018. *See also* Richter, T. Insolvenční právo. 2. vydání. Praha: Wolters Kluwer ČR, 2017, p. 521.

rules (a receivable arising out of credit financing has the status of a preferred receivable) (section 357 of the Insolvency Act). On the other hand, the rights of creditors against co-debtors and guarantors are not affected in any way (section 356(3) of the Insolvency Act).

309. The role of the insolvency administrator in the reorganization is fundamentally different from that in bankruptcy. After the reorganization plan is approved, the insolvency administrator continues his/her previous activities, but he/she is further assigned to a support and supervisory role (section 354 of the Insolvency Act). The insolvency administrator shall ensure that the procedural steps associated with the effectiveness of the reorganization plan are carried out and that the debtor can exercise its rights to the assets. In addition, the insolvency administrator exercises the obligations laid down in the reorganization plan. If the debtor has rights to assets, it is obliged to inform the insolvency administrator about the fulfilment of the reorganization plan, its legal acts and other activities according to the plan. It further informs on common or recurring activities regularly in the time periods specified by the reorganization plan or the decision of the insolvency court.

310. The creditors' committee may control the debtor with the rights to assets in the manner determined by the reorganization plan and on the basis of the reports of the insolvency administrator (section 355(1) of the Insolvency Act). The insolvency administrator shall also inform the creditors' committee of his/her activities. A simple equation applies: if the creditors' control mechanism is not provided for in the reorganization plan, then the creditors have waived their right to control the debtor.[146] In addition, the creditors' committee may reserve in advance that some legal acts of the debtor which are of fundamental importance may be carried out by the debtor only with its prior consent, even if such a restriction is not included in the reorganization plan (section 355(2) of the Insolvency Act). If the creditors' committee finds deficiencies, it may propose measures to the insolvency court to remedy them (section 355(3) of the Insolvency Act).

311. Generally, once the reorganization plan is in force (i.e., approved by the court), the insolvency court's role is limited; it should interfere with the ongoing reorganization only minimally and should limit its activities to the hearing of notifications, complaints, requests submitted and to reviewing the reports on reorganization.[147]

312. During the reorganization, it may prove appropriate to modify the mechanism of reorganization. It is, therefore, possible for the proposer of the plan to propose an amendment to an already-approved reorganization plan so as to make the reorganization's objective(s) more achievable (section 361(1) of the Insolvency Act). The procedure of approving an amendment to a reorganization plan after it is

---

146. Hásová, J., Moravec, T. a kol. Insolvenční zákon, 3. vydání. Praha: C. H. Beck, 2018, p. 1280.
147. Maršíková, J. et al. Insolvenční zákon s poznámkami, judikaturou, nařízením Evropského parlamentu a Rady (EU) č. 2015/848 a prováděcími předpisy. 3. aktualizované vydání. Praha: Leges, 2018, p. 785.

effective is similar to the procedure of its approval. The same rules for voting apply as for voting on the reorganization plan, including the dividing of creditors into groups. However, the consent of all groups of old and new creditors (in principle, also those who originally voted against the reorganization plan) is required, and the insolvency court cannot approve the change despite the disagreement of a group of creditors.[148] Another significant modification is that if the creditor has not voted on the change either by the set deadline or at the hearing, the creditor is deemed to agree with the proposed change (section 361(5) of the Insolvency Act). The insolvency court has the final say and shall approve an amendment if the Insolvency Act's conditions are met (there is no room for discretion).

313. Reorganization may be terminated in several ways (including by successful completion of the reorganization plan).

314. First, if an illegal activity in connection with the reorganization plan comes to the surface, the insolvency court shall revoke the decision approving the reorganization plan (within six months or three years of the plan becoming effective, as the case may be) (section 362 of the Insolvency Act). If the decision approving the reorganization plan is revoked, the rights of the creditors that existed before its approval are restored, and the rights of creditors and third parties established by the reorganization plan remain intact.

315. Sometimes, despite the best of intentions and endeavours, it will be necessary to conclude that reorganization is not an appropriate or even possible solution to a particular debtor's insolvency. In that case, there will be no solution except bankruptcy. The insolvency court is, therefore, empowered to decide to convert the reorganization into bankruptcy even ex officio if it becomes aware of the reasons for the conversion into bankruptcy. These reasons are mainly provided for in the Insolvency Act (section 363(1) of the Insolvency Act). However, the insolvency court may not convert reorganization into bankruptcy if the reorganization plan has already been met in substantial parts (section 363(4) of the Insolvency Act). The insolvency court shall decide to convert the reorganization into bankruptcy if, for example, the insolvency court did not approve the reorganization plan and the time period to propose the reorganization plan already lapsed, or the debtor fails to fulfil its essential obligations following the effectiveness of the reorganization plan, or it becomes apparent that a substantial part of the plan cannot be met.

316. Of course, the best option that can occur after approval of the reorganization plan is that it is fulfilled. During the implementation of the reorganization plan, the insolvency court takes note of the reports of the insolvency administrator and the creditors' committee on its performance and is entitled to impose measures to ensure compliance with the reorganization plan, but only if they are proposed to it

148. Hásová, J., Moravec, T. a kol. Insolvenční zákon, 3. vydání. Praha: C. H. Beck, 2018, p. 1285. Maršíková, J. et al. Insolvenční zákon s poznámkami, judikaturou, nařízením Evropského parlamentu a Rady (EU) č. 2015/848 a prováděcími předpisy. 3. aktualizované vydání. Praha: Leges, 2018, pp. 777–778.

(section 364(1) of the Insolvency Act). The Insolvency Act does not require the reorganization plan to be met in full. Hence, it is completely sufficient if its essential parts are fulfilled; these are interpreted by the insolvency court with regard to the specific circumstances of the case and the form of the reorganization plan (i.e., on a case-by-case basis).

317. If the reorganization plan is fulfilled (in whole or in substantial parts), the insolvency court will take note of its fulfilment by a decision terminating the reorganization, against which an appeal is not admissible, and which terminates the entire insolvency proceedings (section 364(3) of the Insolvency Act). Upon completion of the reorganization and insolvency proceedings, the insolvency court shall decide on the amount of the insolvency administrator's remuneration and reimbursement (section 364(4) of the Insolvency Act).

§5. Debt Discharge

318. Debt discharge is a mode of resolving insolvency that is primarily intended for consumers. Originally, it was intended exclusively for consumers and legal entities that are not entrepreneurs, but over time, Czech courts ruled that persons who are entrepreneurs may also be subject to debt discharge under certain conditions, which are now expressly reflected by the Insolvency Act.[149]

319. Natural persons who are entrepreneurs may be subject to debt discharge on the condition that every creditor of the debtor's debt arising out of entrepreneurship has expressly consented to debt discharge. This general rule is not without exceptions; for example, secured creditors of debts arising out of entrepreneurship need not consent. The same condition applies to legal entities (non-entrepreneurs) who do have a debt arising out of entrepreneurship.[150]

320. The purpose of debt discharge is that, if the specified conditions are met (e.g., eligibility, etc.) and at least part of the debt is satisfied, a substantial part of the debtor's debts will cease to exist.[151] This will, in turn, allow a higher level of satisfaction for the creditors and at the same time, the return of the debtor to active economic life. Before 2019, the debtors' satisfaction could not be lower than 30%; however, this rule was breached by an amendment to the Insolvency Act,[152] and the debtors may not need to repay at least 30% of their debts, provided they exercised all efforts which can be justly required to repay their debts (and the insolvency court has not terminated debt discharge) (section 412a(1) of the Insolvency Act).

---

149. These conditions are laid down in s. 389(2) IA.
150. For example, an association (a legal entity under Czech civil law which is not a business corporation) may conduct business as its secondary activity and, thus, may have debts arising out of entrepreneurship.
151. Winterová, A., Macková, A. et al. Civilní právo procesní. Část druhá: Řízení vykonávací, řízení insolvenční. 1. vydání. Praha: Leges, 2015, p. 296.
152. Amendment by Act No. 31/2019 Coll.

Chapter 5. General Obligations of Economic Operators

321. There are certain obligations that all economic operators have to follow regardless of the form under which they conduct their business. The general obligations and duties of natural and legal entities do not differ per se, although there could be some differences when it comes to specific time limits or the amount of fees or duties. In this chapter, the most important duties[153] will be described in greater detail, namely the obligation to register with the Companies Register and the tax administration, to open and operate a bank account, to maintain bookkeeping and to prevent money laundering.

§1. Companies Register

322. The Companies Register is a public register of economic operators which contains publicly accessible information about the economic operators listed.[154] It is regulated mainly by Act No. 304/2013 Coll., on the Public Registers of Legal and Natural Persons, and the Civil Code. Part of the Companies Register is the Collection of Deeds, where economic operators file the documents prescribed by law (e.g., founding documents, such as articles of association or accounting documents).

323. The Companies Register is accessible online.[155] The information in the Companies Register is searchable by trade name, identification number, registered office, legal form and/or registration number. Information is provided in the form of a current or a full (historical) extract. Part of the search result is also the Collection of Deeds, which has individual documents relating to the economic operator in question.

324. The Companies Register is administered by regional courts. The relevant regional court is determined based on the address of the relevant entity's registered office. If an entrepreneur, who is a natural person, does not have a registered office, he/she is registered by the Companies Register of the court competent under his/her place of residence. Foreign persons are entered in the court which is competent under the location of their enterprise or branch.

153. The Czech Chamber of Commerce recently launched a web portal (https://pespropodnikatele.cz/) with paid access that aims to concentrate all the obligations of economic operators in one place.
154. Generally to the Companies Register, *see*, e.g., Havel, M., Štenglová, I., Dědič, J., Jindřich, M. a kol Zákon o veřejných rejstřících právnických a fyzických osob. Komentář. Praha. C. H. Beck, 2015.
155. https://or.justice.cz/ias/ui/rejstrik.

I. Formal & Material Publicity of the Companies Register

325. The Companies Register is governed by several leading principles.[156] Under the 'formal publicity principle', everyone is entitled to inspect the Companies Register without the need to prove any legal grounds for such inspection. This is ensured by the fact that the Companies Register is freely accessible via the internet. Under the (negative) material publicity principle, a registered corporation cannot claim vis-à-vis third parties that the data registered in the Companies Register does not correspond to reality (e.g., that a board member registered in the Companies Register is, in fact, no longer a board member). Under the (positive) material publicity principle, the information and documents which are made public through the Companies Register are effective vis-à-vis third parties as of the moment of publication unless the registered person proves that the third party knew such data in advance.[157] However, such data and the contents of documents cannot be considered, used and/or relied on until the sixteenth day after its publication provided that the third party proves that it could not have been aware of said information.

II. Listed Entities

326. The following entities are registered in the Companies Register:

(a) business corporations (i.e., commercial companies and cooperatives) established under the Corporations Act;[158]
(b) entrepreneurs (natural persons), provided that their revenue for the two previous accounting periods reached CZK 120,000,000;
(c) other entrepreneurs (natural persons) that file a request to be registered; and
(d) other entities if it is specifically provided for in a special law.

III. Recorded Data

327. The following data shall be entered into the Companies Register (section 25 of the Act on the Public Registers of Legal and Natural Persons):

(a) the name and registered office or address of the registered person;
(b) the object of entrepreneurial activity or the purpose of the entity if it is required by another act;

---

156. On the material and formal publicity principle, *see*, e.g., Lavický, P. a kol Občanský zákoník I. Obecná část (§ 1-654). Komentář. Praha: C. H. Beck, 2014. pp. 633 et seq., Havel, M., Štenglová, I., Dědič, J., Jindřich, M. a kol Zákon o veřejných rejstřících právnických a fyzických osob. Komentář. Praha. C. H. Beck, 2015. pp. 6 et seq., or Mates, P. a Semík, K. Nad zákonem o veřejných rejstřících aneb nihil novi sub sole. Bulletin advokacie. 2014, Vol. 2014, Nos 1–2, pp. 39 et seq.
157. On the material publicity principle, *see*, e.g., Štenglová, I., Dědič, J., Tomsa, M. a kol. Základy obchodního práva. Praha: Leges, 2014, pp. 51 et seq.
158. Including business corporations established under the laws of the European Union.

(c) in the case of a legal person, the legal form thereof;
(d) in the case of a legal person, the date of establishment and termination thereof;
(e) in the case of an entrepreneur – natural person, his/her date of birth, personal identification number (‘*rodné číslo*’) if a personal identification number has been assigned, and address thereof;
(f) the identification number (‘*IČO*’) assigned by the registry court;
(g) the name of the statutory body, if not provided by law, the number of members of the statutory body, the name and address of any person who is a member of the statutory body, the manner in which he/she is acting on behalf of the legal person, and the date of establishment and termination of that person’s office; if a legal person is a member of the statutory body, also the name and address of the person representing him/her during the exercise of his/her office;
(h) if a control body is to be set up, its name unless the name is prescribed by law, the number of members of the control body, the name and address of any person who is a member of the control body, and the date of establishment and termination of that person’s office; if a legal person is a member of the control body, also the name and address of the person representing him/her during the exercise of his/her office;
(i) the name and address of the procurator (‘*prokurista*’ – agent), along with the manner in which the procurator acts, including information about the procuration applying only to a particular branch or particular business enterprise, its identification, and information about whether the procurator is entitled to alienate or encumber real estate;
(j) other facts stipulated by relevant legislation or other important facts whose registration is requested by a registered person if the person has a legal interest in such registration; and
(k) the date on which the registration was performed.

328. The following data shall also be entered into the Companies Register (section 48 of the Act on the Public Registers of Legal and Natural Persons):

(a) the amount of the company’s registered capital (applies to limited liability companies and joint-stock companies); and the extent of its repayment (applies to joint-stock companies);
(b) the amount of each member’s contribution to the registered capital, where registration of such member in the Companies Register is provided for under any other law; and the extent of fulfilment of the contributory obligation;
(c) information about the fact that the business enterprise or part thereof has been transferred, pledged, leased, or usufructuary leased, or, alternatively, information about the extinction of obligations arising out of these contracts, and court resolutions on the acquisition of a business enterprise or part thereof by inheritance;
(d) information about the fact that the business corporation opted to be governed fully by the Corporations Act by the procedure according to section 777(5) of said Act;
(e) information about the fact that the exercise of the office of a member of a company body has been suspended pursuant to the Corporations Act;

(f) existence of a lien on a share in a corporation unless it is represented by a security or a book-entry security, the designation of the pledged share in the corporation, the name and registered office or the address of the pledgee, the name and registered office or address of the shareholder whose share is subject to the pledge, if he/she is not registered in the Companies Register, and an indication of the secured debt;
(g) other rights in rem in respect of a share in a business corporation, unless it is represented by a security or a book-entry security, and the name and registered office or the address of the shareholder in respect of whose share the other right in rem is established, if he/she is not entered in the Companies Register;
(h) concerning an unlimited partnership, the name and registered office or address of its partners;
(i) concerning a limited partnership, the name and registered office or address of its partners, specifying which one of the partners is the general partner and which one is the limited partner; where a limited partner may own more than one interest, the identification of the interest; and the amount of the limited partnership sum of each limited partner and changes thereto;
(j) concerning a limited liability company, the name and registered office or address of its members, the share amount of each member, identification of the share, and where the shareholder may hold more than one share, the name of the type of share and a description of the rights and obligations connected with it, at least by reference to the articles of association filed in the Collection of Deeds, and if the articles of association provide more than one type of share, information that a common certificate was issued on the share;
(k) concerning a joint-stock company, the number, form, and nominal value of shares, or information about the fact that the company issues shares with no nominal value (no-par value shares) and the amount thereof, information about whether the shares will be issued as security or book-entry securities or will be immobilized, the name of the type of shares and a description of rights and obligations associated with it at least by reference to the articles of association filed in the Collection of Deeds if the company issued more types of shares, and potential restrictions on the transferability of bearer shares; if the company has a sole shareholder, the name and registered office or address of the shareholder is registered;
(l) concerning a cooperative, information about whether it is a cooperative, housing cooperative, or social cooperative, and the amount of the basic membership contribution or of the entry membership contribution; and
(m) concerning a state enterprise, the designation of the person that exercises the office of the founder of the state enterprise in the name of the state, the amount of common assets and liabilities, the minimal amount of common assets and liabilities which the state enterprise is obliged to maintain, and designated assets;
(n) information on the commencement of proceedings for the dissolution of the business corporation pursuant to §105a.

329. The Companies Register also contains information on:

(a) in the case of a legal person, the date of declaration of invalidity or the date of dissolution thereof, always included the legal reason therefor;
(b) entry into liquidation, the name and registered office or address of the liquidator; if a legal person is the liquidator, also the name and address of the person representing it during the exercise of its office;
(c) any initiation of insolvency proceedings;
(d) any restriction of the right of the debtor to dispose of the bankrupt entity's estate based on a decision by an insolvency court;
(e) any bankruptcy order and annulment of bankruptcy;
(f) the name and registered office of the insolvency administrator;
(g) any authorization of reorganization, the approval of the reorganizational plan and the execution of the reorganization plan or its essential parts;
(h) any execution order inhibiting a share of a member in a company, as well as a decision on the withdrawal of an execution or communication that the execution ended by means other than withdrawal, including the reason for the decision;
(i) any execution order on the sale of a business enterprise or part thereof, as well as a decision on the withdrawal of an execution or communication that the execution ended by means other than withdrawal, including the reason for the decision;
(j) a decision of the court ordering an interim measure consisting in restricting or prohibiting the disposal of a shareholder's share in the company, an enterprise or a substantial part of the company's assets, as well as the revocation or termination of such interim measure, including the reason for the decision;
(k) the termination of liquidation;
(l) the legal reason for a legal person's deletion from the register; and
(m) the name and registered office or address of the curator of the legal person.

IV. Collection of Deeds

330. Besides all of the above-stated required information, the registered entity also has to submit certain documents, such as articles of association and annual reports, to the Collection of Deeds.[159]

V. Registration

331. Economic operators may apply for registration in the Companies Register in one of two ways, either by application with the relevant registry court or by a

159. For a full list of the documents which must be submitted to the Collection of Deeds, *see* s. 66 of the Act on the Public Registers of Legal and Natural Persons. On the collection of documents, *see*, e.g., Havel, M., Štenglová, I., Dědič, J., Jindřich, M. a kol Zákon o veřejných rejstřících právnických a fyzických osob. Komentář. Praha. C. H. Beck, 2015. pp. 238 et seq. or Plíhal, T. Porušování povinnosti zakládat řádně listiny do sbírky listin jako důvod pro zrušení právnické osoby s likvidací soudem. Bulletin advokacie. 2014, Vol. 2014, Nos 1–2, pp. 46 et seq.

request lodged with the notary. Applications for registration (i.e., requests for registration) are submitted by the person (entity) being registered. In the case of legal persons, the application is submitted by the person authorized to represent the legal person (e.g., chairman of the board).

332. Registration by registry court. The application for registration[160] of an entity into the Companies Register shall be made in Czech and in the prescribed form.[161] The application for registration must be submitted without undue delay after there is a reason therefor (e.g., change in personnel). The application shall be accompanied by documents proving the information to be registered. The application has to be signed, and the signature must be certified.

333. Registry courts examine whether all the statutory requirements for registration have been met. In this respect, the courts primarily examine whether the data to be registered is evidenced by the accompanying documents, whether the name of the entity to be registered is not interchangeable with the name of an already-registered entity, and whether or not it is deceptive.

334. If the application for registration does not meet the statutory requirements, the court will notify the applicant and request he/she remedy the application. If the applicant does not remedy the application, the registry court will reject the registration. The court resolution rejecting the application shall contain the specific reasons why the application was not successful, together with instructions on how the application can be remedied.

335. If all of the statutory requirements for registration have been satisfied, the registry court will register the applicant within five business days after receiving the application. The registry court shall register the applicant as of the application's date of filing, but not earlier than on the registration's date of execution. If the registry court fails to register or issue a decision on the application within five business days, the registration shall be deemed to have been made on the day following the expiry of this period. The registry court shall notify the applicant about the registration by sending an extract from the Companies Register containing the record. The extract shall be sent within three days after the registration.

336. The initial fee for registration in the Companies Register via the registry court is CZK 12,000 for joint-stock companies and CZK 6,000 for other entities. The fee for changing the registered information is CZK 2,000.

337. Registration by a notary. When the Act on the Public Registers of Legal and Natural Persons was adopted, notaries also became empowered to register economic operators into the Companies Register. A notary shall carry out the registration at the request of a person entitled to submit the application for registration if:

160. Or application to change registered information.
161. All such forms are available online at https://or.justice.cz/ias/ui/podani.

(a) the facts to be registered have their basis in a notarial deed prepared for registration in the Companies Register, in a notarial deed prepared for registration in the register of trusts or in a notarial deed verifying the decision of a company body of a legal person, or the recorded facts have been examined by a notary in the context of a review of compliance with the prerequisites for drawing up the underlying notarial record;
(b) in the notarial deed, the notary states that the content of the legal act is in accordance with legal regulations and the founding act of a legal person, or alternatively that the formalities or legal acts to which the legal person or its body are obliged to have been fulfilled; and
(c) all documents required for registration in the Companies Register or for incorporation in the Collection of Deeds have been submitted to the notary.

338. Only the notary who prepared the notarial deed required for registration can register the entity into the Companies Register. If the prerequisites for the registration do not meet the statutory requirements, the notary will refuse to register the entity. If the prerequisites for the registration are met, the notary will register the entity without undue delay after being requested to do so. The initial fee for registration in the Companies Register by a notary is CZK 8,000 for joint-stock companies and CZK 2,700 for other entities. The fee for changing the registered information is CZK 1,000.

§2. Registration with the Tax Administrator

339. Economic operators are required to register with the appropriate tax administrator (tax offices) for the purpose of paying taxes. The appropriate tax administrator is generally[162] determined (i) in the case of natural persons (entrepreneurs), based on his/her permanent residence, or (ii) in the case of legal persons, based on the address listed as its registered office in the Companies Register (*section 13 of the Act No. 280/2009 Coll., Tax Code*). The duty to register with the tax administrator arises for economic operators who are obliged to register for individual tax (*section 125 of the Tax Code*). At the beginning of the first registration, the tax administrator will assign a tax identification number, which is then used in all communications with the tax administration. The tax identification number contains the code 'CZ' and the birth identification number (for natural persons (entrepreneurs)) or a company identification number (for legal persons) (*section 130 of the Tax Code*). The appropriate tax administrator then issues a decision on the registration within thirty days after the date on which the application was filed (*section 129(1) of the Tax Code*). The duty to register for principal[163] taxes is summarized below.

162. There are exceptions to this rule, e.g., if the subject of the tax is real estate, the competent tax administrator is determined based on the territory in which the real estate is located.
163. Economic operators may also be obliged to register in respect of other taxes (such as real estate taxes, consumption taxes, etc.) if the conditions for paying such taxes are met.

340. Income Tax. The tax that nearly every economic entity has to pay is income tax, which is regulated by Act No. 586/1992 Coll., on Income Taxes. *Natural persons (entrepreneurs)* have to register with the competent tax administrator within fifteen days after the date on which they began a gainful self-employed activity or received income from a self-employed activity. This obligation does not arise if the person only has non-taxable income, tax-exempt income, or income from which the tax is collected at a special tax rate (*section 39 of the Act on Income Taxes*). Other income, such as rental income, is also not affected by this obligation. *Legal persons* have to register with the competent tax administrator within fifteen days after being established. The same applies in connection with permanent establishments and foreign entities that have started to operate in the Czech Republic, have received income from local sources, or have obtained permission in the Czech Republic to pursue an activity which is a source of income (*section 39a of the Act on Income Taxes*). The obligation to register does not arise under the same conditions as those for natural persons (entrepreneurs).

341. Natural persons (entrepreneurs) have to tax all of their taxable income (i.e., both from sources in the Czech Republic and abroad) in the Czech Republic if they reside[164] or usually reside[165] in the Czech Republic. Otherwise, only the taxable income which they earned from sources in the Czech Republic is subject to taxation in the Czech Republic (*section 2 of the Act on Income Taxes*).

342. Legal persons have to tax all of their taxable income (i.e., both from sources in the Czech Republic and abroad) in the Czech Republic if they have their registered office or place of management[166] in the Czech Republic. Otherwise, only the taxable income which they earned from sources in the Czech Republic is subject to taxation in the Czech Republic (*section 17 of the Act on Income Taxes*).

343. Economic operators with employees have to register with the competent tax administrator within eight days of becoming obliged to perform the acts stipulated by the Act on Income Taxes for such operators (e.g., the obligations to collect and transfer employee income taxes regarding income from such employment on behalf of such employees) (*section 39b of the Act on Income Taxes*).

344. Value Added Tax (VAT). Issues regarding VAT are mostly regulated by Act No. 235/2004 Coll., on VAT. VAT administration is divided between tax and customs authorities.

---

164. That is, if they have a permanent apartment in circumstances where their intention to stay permanently in such apartment can be inferred.
165. For at least 183 days in a calendar year.
166. Place from which the legal person is controlled.

345. Economic operators domiciled in the Czech Republic[167] whose turnover exceeds CZK 1,000,000 in the immediately preceding maximum of twelve calendar months, with the exception of persons who only perform exempt transactions, are obliged to register for VAT within fifteen days after the end of the calendar month in which it exceeded the determined turnover (*sections 6 and 94 of the Act on VAT*).

346. Any economic operator domiciled in the Czech Republic who carries out or will carry out a transaction with the right to a VAT deduction, or an economic operator domiciled outside the Czech Republic who carries out or will carry out a transaction with the right to a VAT deduction in the Czech Republic, may register voluntarily for VAT (*section 94a of the Act on VAT*).

347. In the VAT registration application, the economic operator is obliged to list all of its bank accounts that will be used for business, and it may also choose to have some of them made public (*section 96 of the Act on VAT*).

§3. Accounting

I. Legislation

348. The duty of economic entities to keep accounts is prescribed and regulated by the Civil Code and by the Accounting Act. The Accounting Act incorporates not only the provisions of the International Accounting Standards (IAS) and International Financial Reporting Standards but also the applicable EU legislation on accounting.

349. The Ministry of Finance has also issued several decrees that regulate the specifics of keeping accounts (such as the precise scope of yearly financial statements) for various entities (e.g., entrepreneurs, banks, insurance companies, etc.). Accounts should also be kept in accordance with the Czech Accounting Standards (CAS).

II. Scope of the Obligation to Keep Accounts

350. All legal persons have to keep accounts. Natural persons have to keep accounts: (1) if they are registered in the Companies Register; (2) if their turnover in the course of their business activities exceeded the amount of CZK 25,000,000 for the immediately preceding calendar year; or (3) if the duty to keep accounts is

167. In the meaning of operators whose address, i.e., the place of management, which is the place where the principal decisions concerning the management of the taxable person are taken or, where appropriate, the place where its management meets, is in the Czech Republic; if the natural person does not have his/her place of management, the registered office of the natural person means the place of his/her usual stay.

prescribed by another act. Trust funds, investment funds and pension funds also have to keep accounts. These entities are accounting units in the meaning of the Accounting Act.

351. Legal persons are obliged to keep accounts from the moment they are first established until termination. Natural persons have to keep accounts once they are registered in the Companies Register, as of the first day of the year in which their turnover exceeded CZK 25,000,000, or as of the day prescribed in another act.

352. Accounting units have to perform double-entry bookkeeping in accordance with the Accounting Act, the relevant decree of the Ministry of Finance, and the CAS. Double-entry bookkeeping records the state and movement of assets, liabilities including debts, as well as costs and revenues, and the profit or loss.

353. Single-entry bookkeeping is permitted only for associations ('*spolek*'), labour unions, employers' organizations, churches, and gamekeeper's associations. The subject of single-entry bookkeeping is to record the state of expenditures and income, and assets and liabilities.

III. Accounting Period

354. Accounting units shall continuously record accounting entries during the accounting period. The accounting period is generally equivalent to the calendar year, but it also may be equivalent to the financial year, which is a period of twelve consecutive calendar months that starts on the first day of a month other than January.

§4. Prevention of Money Laundering and Terrorist Financing

355. The following economic operators are subject to the obligations imposed by Act No. 253/2008 Coll., on certain measures against money laundering and terrorist financing[168] ('AML Act'):

(a) banks;
(b) financial institutions, other than banks;[169]
(c) providers of gambling services;

168. This act incorporates the relevant European Union legislation, such as Directive (EU) 2015/849, on the prevention of the use of the financial system for the purposes of money laundering and terrorist financing.
169. These include savings and credit cooperatives, the Central Securities Depository Prague, stock exchanges, commodity exchanges, securities dealers, investment companies, foreign collective investment companies, insurance undertakings, etc.

(d) persons who are entitled to sell or purchase real estate; who are real estate agents[170]; who are auctioneers[171];
(e) auditor, tax advisor, another person authorized to provide legal assistance or financial and economic advice in matters of taxes, fees and other similar monetary benefits, as well as in matters directly related thereto, pursuant to another legal regulation, and a person authorized to carry out the business of accounting consultants, bookkeeping and tax record-keeping pursuant to the Trade Licensing Act;
(f) bailiffs (court executors);
(g) attorneys or notaries;
(h) providers of asset management services;[172]
(i) persons trading in works of art[173] if their value reaches at least EUR 10,000; cultural monuments or objects of cultural value or persons arranging such transactions;
(j) persons authorized to trade in used goods or to pledge things;
(k) administrators of the registry of permits trading pursuant to Act No. 383/2012 Coll., on Conditions of Trading in Greenhouse Gas Emission Permits;
(l) persons providing services related to virtual assets;
(m) a trustee or a person in a similar position in a trust similar in structure or function to a trust governed by the law of another state;
(n) a foreign legal or natural person who is a person referred to in (a) to (m), which operates in the Czech Republic through its branch or establishment;
(o) a foreign person operating in the territory of the Czech Republic if, as an entrepreneur, it carries out the activities referred to in (a) to (m);
(p) entrepreneurs with regard to cash transactions worth EUR 10,000 or more;
(q) a legal person which is not an entrepreneur, if it is authorized to provide as a service any of the activities referred to in (a) to (m), or in cash transactions of EUR 10,000 or more.

356. The main obligation for the above-mentioned subjects is the KYC duty to identify their clients (business partners). Every obliged subject shall identify its clients at the start of a business relationship, in the case of suspicious transactions, when it is clear that the value of the transaction exceeds EUR 10,000, and in some other instances stated in the AML Act (*section 7 of the AML Act*). The client shall be identified by the obliged person for the first time in person (or in the case of legal persons, it's representative). Natural persons shall be identified via ID cards; legal persons shall be identified via a document proving their existence (extract from the Companies Register) together with the natural person acting on its behalf. Trust funds shall be identified by the identification data from the document providing their

170. In the case of mediation of a real estate contract pursuant to Section 2(d)(2) of the Real Estate Mediation Act; however, in the case of a lease, sublease or leasehold, only if the amount of the monthly payment or the proportionate part of the proceeds of the immovable property provided to the lessor on a monthly basis, or the sum of the two, amounts to at least EUR 10,000.
171. According to the Public Auctions Act for activities related to the auction of immovable property.
172. Such as establishing legal entities, acting on behalf of a legal entity, providing a registered office, address, or other related services for another legal entity and similar activities.
173. According to Annex 3 of the AML Act.

existence together with the natural person acting on their behalf. As part of identifying the client, the obliged subject shall also ascertain and record whether the natural person acting on behalf of the client in the transaction or business relation and the client's ultimate beneficiary owner is a politically exposed person or whether it is a person against whom the Czech Republic applies international sanctions.

357. Those to whom the AML obligations apply also have to verify their clients at the start of the business relationship, in the case of suspicious transactions, when it is clear that the value of the transaction exceeds EUR 15,000, and in some other instances stated in the AML Act (*section 9(1) of the AML Act*). Verification includes obtaining and evaluating the information on the purpose and intended nature of the trade or business relationship and the information about the nature of the client's business, ascertaining the identity of the ultimate beneficial owner and ascertaining whether the ultimate beneficiary owner is a politically exposed person or a person against whom the Czech Republic applies international sanctions. In the case of legal persons, verification includes ascertaining the ownership and management structure of the client and ascertaining whether in the structure there is a person against whom the Czech Republic applies international sanctions. Verification also includes continuous monitoring of the business relationship, including reviewing transactions conducted during the relationship, reviewing sources of funds or other assets to which the trade or business relationship relates, and in the case of a business relationship with a politically exposed person, also taking appropriate measures to establish the origin of his/her property.

358. The obliged subject shall refuse to execute a transaction or establish a business relationship or – unless excluded by special legislation – shall terminate the business relationship if the client refuses to undergo identification or verification, if it cannot be performed for other reasons, or if the obliged subject has reason to doubt the authenticity or accuracy of the information (*section 15 of the AML Act*).

359. If an obliged subject identifies a suspicious transaction in connection with its activity, it shall notify the Financial Analytical Office. Obliged subjects shall also postpone the execution of suspicious transactions unless such postponement would compromise an investigation into such suspicious transaction. Suspicious transaction means any transaction carried out in the circumstances giving rise to suspicion of money laundering or suspicion that the funds used in the trade are intended to finance terrorism.[174] A transaction is always suspicious if:

(a) the client or the ultimate owner is a person against whom the Czech Republic applies international sanctions;
(b) the subject of trade is or is intended to be goods or services which are subject to sanctions applied by the Czech Republic; or

174. Circumstances that can raise suspicion include: making withdrawals or transfers to other accounts immediately after a cash deposit, the number of accounts opened by the client is disproportionate with regard to the subject of its business or its property, funds are transferred without a clear economic reason, etc.

(c) the client refuses to undergo verification or refuses to present the identification of the person for whom he/she acts.

360. Persons to whom the AML obligations apply also have to keep the following documents/information for a period of ten years after executing a transaction which gave rise to AML obligations or to terminate the business relationship with the client (*section 16 of the AML Act*):

(a) information obtained when identifying the client;
(b) copies of documents obtained as part of identifying the client;
(c) indication of who first identified the client, and when;
(d) information and copies of documents obtained as part of verifying the client;
(e) records of all steps taken when verifying the client;
(f) records of the process of assessing and determining the risk profile of the client;
(g) documents justifying an exception to identifying and/or verifying the client;
(h) in the case of representation, the original or a certified copy of the power of attorney; and
(i) information and evidence regarding the transactions associated with the obligation of identification.

361. Moreover, persons to whom the AML obligations apply shall identify and assess the risks of money laundering and terrorist financing that may arise in the course of their activities. As a result of this identification and assessment, the obliged subject shall implement appropriate internal control and communication strategies and procedures to mitigate and effectively manage the risks of money laundering and terrorist financing. The obliged subject shall also develop a system of internal principles, procedures and control measures[175] to fulfil the obligations set out in the AML Act.

362. Fines for breaching the obligations imposed by the AML Act can range from CZK 200,000 (breach of the duty of confidentiality) to CZK 130,000,000 (e.g., breach of the duty of identification, verification or duty to deny execution of a transaction).

175. Including: a detailed list of the features of suspicious transactions that may occur in the activity of a particular obliged subject, a method of client identification, including measures to identify politically exposed persons and entities against whom the Czech Republic applies international sanctions, etc.

Chapter 6. Intellectual Property Rights

§1. Intellectual Property

I. General Observations

363. Intellectual property refers to creations of the mind, such as inventions, literary and artistic works, designs, and symbols, names and images used in commerce.

364. Intellectual property is protected in law by, for example, patents, copyright and trademarks, which enable people to earn recognition or financial benefit from what they invent or create. By striking the right balance between the interests of innovators and the wider public interest, the intellectual property system aims to foster an environment in which creativity and innovation can flourish.[176]

365. In the Czech Republic, intellectual property comprises industrial property rights on the one hand and copyright (including software and database protection) and neighbouring rights (rights of producers, broadcasters and performing artists) on the other hand. Industrial property rights include protection of the results of technical, creative work (patents and utility models), protection of design (industrial designs), rights to mark (trademarks, geographical indications and appellations of origin) and topography of semiconductor products.

366. The Czech Republic is a contracting party of the Agreement on the Visegrad Patent Institute (VPI), a member of the World Intellectual Property Organization (WIPO), which is an important international organization in the industrial property protection field, and contractor of many multilateral international treaties concerning the protection of industrial property administered by this organization. The Czech Republic is also a member of the European Patent Organization (EPO) and contractor of the European Patent Convention, which is administered by the EPO. It is also a contractor of the Agreement on Trade-Related Aspects of Intellectual Property Rights (TRIPS) administered by the World Trade Organization (WTO).[177]

367. The relationship between international and domestic law is defined in Article 10 of the Constitution of the Czech Republic. According to the Constitution, promulgated treaties which the Czech Parliament has given its consent to ratifying, and by which the Czech Republic is bound, form a part of the legal order. If a treaty provides something other than that which a statute provides, the treaty shall apply (*Article 10 of the Constitution*).

368. An intellectual property right is constitutionally enshrined in the CHRF which was adopted from Czechoslovak law in 1991. The Charter contains both the

---

176. *See* https://www.wipo.int/about-ip/en/.
177. *See* https://www.upv.cz/en/legislation/international.html.

constitutional right to own property, including intangible property, and the right to creations (*Article 11 and Article 34(1) of the Charter*).

II. Patents

A. General Observations

369. Czech patent law is primarily governed by the Patent Act.[178] Further, patent legislation includes the Paris Convention for the protection of Industrial Property, the Patent Cooperation Treaty, Strasbourg Agreement Concerning the International Patent Classification, the Budapest Treaty on the International Recognition of the Deposit of Micro-organisms for the Purposes of Patent Procedure, and the Agreement on TRIPS, the Agreement on the VPI, and contractor of the European Patent Convention which is administered by the EPO.

370. The Patent Act outlines the criteria for patentable inventions. Patents shall be granted for any inventions which are new, which involve an inventive step, and which are susceptible of industrial application (*section 3/1 of the Patent Act*).

371. A patent is an exclusive right granted for an invention, which is a product or a process that provides, in general, a new way of doing something, or offers a new technical solution to a problem. To obtain a patent, technical information about the invention must be disclosed to the public in a patent application.[179]

372. Besides new products and technologies, chemical substances, pharmaceuticals and microorganisms used in industrial production, as well as biotechnological processes and products resulting from them, can be patented. On the other hand, what cannot be patented are discoveries and/or scientific theories, computer programs, plant or animal varieties, and methods of medical treatment of the human body or animals.

373. The right to a patent shall belong to the inventor or his/her successor in title. The inventor is the person who has made the invention by means of his/her own creative work. Joint inventors shall be entitled to a patent in the proportion in which they have participated in creating the invention (*section 8 of the Patent Act*).

374. Once a patent has been granted, it shall have effect as from the date of publication in the Official Bulletin of the IPO (*section 11/2 of the Patent Act*).

178. Generally on the Czech patent law, *see*, e.g., Horáček, R., Čada, K., Hajn, P. Práva k průmyslovému vlastnictví. 3. vydání. Praha. C. H. Beck, 2017, pp. 71 et seq., Chloupek, V., Hartvichová, K. a kol. Patentový zákon. Komentář. Praha. C. H. Beck, 2017, Krausová, A. Patentové právo a jeho strategické využití. Revue pro právo a technologie. 2013, Vol. 4, No. 7, pp. 27 et seq. Or Kasl, F. Obhajitelnost softwarových patentů. Revue pro právo a technologie. 2017, Vol. 8, No. 16, pp. 25 et seq.

179. *See* https://www.wipo.int/patents/en/.

375. A patent granted in the Czech Republic is valid for twenty years from the filing date of the application, and its basic effect represents the right for the patentee to prevent anybody from using it without preliminary agreement.[180]

B. Exclusions from Patents

376. Patents shall not be granted in respect of:

(a) inventions the exploitation of which would be contrary to the public order or morality; being contrary to the public order or morality may not be deduced merely because the exploitation of the given invention is prohibited by law;
(b) plant or animal varieties or essentially biological processes for the production of plants or animals; this provision shall not apply to microbiological processes and the products thereof (*section 4 of the Patent Act*).

C. Substantive Requirements

Novelty

377. The novelty of the invention is one of the basic substantive requirements of patentability. An invention shall be considered to be new if it does not form part of the state of the art.

378. The state of the art shall be held to comprise everything made available to the public by means of a written or oral description, by use, or in any other way, prior to the date from which the right of priority belongs to the applicant (*section 5/2 of the Patent Act*). In addition to this basic definition, the Patent Act regulates further details of what is or is not state of the art.

379. The disclosure of an invention which took place no earlier than six months prior to the filing of the application shall not be considered as being part of the state of the art if it was due to or in consequence of:

(a) evident abuse in relation to the applicant or his/her legal predecessor;
(b) the fact that the applicant or his/her legal predecessor displayed the invention at an official or officially recognized exhibition within the terms of the relevant international treaty. In such a case, it shall be for the applicant to declare, when filing the application, that the invention has been displayed and to produce in support of his/her declaration, within a period of four months as from filing, a certificate attesting that the invention has been displayed in compliance with the provisions of the international treaty (*section 5/5 of the Patent Act*).

---

180. *See* https://upv.cz/en/ip-rights/patents.html.

380. The IPO is the only competent authority to assess the fulfilment of this substantive requirement of patentability in the Czech Republic. An invention's novelty cannot be reliably assessed by experts, nor can a court decide in the Czech Republic on this substantive requirement, even as a preliminary question.[181]

Inventive step

381. An invention shall be considered as involving an inventive step if, having regard to the state of the art,[182] it is not obvious to a person skilled in the art (*section 6/1 of the Patent Act*).

382. Having an inventive step is another necessary substantive requirement for patentability. The reason for including this condition among the patentability criteria is to prevent patents from being granted for inventions that are formally new but whose novelty is ensured only by features that are evident to those skilled in the art. A patentable invention must be of benefit to the state of the art as a whole or to the prior art by enriching this state.[183]

Industrial applicability

383. Another legal condition of patentability is the invention's industrial applicability, which is an objective feature of the subject of the invention to be manufactured or otherwise economically used (i.e., in industry, agriculture or other areas of economy). This characteristic is usually associated with the so-called reproducibility or feasibility of the invention, that is to say, the possibility of repeatedly making or using the object of the invention.[184]

D. Formal Requirements

384. The IPO carries out the patent granting procedure resulting from a patent application, which can be filed by the inventor or by a person to whom this right was transferred by the inventor. Patent applications ordinarily follow a set form, which also must include a description of the invention and/or related drawings and so-called patent claims. The claims precisely define the subject matter for which the protection is requested. Application forms are available in the IPO's filing room and can also be downloaded from the IPO's website. Applications can be filed in person, by post or electronically.

---

181. Chloupek, V., Hartvichová, K. a kol. Patentový zákon. Komentář. 1. vydání. Praha: C. H. Beck, 2017.
182. However, the content of the applications that have only been published as of the date on which the applicant's priority right began shall not be taken into consideration in assessing the inventive step.
183. Chloupek, V., Hartvichová, K. a kol. Patentový zákon. Komentář. 1. vydání. Praha: C. H. Beck, 2017.
184. *Ibid.*

385. Every filed application undergoes a preliminary examination to eliminate those containing matters evidently non-patentable, lacking unity, and/or containing defects which prevent it from being published. An applicant is notified of all the deficiencies by an official letter. The IPO publishes applications and any notes on disclosure in the Official Bulletin, eighteen months after the priority date. The system of deferred examination is also valid in the Czech Republic. In compliance with the European patent system, a substantive examination is carried out upon the applicant's request. This request must be filed within thirty-six months after the filing date. The patent is granted by the IPO only after the substantive examination has been carried out and on condition that the invention complies with all requirements on patentability. Administration fees are tied to the patent procedure. The patent owner must also pay maintenance fees to keep the patent valid.[185]

386. Applicants with neither residence nor principal place of business on the territory of the Czech Republic should be represented by a patent attorney or a legal practitioner.[186]

E. Rights of the Patentee

387. The patent owner has the exclusive right to use the invention, to authorize others to use the invention, or to assign the patent to others.

388. Nobody shall be allowed to do the following without the patent owner's consent:

(a) to make, offer, put on the market or use a product which is the subject matter of the patent, or to import or stock the product for this purpose, or to dispose of it by another manner;
(b) to use a process which is the subject matter of the patent or to offer the process for use;
(c) to offer, put on the market, use or import or stock for this purpose the product obtained directly by a process which is the subject matter of the patent; identical products shall be held to have been obtained by means of the process which is the subject matter of the patent when it is highly probable that the product was obtained by means of the process which is the subject matter of the patent, and in spite of reasonable effort, the patent owner was not able to determinate the process actually used, unless the contrary is proven. In proving the contrary, rights conferred by trade secret protection shall be respected (*section 13 of the Patent Act*);

185. *See* https://upv.cz/en/ip-rights/patents.html.
186. *See* https://www.epo.org/law-practice/legal-texts/html/natlaw/en/iv/cz.htm.

(d) to supply or offer to supply a person other than the person authorized to use the patented invention with the means relating to an essential element of the invention and, serving in this sense, to put it into effect when it is obvious in the circumstances that these means are suitable and intended for putting the patented invention into effect[187] (*section 13a of the Patent Act*).

389. The patent owner shall not be entitled to prohibit third persons from disposing of the product which is the subject matter of the protected invention if the product has been put on the market in the Czech Republic by the patent owner or with his/her consent unless there exist reasons for extending patent rights to the mentioned activities (*section 13a of the Patent Act*).

390. The authorization to exploit an invention protected by a patent (licence) shall be given by written contract (licence contract). A Licence contract shall have effect in respect of third parties as from its entry in the Patent Register (*section 14 of the Patent Act*).

F. Inventions by Employees

391. Under Czech patent law, if an inventor has created an invention as part of his/her tasks deriving from an employment relationship, by reason of the fact that he/she is a member of an organization or of any other similar employment relationship (employment relationship), the right to the patent shall pass to the employer, unless otherwise laid down by contract. The right of inventorship as such shall remain unaffected.

392. An inventor who has made an invention within the framework of an employment relationship shall be required to report the fact without delay, in writing, to his/her employer and to communicate to his/her employer the documents required for assessing the invention.

393. If the employer does not claim the right to the patent within a period of three months after receiving the communication referred to above, the right to the patent shall revert to the inventor. Both the employer and the employee shall be required to maintain the secrecy of the invention with respect to third parties. Any inventor who has made an invention under an employment relationship shall be entitled, where the employer claims the right to the patent, to appropriate remuneration from the employer (*both section 9 of the Patent Act*).

---

187. This shall not apply when the means are products commonly existing on the market, unless a third person induces the purchaser to commit an act which is prohibited by s. 13 of the Patent Act.

G. Lapse of a Patent

394. A patent shall lapse:

(a) on expiry of its term of validity;
(b) if the patent owner has not paid the respective maintenance fees in force within the prescribed time limit;
(c) on relinquishment by the proprietor of the patent; in such a case, the patent shall terminate as from the date on which the IPO receives a written declaration by the proprietor of the patent (*section 22 of the Patent Act*).

Revocation of the patent

395. The IPO shall revoke a patent (section 23 of the Patent Act) if it is subsequently ascertained that:

(a) the invention did not meet the conditions of patentability;
(b) the invention is not disclosed clearly and completely in the patent, which should be carried out by a person skilled in the art;
(c) the subject matter of the patent extends beyond the content of the invention application as filed, or the subject matter of the patents granted on a divisional application extends beyond the content of the invention application as filed, or the extent of the protection arising from the patent was extended;
(d) the patent owner has no right to the invention under section 8 of the Patent Act. This reason for revocation applies only upon the request of the authorized person pursuant to section 29 of the Patent Act.

III. Utility Models

A. General Observations

396. Czech utility models law is governed by the Utility Models Act.[188] Technical solutions which are new, exceed the framework of mere professional skill, and are industrially applicable shall be protected as utility models (*section 1 of the Utility Models Act*).

397. The following, in particular, shall not be deemed technical solutions:

(a) discoveries, scientific theories and mathematical methods;

188. Generally on the Czech utility models law, *see*, e.g., Horáček, R., Čada, K., Hajn, P. Práva k průmyslovému vlastnictví. 3. vydání. Praha. C. H. Beck, 2017, pp. 242 et seq., Pecková, A. Vliv institutu užitného vzoru dle německé předlohy ve vybraných mimoevropských zemích. Acta MUP. 2018, Vol. 9, No. 2, pp. 5 et seq. or Čada, K. K některým otázkám moderní české judikatury v oblasti práv k technickým řešením. Acta MUP. 2015, Vol. 6, No. 2, pp. 59 et seq.

(b) the mere appearance of products;
(c) schemes, rules and methods for performing mental acts;
(d) computer programs; and
(e) the mere presentation of information (*section 2 of the Utility Models Act*).

398. A utility model system provides protection of so-called minor inventions through a system similar to the patent system. Recognizing that minor improvements of existing products which do not fulfil the patentability requirements may have an important role in a local innovation system, utility models protect such inventions through granting an exclusive right which allows the right holder to prevent others from commercially using the protected invention without his/her authorization for a limited period of time.

399. In general, compared with patents, utility model systems require compliance with less stringent requirements (e.g., a lower level of inventive step), have simpler procedures, and offer a shorter term of protection. Designed primarily to respond to the needs of local innovators, the requirements and procedures for obtaining protection and the duration of that protection vary from one country to another.[189]

400. Utility model protection can be used for new technical solutions susceptible of industrial application, exceeding common technical skill. As stated above, the conditions for utility model protection are different from the patent procedure at the inventive level.

401. This protection is not suitable for cases in which the subject of protection is to be utilized at a later stage, but it is ideal for items with a shorter lifespan because the effect of registering a utility model is the same as that of a patent. However, due to the fact that there is no novelty and no inventive level examination performed, protection under a utility model is much more fragile, and the owner's position is less confident. The utility model fees, on the other hand, are much lower.[190]

402. The right to utility model protection shall belong to the author or his/her successor in title. The author of the utility model shall be the person who created the utility model by means of his/her own creative work (*section 6 of the Utility Models Act*).

403. The protection under a utility model lasts four years but may be extended twice upon the owner's request for three years in each case. Protection under the utility model granted in the Czech Republic is valid for up to ten years.

---

189. *See* https://www.wipo.int/patents/en/topics/utility_models.html.
190. *See* https://upv.cz/en/ip-rights/utility-models.html.

B. Exclusions from Utility Models

404. The following shall not be protected as utility models:

(a) technical solutions contrary to the public interest, particularly the principles of humanity and public morality;
(b) plant or animal varieties and biological reproductive materials; and
(c) production processes or work activities (*section 3 of the Utility Models Act*).

C. Substantive Requirements

Novelty

405. The novelty of a technical solution is one of the basic substantive requirements. A technical solution shall be considered new if it does not form part of the state of the art. For the purposes of the Utility Models Act, the state of the art shall be deemed to comprise everything made available to the public prior to the date from which the applicant claimed the right of priority. The state of the art shall not be held to comprise any disclosure of the applicant's work or that of his/her predecessor in title which took place within six months before the filing of the utility model application (*section 4 of the Utility Models Act*).

Industrial applicability

406. A technical solution shall be considered susceptible of industrial application if it can be used repeatedly in economic activities (*section 5 of the Utility Models Act*).

Formal requirements

407. Registration of a utility model shall be subject to the filing of a written application for a utility model with the IPO. The application shall relate to one technical solution only or to a group of technical solutions so linked as to form a single inventive concept (*section 8 of the Utility Models Act*).

408. The application requirements for utility models are analogical to those of patent applications except the procedure is different. Based on the so-called registration principle, the IPO examines whether the basic conditions are fulfilled and then enters the utility model in the Patent Register without any examination on its novelty and creative level or whether it is eligible for protection. As opposed to patents, the registration of a utility model can be carried out quickly, usually three to four months after the application has been filed.

409. A utility model application can – under certain circumstances – branch off the original patent application while maintaining its original priority.[191]

D. Rights Conferred by Utility Models

410. Nobody may manufacture, place on the market, or use in his/her economic activities a technical solution that enjoys utility model protection without the consent of the owner of the utility model.

411. The owner of the utility model shall be entitled to give his/her consent (licence) to use a technical solution's utility model protection to other persons or to assign the utility model to them.

412. Rights conferred by a patent granted on the basis of a patent application having later priority may not be asserted in the event of a dispute without the consent of the owner of the utility model (*section 12 of the Utility Models Act*).

E. Lapse of a Utility Model

413. A utility model shall lapse:

(a) on expiry of its term of validity;
(b) on relinquishment by the owner of the utility model; in such a case, protection shall terminate as from the date on which the IPO receives a written declaration to such effect by the owner of the utility model (*section 16 of the Utility Models Act*).

F. Revocation of a Utility Model

414. The IPO shall, upon request, revoke the utility model protection if a court decision determines that the owner of the utility model was not entitled thereto under the Utility Models Act.

415. A request for revocation of utility model protection may only be filed by the person (or such person's successor in title) who has been determined by the court decision to be entitled to utility model protection.

416. At the request of the person entitled to utility model protection, which shall be filed within one month after the final court decision, the IPO shall register such

191. *See* https://www.upv.cz/en/ip-rights/utility-models.html.

person as the owner of the utility model. If no request for transfer is filed, the IPO shall cancel the utility model registration ex officio (*section 19 of the Utility Models Act*).

G. Cancellation of the Utility Model

417. At the request of any person, the IPO shall cancel the registration of a utility model if:

(a) its technical solution does not qualify for protection under the Utility Models Act;
(b) the subject matter of the utility model is already protected by a patent with effects on the territory of the Czech Republic or utility model enjoying earlier priority;
(c) the subject matter of the utility model extends beyond the content of the application as filed.

418. The effect of a cancelled registration shall be as if the utility model had not been recorded in the register.

419. If the grounds for the cancellation only relate to part of the utility model, the utility model shall be cancelled partially.

420. A utility model may also be even cancelled after the lapse of the utility model if the person filing the request can prove a legal interest (*section 17 of the Utility Models Act*).

IV. Industrial Designs

A. General Observations

421. This area is governed by the Industrial Designs Act[192] and Decree No. 550 of the Federal Office for Inventions on the Procedure in Matters of Inventions and Industrial Designs. Industrial designs are applied to a wide variety of products of industry and handicraft items: from packages and containers to furnishing and household goods, from lighting equipment to jewellery, and from electronic devices to textiles. Industrial designs may also be relevant to graphic symbols, graphical user interfaces (GUI), and logos.[193]

192. Generally to the Czech regulation of industrial designs, *see*, e.g., Horáček, R., Čada, K., Hajn, P. Práva k průmyslovému vlastnictví. 3. vydání. Praha. C. H. Beck, 2017, pp. 257 et seq. or Chloupek, V., Hartvichová, K. a kol. Patentový zákon. Komentář. Praha. C. H. Beck, 2017, pp. 311 et seq.
193. *See* https://www.wipo.int/designs/en/.

422. Legal protection of an industrial design by its registration in the Industrial Design Register is intended for designer solutions. Industrial design is understood to mean the appearance of a product or its part, consisting particularly of signs of lines, contours, colours, shape, material structure of the product per se or ornamentation. It involves a visually perceivable feature or component of a product. It does not involve engineering, structural, functional, material or another nature of it.

423. A product means an industrially or handmade object, including parts intended for assembly into a single compound product, as well as a graphic symbol or typographic sign, except for computer programs.

424. Industrial designs are considered identical if their features can be distinguished from each other only in non-essential details. Industrial design has an individual character if the general impression that it invokes in a well-informed user distinguishes from a general impression being invoked in the same user by another industrial design that has been made accessible to the public prior to the filing date of the application.[194]

425. An industrial design may consist of three-dimensional features, such as the shape of an article, or two-dimensional features, such as patterns, lines or colour.

426. The protection of a registered industrial design lasts five years, starting from the filing date. It can be renewed repeatedly by five years up to a total of twenty-five years (*section 11 of the Industrial Designs Act*).

B. Exclusions from Industrial Designs

427.

(a) The IPO shall not enter into the register any industrial design which is contrary to public policy or to principles of morality.
(b) The IPO shall not enter into the register an industrial design if an identical industrial design with a prior right of priority has already been registered in the Czech Republic (*section 8, 9 of the Industrial Designs Act*).

C. Substantive Requirements

428. Not every industrial design can be protected. An industrial design is qualified for protection if it is new and is of an individual nature.

194. *See* https://upv.cz/en/ip-rights/industrial-designs/national-application-information.html.

Novelty

429. An industrial design shall be considered new if no identical design has been made available to the public before the filing date of the application for registration or the date of priority. Industrial designs shall be deemed to be identical if their features differ only in immaterial details (*section 4 of the Industrial Designs Act*).

430. Industrial designs that are made accessible to the public by the author or legal representative within twelve months prior to the application's filing date are not considered as officially being made available to the public.[195]

Individual nature

431. An industrial design shall have an individual nature if the overall impression it produces on an informed user differs from the overall impression produced on such user by any industrial design which has been made available to the public before the filing date of the application for registration or the date of priority.

432. In assessing the individual nature of an industrial design, the degree of freedom of the designer in developing the design shall be taken into consideration (*section 5 of the Industrial Designs Act*).

D. Formal Requirements

433. Industrial design registration is applied for by filing an industrial design application, best by making use of the form that can be obtained in the IPO filing room or online. Industrial design applications may be filed by the person(s) having the right thereto (*section 12 of the Industrial Designs Act*).

434. Applications can be submitted either by post, in electronic form, or handed over in person. They must contain information about the applicant, display of his/her willingness to register the design, and design representation that provides an unambiguous idea of the product's appearance. The representation of the industrial design is the most important attachment to the application and, therefore, proper attention should be paid to ensuring it is of high quality, as only the representation defines the subject matter of the protection as well as the protection range. The representation can be made in the form of a photograph or a drawing. There are single applications for one industrial design or multiple applications for two or more industrial designs. All industrial designs within a multiple application must be classified under a single class of the international classification for industrial designs.[196]

195. *Ibid.*
196. *Ibid.*

E. *Rights Conferred by Industrial Designs*

435. The registration of an industrial design shall confer on its holder the exclusive right to use it, to prevent any third party not having his/her consent from using it, to afford his/her consent to use the industrial design to other persons or to assign the design right to them. The aforementioned use of an industrial design means, in particular, the making, offering, putting on the market, importing, exporting or using of a product in which the design is incorporated or to which it is applied, or stocking such a product for these purposes.

436. Rights conferred by the design right upon registration shall have effects from the filing date of the application. If the industrial design has not been made available to the public, the holder can assert his/her rights arising from the registration against third persons only in cases where the industrial design has not been used in good faith (*section 19 of the Industrial Designs Act*).

F. *Lapse of an Industrial Design*

437. The right conferred by a design right upon registration shall lapse:

(a) if the time of protection has expired; or
(b) if the holder of the design right surrenders it; in this case, the right shall lapse on the day when this fact is registered in the register. If the rights of third persons are attached to the industrial design, the IPO shall not indicate the lapse of the industrial design until it obtains from the holder of the design right the evidence that these third persons have been informed of this intention by the holder of the design right (*section 26 of the Industrial Designs Act*).

G. *Cancellation of Industrial Design*

438. The IPO shall cancel the registered industrial design from the register if:

(a) the industrial design does not correspond to the industrial design definition within the meaning of the Industrial Designs Act;
(b) the industrial design does not fulfil the requirements posed on it in terms of the Industrial Designs Act;
(c) its holder is not entitled to the industrial design in terms of the Industrial Designs Act;
(d) the industrial design has already been protected in the Czech Republic by a registered industrial design with a prior right of priority;
(e) in the industrial design a distinctive sign is used, which – before the right of priority is created – confers on the right holder of the sign the right to prohibit such use;

(f) the design constitutes an unauthorized use of work protected under a copyright; or

(g) the design constitutes an improper use of any of the items listed in Article 6ter of the Paris Convention for the Protection of Industrial Property (the Paris Convention) or of other symbolic signs, flags, escutcheons other than those covered by Article 6ter of the Paris Convention, which are of particular public interest in the Member State concerned (*section 27 of the Industrial Designs Act*).

439. Cancellation of a registered industrial design in the Industrial Design Register shall have the same effects as if the industrial design had not been registered in the Industrial Design Register (*section 28 of the Industrial Designs Act*).

V. Topographies of Semiconductor Products

A. Legislation

440. This area is governed by Act No. 529 /1991 Coll., on the Protection of Topographies of Semiconductor Products as amended.

B. Definition and General Observations

441. In the semiconductor industry, the key solution for the chip to be manufactured is the location of circuit elements in the integrated circuits and their interconnection. This solution and/or its representing carries no doubt the features of creative work that must be protected against pirating and unjustified enrichment.

442. The entry of certain topography of semiconductor products to the national register serves for this purpose. The entry can be done only based on an application filed with the IPO. The right to the protection of topography can only be claimed by citizens of the Czech Republic or those residing in the Czech Republic. Others can only on the condition of reciprocity.

443. The application procedure is carried out on the basis of the registration principle. The IPO thus does not examine the material conditions of protection. The IPO administers the register of topographies, which contains all conclusive statements. The register is accessible to the public.[197]

444. However, the last topography of a semiconductor product was registered in 1994.

---

197. *See* https://upv.cz/en/ip-rights/topographies-of-semiconductor-products/national-application-information.html.

VI. Trademarks

A. General Observations

445. Trademark Act governs Czech trademark law.[198] The Trademark Act implements the Directive of the European Parliament and of the Council (EU) 2015/2436 of 16 December 2015 to approximate the laws of the Member States relating to trademarks (Trademark Directive).

446. The Trademark Directive contains provisions further approximating the laws of the Member States relating to trademarks, with regard to both substantive and procedural matters. One of the key changes brought about by the new legislative instruments is the elimination of the graphic representation requirement from the definition of both EU and national trademarks. Such elimination gives rise to the possibility of accepting new types of trademarks, filed in formats not previously provided for by national or regional systems.[199]

447. Under the conditions defined in the Trademark Act, a trademark may consist of any signs, in particular, words, including personal names, colours, designs, letters, numerals, the shape of goods or the packaging of goods, or sounds, provided that such signs are capable of:

(a) distinguishing the goods or services of one undertaking from those of another; and
(b) being represented in the Register of Trademarks in a manner which enables the competent authorities and the public to determine the clear and precise subject matter of the protection afforded to its proprietor (*section 1a of the Trademark Act*).

448. The right to use a trademark may be licensed through a licensing contract concluded pursuant to other laws for all or some of the goods or services for which the trademark is registered. A licence may be exclusive or non-exclusive. The licence shall take effect towards third parties upon its entry in the Register of Trademarks. Any of the contracting parties may request entry in the Register of Trademarks (*section 18 of the Trademark Act*).

449. The term of protection is ten years and can be renewed repeatedly for another ten years upon request of the trademark owner and payment of the renewal fee (*section 19 of the Trademark Act*).

---

198. Generally on the Czech trademarks law, *see*, e.g., Pullmannová, H. Vztah a limity používání obchodního jména a ochranné známky v judikatuře SDEU. Právní rozhledy. 2018, Vol. 26, No. 19, pp. 649 et seq. or Kopcová, M. Moderní funkce ochranných známek a jejich vliv na posouzení konfliktu ochranné známky s obchodní firmou v judikatuře SDEU. Právní rozhledy. 2019, Vol. 27, No. 8, pp. 282 et seq.

199. *See* https://upv.cz/en/ip-rights/trade-marks/cc_representation_tm.html.

B. Exclusions from Trademarks

450. The Trademark Act excludes, e.g., the following signs from the registration:

(a) a sign which cannot constitute a trademark within the meaning of the Trademark Act;
(b) a sign which is devoid of any distinctive character;
(c) a sign which consists exclusively of signs or indications which may serve, in trade, to designate the kind, quality, quantity, intended purpose, value, geographical origin or the time of production of goods or of the rendering of services, or other characteristics of goods or services;
(d) a sign which consists exclusively of signs or indications which have become customary in the current language or in bona fide and established practices of the trade;
(e) a sign which consists exclusively of the shape, or another characteristic, which results from the nature of the goods themselves, or which is necessary to obtain a technical result, or which gives substantial value to the goods;
(f) a sign which is contrary to public policy or accepted principles of morality; or
(g) a sign which is of such a nature as to deceive the public, for instance, as to the nature, quality or geographical origin of the goods or services (*section 4 of the Trademark Act*).

C. Types of Trademarks

Word

451. A trademark that consists exclusively of words or letters, numerals, other standard typographic characters or a combination thereof.[200]

452. The mark shall be represented by submitting a reproduction of the sign in standard script and layout, without any graphic feature or colour.

Figurative

453. A trademark where non-standard characters, stylization or layout, or a graphic feature or a colour are used, including marks that consist exclusively of figurative elements or a combination of verbal and figurative elements.

454. The mark shall be represented by submitting a reproduction of the sign for which registration is sought, showing all its elements and, where applicable, its colours.

200. *See* https://upv.cz/dms/pdf_dokumenty/oz_pdf/cc/cc_representation201905.pdf.

Shape

455. A trademark that consists of or extends to a three-dimensional shape, including containers, packaging, the product itself or their appearance.

456. The mark shall be represented by submitting either a graphic reproduction of the shape, including computer-generated imaging, or a photographic reproduction. Graphic or photographic reproduction may contain different views.

Position

457. A trademark that consists of the specific way in which the mark is placed or affixed on the product.

458. The mark shall be represented by submitting a reproduction which appropriately identifies the position of the mark and its size or proportion with respect to the relevant goods. The elements which do not form part of the subject matter of the registration shall be visually disclaimed, preferably by broken or dotted lines. The representation may be accompanied by a description detailing how the sign is affixed on the goods.

Pattern

459. A trademark that consists exclusively of a set of elements which are repeated regularly.

460. The mark shall be represented by submitting a reproduction showing the pattern of repetition. The representation may be accompanied by a description detailing how its elements are repeated regularly.

Colour

461. A trademark that consists: (i) exclusively of a single colour without contours; or, (ii) exclusively of a combination of colours without contours.

462. The mark shall be represented by submitting (i) a reproduction of the colour and an indication of that colour by reference to a generally recognized colour code; or (ii) a reproduction that shows the systematic arrangement of the colour combination in a uniform and predetermined manner, and an indication of those colours by reference to a generally recognized colour code. A description detailing the systematic arrangement of the colours may also be added.

Sound

463. A trademark that consists exclusively of a sound or combination of sounds.

464. The mark shall be represented by submitting an audio file reproducing the sound or by an accurate representation of the sound in musical notation.

Motion

465. A trademark that consists of or extends to a movement or a change in the position of the elements of the mark.

466. The mark shall be represented by submitting a video file or by a series of sequential still images showing the movement or change of position. Where still images are used, they may be numbered or accompanied by a description explaining the sequence.

Multimedia

467. A trademark that consists of or extends to the combination of image and sound.

468. The mark shall be represented by submitting an audiovisual file containing the combination of the image and the sound.

Hologram

469. A trademark that consists of elements with holographic characteristics.

470. The mark shall be represented by submitting a video file or a graphic or photographic representation containing the views which are necessary to sufficiently identify the holographic effect in its entirety.

Other

471. A trademark that is not covered by any of the types listed above.

472. The mark shall be represented in any appropriate form using generally available technology, as long as it can be reproduced on the register in a clear, precise, self-contained, easily accessible, intelligible, durable and objective manner so as to enable the competent authorities and the public to determine with clarity and precision the subject matter of the protection afforded to its proprietor. The representation may be accompanied by a description.

D. Formal Requirements

473. Applications for registering a trademark shall be filed with the IPO. Each application may concern only one trademark (*section 19 of the Trademark Act*).

474. The IPO shall record the application's filing date. With the application's filing date, the applicant acquires the right of priority against any third person who later files an application for an identical or similar trademark for identical or similar goods or services (*section 20 of the Trademark Act*).

475. The IPO carries out a formal examination to find out whether the application has all necessary particulars stipulated by the law, which is followed by a substantive examination to find out whether the designation applied for is qualified for registration, for instance, if it is not identical to an already-registered trademark or whether it is not a generic name or descriptive denomination, misleading or false indication, etc. The IPO operates a fully automated system of trademark procedures and a search system using random criteria (e.g., text wording of the trademark, type of trademark, classification of the figurative elements of trademark, trademark owner's name or classes of goods and services). All records of trademarks registered through the national and international procedure are recorded in the system. By registering in the Trademark Register, the owner acquires an exclusive right to use the trademark.[201]

E. Rights by Trademarks

476. The proprietor of a trademark shall have the exclusive right to use the trademark in relation to the goods or services covered by the trademark. The proprietor of the trademark shall prove his/her rights by means of an abstract from the Trademarks Register, or by means of a certificate of registration. The proprietor of the trademark shall have the right to use the sign ® together with the trademark.

477. Unless otherwise provided by the Trademark Act,[202] third parties may not use the following without the consent of the proprietor of the trademark in the course of trade:

(a) any sign identical to the trademark for goods or services identical to those for which the trademark is registered;
(b) any sign where, because of its identity or similarity to the trademark and because of the identity or similarity of the goods or services covered by the trademark, there exists a likelihood of confusion on the part of the public, including the likelihood of association between the sign and the trademark;
(c) any sign identical or similar to the trademark, irrespective of whether the goods or services for which it is used are identical, similar or not similar to those for which the trademark is registered, where the trademark has a reputation in the Czech Republic, and the use of the sign without due cause would take unfair advantage of, or be detrimental to, the distinctive character or the repute of the trademark (*section 8 of the Trademark Act*).

---

201. *See* https://upv.cz/en/ip-rights/trade-marks.html.
202. For example, in ss 10–11 of the Trademark Act.

F. Revocation of a Trademark

478. The IPO shall revoke a trademark in proceedings initiated upon an application filed by the third party if:

(a) within a continuous period of five years prior to the application for revocation, the trademark has not been put to genuine use in connection with the goods or services in respect of which it is registered, and there are no proper reasons for non-use; the use which commenced or which was resumed following five years of non-use of the trademark within three months preceding the filing of the application for revocation shall be disregarded where the preparations for the commencement or the resumption of the use occurred only after the proprietor becomes aware that the application for revocation may be filed;
(b) in consequence of acts or inactivity of the proprietor, the trademark has become a common name in the trade for a product or service in respect of which it is registered;
(c) in consequence of the use made of the trademark by the proprietor of the trademark or with his/her consent in respect of the goods or services for which it is registered, the trademark is liable to mislead the public, particularly as to the nature, quality or geographical origin of those goods or services (*section 31 of the Trademark Act*).

Invalidity of a Trademark

479. The IPO shall declare a trademark invalid in proceedings initiated upon an application filed by a third party, where the trademark has been registered contrary to the provisions of the Trademark Act or where the trademark application was not filed in good faith (*section 32 of the Trademark Act*).

VII. Protection of Biotechnological Inventions

A. General Observations

480. The area of protection of biotechnological inventions is governed by the Biotechnological Inventions Act,[203] and by the Patent Act. Biotechnological inventions are patentable if they concern:

203. Generally on the protection of biotechnological inventions, *see*, e.g., Doležal, T. Patentovat či nikoliv? Právní a morální dilemata spojená s komerční využitelností výstupů výzkumu na lidských embryonálních kmenových buňkách. Právní rozhledy. 2012, Vol. 20, No. 18, pp. 640 et seq. or Mišúr, P. Evropský parlament: Produkty získané biologickými procesy nesmějí být patentovatelné. Obchodněprávní revue. 2019, Vol. 11, No. 10, pp. 263 et seq.

(a) biological material,[204] which is isolated from its natural environment or produced by means of a technical process, even if it previously occurred in nature;
(b) plants or animals, if the technical feasibility of the invention is not confined to a particular plant or animal variety; or
(c) microbiological[205] or other technical process and a product, other than a plant or animal variety, obtained by this way (*section 2 of the Biotechnological Inventions Act*).

B. Exclusions of Patentability

481. Patents shall not be granted to:

(a) inventions whose commercial exploitation would be contrary to public policy or to principles of morality, namely to processes for cloning human beings, processes for modifying the germ line genetic identity of human beings, processes of using human embryos for industrial or commercial purposes or processes for modifying the genetic identity of animals which are likely to cause them to suffer without any substantial medical benefit to man or animal, and also to animals resulting from such processes; however, the contradiction to public policy or to principles of morality shall not be deduced merely from the fact that the exploitation of the invention is prohibited by legal regulations;
(b) a human body at various stages of its formation and development, and the simple discovery of one of its elements, including the sequence or partial sequence of a gene; this does not apply to an element isolated from the human body or otherwise produced by means of a technical process, including the sequence or partial sequence of a gene, even if the structure of that element is identical to that of a natural element; and
(c) plant and animal varieties or essential biological processes for the production of plants or animals (*section 3 of the Biotechnological Inventions Act*).

C. Scope of Protection

482. The protection conferred by a patent on a biological material possessing specific characteristics as a result of the invention shall extend to any biological material derived from that biological material through propagation or multiplication in an identical or divergent form and possessing those same characteristics.

---

204. Section 1(a) of the Biotechnological Inventions Act: biological material means any material containing genetic information and capable of reproducing itself or being reproduced in a biological system.
205. Section 1(b) of the Biotechnological Inventions Act: microbiological process means any process involving or performed upon or resulting in microbiological material.

483. The protection conferred by a patent on a process that enables a biological material to be produced possessing specific characteristics as a result of the invention shall extend to biological material directly obtained through this process and to any other biological material derived from the directly obtained biological material through propagation or multiplication in an identical or divergent form and possessing those same characteristics.

484. The protection conferred by a patent on a product containing or consisting of genetic information shall extend to all material in which the product is incorporated or in which the genetic information is contained and performs its function, except the human body at the various stages of its formation or development (*section 6 of the Biotechnological Inventions Act*).

VIII. Plant Breeders' Rights

A. General Observations

485. Czech plant breeders' rights are governed by the Plant Breeders Rights Act together with European legislation. Plant breeders' rights are a form of intellectual property designed specifically to protect new varieties of plants. As mentioned above, plant varieties as such are excluded from Czech patent law. The Plant Breeders Rights Act provides for the protection of plant varieties of all plant genera and species by plant breeder's rights.[206]

486. The plant variety right may be granted to varieties of all plant genera and species, including hybrids between genera and species (*section 3/1 of the Plant Breeders Rights Act*).

487. The Plant Breeders Rights Act does not define the term '*variety*' and, in this case, refers to the International Convention for the protection of new varieties (Convention). The Convention defines '*variety*' as a plant grouping within a single botanical taxon of the lowest known rank, which grouping, irrespective of whether the conditions for the grant of a breeder's right are fully met, can be:

(a) defined by the expression of the characteristics resulting from a given genotype or combination of genotypes;
(b) distinguished from any other plant grouping by the expression of at least one of said characteristics; and
(c) considered as a unit with regard to its suitability for being propagated unchanged (*Article 1(iv) of the Convention*).

---

206. *See* http://eagri.cz/public/web/en/ukzuz/portal/plant-varieties/plant-variety-rights/ohter/plant-variety-rights.html.

488. For the period from filing the application to the grant of plant variety rights until the variety becomes legally effective, the holder is entitled to reasonable compensation from each person who during such period exploited the variety in a manner which would require a licence granted by the holder after such rights have been granted (*section 23 of the Plant Breeders Rights Act*).

489. The holder may transfer the plant variety rights to the protected variety to a third person based on a written contract. If plant variety rights to the same protected variety belong to more persons, the share in such rights may be transferred to any of the co-holders without the others' consent; a co-holder may transfer his/her share to a third person only provided that none of the other co-holders accepts his/her written offer for transfer within one month upon its delivery.[207] A contract on the transfer of the plant variety rights to the protected variety or on the transfer of a share of the plant variety rights to the protected variety becomes effective on the day of its entry in the Register of Protected Varieties kept by the Central Institute for Supervising and Testing in Agriculture (the Institute). The Institute will make the entry after the administrative fee[208] under special legal regulation has been paid.

490. The plant variety rights may be maintained until the end of the twenty-fifth year after the year in which the granting of such rights came into effect; for protected varieties of trees, hops, vines and potatoes, the plant variety rights may be maintained until the end of the thirtieth year following the year in which the granting of such rights came into effect (*section 24 of the Plant Breeders Rights Act*).

B. Substantive Requirements

491. Plant variety rights may be granted to any variety which satisfies the conditions of novelty, distinctness, uniformity and stability (*section 3/2 of the Plant Breeders Rights Act*).

Novelty

492. The variety shall be deemed to satisfy the condition of novelty if, on the application's filing date, the propagating material or material from the variety harvest has not been sold or otherwise disposed of to others by or with the consent of the breeder, for purposes of exploitation of the variety:

(a) on the territory of the Czech Republic earlier than one year before the application has been filed; or
(b) outside the Czech territory earlier than four years before the application has been filed or, in the case of trees or vines, earlier than six years before the application has been filed (*section 4 of the Plant Breeders Rights Act*).

207. Unless the Plant Breeders Rights Act stipulates otherwise, the relations between the co-holders shall be governed by the Civil Code.
208. In the amount of CZK 1,000.

Distinctness

493. The variety shall be deemed to satisfy the condition of distinctness if it is clearly distinguishable from any other variety whose existence is a matter of common knowledge as of the application's filing date by reference to the expression of at least one characteristic resulting from its genotype or combination of genotypes (*section 5 of the Plant Breeders Rights Act*).

Uniformity and Stability

494. The variety shall be deemed to satisfy the conditions of uniformity and stability if it meets the requirements for uniformity and stability of the variety as set in a special legal regulation[209] (*section 6 of the Plant Breeders Rights Act*).

C. Formal Requirements

495. The Institute will examine whether the variety meets the conditions of novelty, distinctness, uniformity and stability and whether the proposed variety denomination complies with the conditions stipulated under the Plant Breeders Rights Act.[210] Compliance with the requirements of distinctness, uniformity and stability is ascertained using field and laboratory tests. When examining varieties to ascertain compliance with the conditions, the Institute may use the results of examinations of distinctness, uniformity and stability performed by professional institutions abroad (*section 14 of the Plant Breeders Rights Act*).

496. The Institute shall grant the applicant the plant variety rights to the variety and shall approve the proposed variety denomination by issuing a breeder's certificate,[211] provided all conditions stipulated by the Plant Breeders Rights Act have been met (*section 16 of the Plant Breeders Rights Act*).

D. Rights Conferred by Plant Variety Rights

497. The holder has the sole authority to use the protected variety on the territory of the Czech Republic, which consists of the right to exploit the propagating material of such variety as follows:

---

209. Section 26 of Act No. 219/2003 Coll., on marketing of seeds and planting material and on the amendments to some Acts (the Act on marketing of seeds and planting material), as last amended.
210. Conditions stipulated under s. 7 of the Plant Breeders Rights Act.
211. Section 16/2 of the Plant Breeders Rights Act: 'The breeder's certificate shall include the denomination of the species to which the variety belongs, variety denomination, name, surname, permanent residence address or business name, registered office and legal form of the holder. The certificate will also include the variety description prepared on the basis of the results of tests of distinctness, uniformity and stability'.

(a) production or propagation;
(b) conditioning for the purpose of propagation;
(c) offering for sale;
(d) sale or other marketing;
(e) import to Member States and export to third countries;
(f) export from the Member States and import to third countries;
(g) stocking for the purposes specified under letters (a)–(f).

498. The holder may provide his/her consent to a third person for using the protected variety (licence). The licence is provided in writing and must include an agreement on the licence fee (*section 19 of the Plant Breeders Rights Act*).

499. Termination and Cancellation of the Plant Variety Rights:

(a) The plant variety rights shall terminate upon the expiry of the period stipulated by this Act or if the holder fails to pay the maintenance fee even after a written notification by the Institute within a period specified by the Institute, or if the holder renounces his/her plant variety rights in writing to the Institute.
(b) Before the expiration of the plant variety rights, the Institute shall terminate such rights if the protected variety no longer meets the condition of uniformity and stability or if the holder fails to comply with his/her obligation under the Plant Breeders Rights Act concerning Variety Maintenance Control.
(c) If it is revealed that, at the time of the issue of the breeder's certificate effectively granting the plant variety rights, not all the conditions for the granting thereof have been met, the Institute shall cancel the breeder's certificate; in such a case, the plant variety rights granted shall be regarded as null and void (*section 25 of the Plant Breeders Rights Act*).

IX. Copyright

A. General Observations

500. Copyright and neighbouring rights are governed in the Czech Republic by the Copyright Act.[212] The subject matter of copyright shall be a literary work or any other work of art or a scientific work which is a unique outcome of the creative activity of the author and is expressed in any objectively perceivable manner including electronic form, permanent or temporary, irrespective of its scope, purpose or significance ('work') (*section 2 of the Copyright Act*).

212. Generally to the copyright law, *see*, e.g., Telec, I., Tůma, P. Autorský zákon, Komentář. Praha. C. H. Beck, 2019, Chaloupková, H., Holý, P., Urbánek, J. Mediální právo. Komentář. Praha. C. H. Beck, 2019. pp. 395 et seq., Zibner, J. Otázky odpovědnosti umělé inteligence za zásah do autorského práva. Revue pro právo a technologie. 2019, Vol. 10, No. 20, pp. 65 et seq., Salač, J. Autorská a průmyslová práva z pohledu zaměstnance a zaměstnavatele. Práce a mzda. 2019, Vol. 67, Nos 7–8, pp. 25 et seq. or Pavelcová, A. Autorská směrnice: nejasnosti převažují. Právní rádce. 2019, Vol. 27, No. 5, pp. 66 et seq.

501. Each and every work is unique. The existence of two identical works is, therefore, out of the question because one of them will be a forgery of the other. Only a natural person has the ability to create works as a unique outcome of the creative activity. On the contrary, legal persons lack such ability, and they can only execute the economic rights of the authors on the grounds of the law[213] or under a licence[214] granted by the author.

502. The work has to be expressed in any objectively perceivable manner. This means that other persons than the author may perceive the work; i.e., the copyright in a work shall arise at the moment when the work is expressed in any objectively perceivable form. The work cannot exist only in the author's mind.

503. In the light of the above, the protection of copyright is informal; i.e., no formal requisites need to be fulfilled to obtain protection because copyright exists from the moment the work is expressed in any objectively perceivable manner. It differs from industrial property rights, where, on the contrary, protection is subject to registration.[215]

B. Author

504. As mentioned above, the author is a natural person who created the work (*section 5/1 of the Copyright Act*). The Copyright Act lays down the legal presumption of authorship. Pursuant to the provision of section 6 of the Copyright Act, the author shall be the natural person whose real name is indicated in a usual manner on the work or is indicated with the work in the register administrated by the relevant collective rights manager, unless proven otherwise. This shall not apply in cases where such information is in conflict with other information so indicated. This provision shall also apply if such a name is a pseudonym, provided that the pseudonym used by the author evokes no doubts as to the author's identity.

C. Content of Copyright

505. Copyright shall include exclusive moral rights and exclusive economic rights.

Moral (Individual) Rights

506. Individual moral authors' rights include:

(a) right to decide about making his/her work public;

---

213. For example, Employee Work under s. 58 of the Copyright Act.
214. Under s. 2358 of the Civil Code.
215. *See* https://www.mkcr.cz/frequently-asked-questions-953.html?lang=en.

(b) right to claim authorship, including the right to decide whether and in what way his/her authorship is to be indicated when his/her work is made public and further used, provided that the indication of authorship is normal in such use; and
(c) right to inviolability of his/her work, in particular, the right to grant consent to any alteration of, or other intervention in his/her work, unless otherwise stipulated herein. Where the work is used by any other person, such use may not be executed in a way that detracts from the value of the work. The author shall have the right of supervision over such other person's compliance with this obligation (author's supervision) unless the nature of the work or its use implies otherwise, or unless it is not possible to fairly require the user to enable the author to exercise his/her right to supervision.

507. The author may not waive his/her moral rights. These rights are non-transferable and shall become extinct on the author's death (*section 11 of the Copyright Act*).

Economic Rights

508. The author shall have the right to use his/her work in its initial form or in a form adapted by another person or otherwise modified, whether separately or in a collection or connection with any other work or elements, and to grant authorization on a contractual basis to any other person to exercise that right.

509. The right to use a work shall mean:

(a) the right to reproduce a work;
(b) the right to distribute an original or a copy of the work;
(c) the right to rent an original or a copy of the work;
(d) the right to lend an original or a copy of the work;
(e) the right to exhibit an original or a copy of the work;
(f) the right to communicate the work to the public, including, but not limited to:
   (i) the right to perform the work live or from a fixation, and the right of transmitting the performance of the work;
   (ii) the right to broadcast the work;
   (iii) the right to retransmit the broadcast of the work;
   (iv) the right of performing the broadcast of the work (section 12 of the Copyright Act).

510. Economic rights may not be waived by the author; such rights are not transferable and are not subject to the execution of a decision (*section 26/1 of the Copyright Act* [216]). Economic rights are inheritable. Economic rights shall run for the life of the author and seventy years after his/her death. If a work has been created as the work of joint authors, the period of duration of economic rights shall be calculated from the death of the last surviving author. The period of duration of economic

216. This provision shall not apply to claims arising from such economic rights.

rights shall always be calculated from the first day of the year following the year in which the event decisive for its calculation occurred (*section 27 of the Copyright Act*).

D. Neighbouring Rights

511. According to the Copyright Act, neighbouring rights include the following:

(a) Rights of the Performer to his/her Artistic Performance.
(b) Right of the Phonogram Producer to his/her Phonogram.
(c) Right of the Audiovisual Fixation Producer to his/her First Fixation.
(d) Right of the Radio and Television Broadcaster to his/her Broadcasting.
(e) Right of the Publisher.
(f) Right of the First Publisher.

X. Know-How

A. General Observations

512. Czech law does not specially regulate know-how.[217] Know-how refers to unpatented knowledge of manufacture-technical information, organizational and business information, recipes, etc., resulting from experience. The term has no Czech equivalent. The term is not uniformly used even in theory; sometimes, it is understood broadly and includes not only non-patented inventions and other creative results of development but also databases and data, sometimes only as manufacturing and technological experience, which can be classified as industrial property.[218]

B. Protection of Know-How

513. Know-how could be part of a trade secret. Then we can apply the means of protecting trade secrets to protecting know-how. Therefore, unfair competition protection within the meaning of section 2985 of the Civil Code applies.[219] There are also other opinions on the possible protection of know-how that depend on, e.g., whether the author of the theory admits the possibility of owning know-how.

---

217. Generally on the know-how under Czech law, *see*, e.g., Horáček, R., Čada, K., Hajn, P. Práva k průmyslovému vlastnictví. 3. vydání. Praha. C. H. Beck, 2017. p. 305, Hajn, P. Když nevíme, jak právně vymezit 'know-how'. Obchodněprávní revue. 2010, Vol. 2, No. 11, pp. 313 et seq. or Lisse, L. Know-how v českém právním řádu. Právní rozhledy. 2003, Vol. 11, No. 10, pp. 503 et seq.
218. Hendrych, D. a kol. Právnický slovník. Praha: C. H. Beck, 2009.
219. Konstantin Lavrushin: Know-how after recodification, *see* https://www.epravo.cz/top/clanky/know-how-po-rekodifikaci-101436.html.

§2. TRADE NAMES (BUSINESS NAMES)

I. Definition and General Observation

514. The legal regulation of business names is contained primarily in the Civil Code. Pursuant to the provision of section 423 paragraph 1 of the Civil Code: '*A business name is a name under which the entrepreneur is registered in the Companies Register. An entrepreneur may not have several corporate names.*'[220]

515. The right to a business name lasts from the moment the entrepreneur acquires the business name, i.e., at the moment of its registration in the Companies Register, and lasts for the time when the entrepreneur is registered in the Companies Register (this is a formal condition for the existence of the business name). Entrepreneurs can change their business name and have a new business name registered in the business register. In the case of legal entities, this change requires a change in the founding document of the legal entity, as the name of the legal entity is a mandatory part of the founding legal act under the Civil Code.[221] In such a case, the change of the business name comes into effect when the new business name is registered in the Companies Register.

II. Requirements

516. An entrepreneur cannot choose any business name. In its creation, it is necessary to comply with certain rules, which include mainly the following:

(a) the business name must not be interchangeable with another business name;
(b) the business name must not be deceptive; and
(c) the business name must clearly and surely distinguish entrepreneurs from other entrepreneurs.

III. Protection of Business Names

517. The protection of the rights to the business name pertains to the first person to have lawfully used it. A person whose right to the business name has been affected has the same rights as in the case of protection against unfair competition (*section 423/2 of the Civil Code*).

---

220. On trade names under Czech law, *see*, e.g., Lavický, P. a kol. Občanský zákoník I. Obecná část (§ 1-654). Komentář. Praha. C. H. Beck, 2014. pp. 1614 et seq., Pullmannová, H. Název podnikatele jako věc a převod práv k němu se vztahujících. Obchodní právo. 2019, Vol. 28, No. 10, pp. 2 et seq. or Kopcová, M. Moderní funkce ochranných známek a jejich vliv na posouzení konfliktu ochranné známky s obchodní firmou v judikatuře SDEU. Právní rozhledy. 2019, Vol. 27, No. 8, pp. 282 et seq.
221. Specifically under s. 123/1 of the Civil Code.

518. The means of protection against unfair competition are regulated by section 2988 of the Civil Code. Under section 2988 of the Civil Code: '*A person whose right has been threatened or violated by unfair competition may request the violator to refrain from competing unfairly or to remove a defective state. This person may also request adequate satisfaction, compensation for damage and restitution of unjust enrichment.*'

Chapter 7. Securities

§1. General Introduction to Securities

519. Czech law defines the term 'security' in section 514 of the Civil Code as 'an instrument incorporating a right in such a manner that after issuing the security the right cannot be asserted or transferred without the relevant instrument'.[222] This general definition is, however, rather misleading as certain rights can be asserted or transferred without the relevant instrument. For example, a right to profit incorporated in a share may be transferred separately from a different security (a coupon), provided that certain criteria are met. The Civil Code provides basic legal criteria which every security has to meet, but only certain (and the most common) types of securities are defined in greater detail. As a result, there is no numerus clausus of securities governed by Czech law.

520. Corresponding to the standards of most European countries, securities may be issued in three different forms: bearer securities (au porteur); securities to order (ordre); or registered securities (au nom).

Au Porteur Securities

521. In accordance with section 1103 of the Civil Code, bearer securities are transferable indefinitely by mere handover. The law does not require the name of the owner of the security to be stated on the security itself.[223] A coupon (security in which a right to yield is incorporated) is a common example of a bearer security.

Ordre Securities

522. In the case of securities to order, the person authorized by the ordre security in its text is directly identified, either as the person in whose name the document was issued or one establishes his/her title to the bill through an uninterrupted series of endorsements (e.g., security).

Au Nom Securities

523. If the form of the security is not specified on the security itself, section 518 paragraph 2 of the Civil Code codifies that securities that indicate the name of the obligee are presumed to be securities to order, while securities that do not indicate

222. Generally on the Czech securities law, *see*, e.g., Marek, R., Ježek, V. Cenné papíry v novém občanském zákoníku. Komentář. Praha. C. H. Beck, 2013, Kotásek, J., Pihera, V., Pokorná J. Právo cenných papírů. Praha. C. H. Beck, 2013, Polišenská, P., Hrabalová, M., Perejdová A. Právo cenných papírů: výběr z důležitých soudních rozhodnutí v právu cenných papírů za období let 2002 až 2015. Praha. Wolters Kluwer, 2016 or Kříž, R. Několik poznámek k přeměně cenných papírů na zaknihované cenné papíry. Obchodněprávní revue. 2017, Vol. 6, No. 6, pp. 161 et seq.

223. Lavický, P. a kol.: Občanský zákoník I. Obecná část (§ 1-654). Komentář. 1. Edition, Praha: C. H. Beck, 2014, commentary on s. 519 of the Civil Code.

the name of the obligee are conclusively presumed to be bearer securities. The actual use of this provision is, however, limited as most types of securities cannot be issued in all three forms.

Book-entry securities

524. Securities which may be replaced by registration in a register and may not be transferred in a manner other than by changing the record in the register represent book-entry securities. Pursuant to section 525 of the Civil Code, book-entry securities may be fungible if delivered by the same issuer and if they create the same rights. Furthermore, the regulation which applies to material (paper form) securities applies to book-entry securities *mutatis mutandis*. However, all Czech book-entry securities are registered in the property and client's accounts governed by a single legal entity, namely the Central Depository of Securities (in Czech: Centrální depozitář cenných papírů). Moreover, the general principles applied to movables under Czech law may also apply to book-entry securities since book-entry securities are deemed to be movables, despite the lack of material substrate.[224]

Immobilized securities

525. Immobilized securities may be considered an alternative to book-entry securities. Immobilized securities are formed if an issuer hands over the securities to the depositary for the benefit of their owner as the initial acquirer. Pursuant to section 2413 of the Civil Code, if registered securities or securities to order are placed in deposit, the name of the owner of the securities is not provided on the securities when they are deposited. Both the issuer and the owners of immobilized securities may exercise rights vis-à-vis the depositary separately to the extent required by law, as regulated in the issue conditions, or otherwise agreed.[225] The issuer is obliged to hand over all the securities issued in the same emission to the depositary.[226] The securities may also be deposited after they have been issued (as a paper document).

526. One of the key aspects of immobilized securities is that similar rules apply to them and to book-entry securities. On the other hand, the main difference between the two is that immobilized securities keep their material substrate, and thus they can be released from deposit to be used as a common security. However, this process may be subject to regulation, depending on the nature of the securities. For example, subject to section 93a paragraph 6 of Act No. 256/2004 Sb., Coll, on Capital Markets, as amended, shareholders of certain joint-stock companies may not

224. Šovar, J. Úvaha nad některými aspekty práva nedržícího vlastníka na vydání zaknihovaných cenných papírů. Obchodněprávní revue, No. 3/2015, C. H. Beck, p. 81.
225. Pihera, V. in Hulmák, M. a kol.: Občanský zákoník VI. Závazkové právo. Zvláštní část (§ 2055–3014). Komentář. 1. Edition. Praha: C. H. Beck, 2014, p. 766.
226. This conclusion corresponds to the fact that the provisions on the register of immobilized securities governing the register of issues of book-entry securities shall be applied *mutatis mutandis* for the register of immobilized securities (s. 93a para. 7 of Act No. 256/2004 Sb., Coll, on Capital Markets, as amended).

demand the issuance of immobilized shares to owners from the depository. Excluding immobilized shares from the holders of the collective depository is permissible only if they change their form at the same time or if they are simultaneously entrusted to another depositary by the procedure in accordance with this provision.

Regulation of securities

527. Under Czech law, securities are mainly governed by the following statutory acts:

(a) Act No. 89/2012 Coll., the Civil Code, as amended, provides the basic legal background for the transferability and issuance of securities and book-entry securities issued under Czech law. Furthermore, certain securities (such as coupons) are closely specified by the Civil Code itself.
(b) Act No. 90/2012 Coll., on Commercial Companies and Cooperatives (Business Corporations Act), as amended (the 'Corporations Act'), provides a rather complex legal background for certain securities related to business corporations, such as shares, common certificates, convertible bonds, preferential bonds, interim certificates and warrants (in order for the preferential right).
(c) Act No. 240/2013 Coll., on Investment Corporations and Investment Funds, as amended, provides *inter alia* the codification of investment certificates issued by the Investment Certificates Limited Partnership (in Czech: komanditní společnost na investiční listy) and share certificates.
(d) Act No. 190/2004 Coll., Act on Bonds.
(e) Act No. 191/1950 Coll., Act on promissory notes and cheques.
(f) Act No. 307/2000 Coll., Act on Agricultural Stock Certificates and Agricultural Public Warehouses.

Different kinds of securities

528. The following securities are the most frequently used securities issued under Czech law; they are analysed in greater detail below:

(a) share;
(b) common certificate;
(c) convertible bond;
(d) preferential bond;
(e) interim certificate;
(all (a) to (e) are regulated mainly by the Corporations Act)
(f) bond (regulated mainly by the Act on Bonds);
(g) promissory note; and
(h) cheque.
Both (g) and (h) are regulated by the Act on promissory notes and cheques.

529. A *share* [227] is a security or a book-entry security to which the right of the shareholder to participate as a member in managing the company and its profits or liquidation balance in the case of its dissolution with liquidation are attached (*see* section 256 paragraph 1 of the Corporations Act). The exact rights and obligations incorporated in a share are listed in the Corporations Act as well as in the company's articles of association that issued the respective share. Shares may be in the form of a security in registered form, which is referred to as a registered share, or in bearer form, which is referred to as a bearer share. This applies similarly to book-entry shares. The transferability of registered shares may be limited by the statutes. A restriction on the transferability of registered shares or a change thereto shall take effect on the date of entry of this fact in the Companies Register. Such a restriction may never lead to the complete exclusion of the transferability of the shares. The second general limit to transferability is set by section 244 of the Corporations Act, which states that '[a] company shall treat all of its shareholders in the same manner under the same circumstances'. Nevertheless, this limitation cannot be strictly understood as a prohibition of restricting the transferability of shares with respect to only certain shares. As the Corporations Act allows a joint-stock company to issue various types of shares, certain types of shares may be transferable without any limitation, while certain restrictions may apply to other types of shares. Accordingly, the right of shareholders to be treated in the same manner under the same circumstances with respect to said restriction means that within the single type of shares, there cannot be any difference as far as the restriction of transferability is concerned. Consequently, the possibility of restricting the transferability is to be decided case by case while taking into account all the relevant factors relating to the company. It is safe to point out, however, that approval by the company's general meeting as a condition precedent for transferring shares is allowed (and rather common) in the Czech Republic if specified in the articles of association.

530. Shares commonly include their par value, which corresponds to the participation (i.e., the rights and obligations) in the joint-stock company related to the respective share. Where so provided in the articles of association, a company may issue no-par value shares. In such a case, the share in the share capital of a no-par value share is determined by the number of shares. If a company issues no-par value shares, it cannot issue or have issued shares with a nominal value. The use of no-par value shares may be beneficial both for joint-stock companies incorporated in the Czech Republic and for their shareholders. One of the main benefits of no-par value shares becomes apparent when it comes to the process of increasing the company's registered capital from the company's own resources (or alternatively for reducing

---

227. Generally on shares under Czech law, *see*, e.g., Štenglová, I., Havel, B., Cileček, F., Kuhn, P., Šuk, P. Zákon o obchodních korporacích. Komentář. 2. vydání. Praha. C. H. Beck, 2017, pp. 510 et seq., Dědič, J., Štenglová, I., Kříž, R., Čech, P. Akciové společnosti. 7., přepracované vydání. Praha. C. H. Beck, 2012, pp. 101 et seq., Lasák, J., Dědič, J. Pokorná, J., Čáp, Z. a kol. Zákon o obchodních korporacích. Komentář. 2. vydání. Praha. Wolters Kluwer, 2021, pp. 1202 et seq. or Kříž, R. Několik poznámek k formě a omezené převoditelnosti zaknihovaných akcií. Bulletin Advokacie. 2019, Vol. 2019, No. 6, pp. 26 et seq.

its registered capital). As there is no need to change[228] the no-par values as a result of increasing the registered capital, considerable transaction costs are reduced as it is not necessary to collect and reissue new shares. Another advantage is related to currency changes. If a joint-stock company decides to change to EUR as its accounting currency (if allowed by accounting regulation), or if the Czech Republic decides to adopt the Euro as its currency, this change would cause the registered capital to be set in EUR rather than in CZK.[229] Consequently, all the par value would have to be changed. Such change would once again not influence no-par value shares.

531. A share shall include: (a) its designation as a share; (b) an unambiguous identification of the company; (c) its par value (or information that no-par value shares were issued – in such a case, the words 'no-par value' (in Czech: kusová akcie) have to be included); (d) indication of the form of share; (e) in the case of a registered share, an unambiguous identification of the shareholder; and (f) information about the type of share, and a description of the rights attached to it, at least by reference to the articles of association, if shares of different types are to be issued. The no-par value share must contain the designation 'no-par share'. Where a book-entry share is issued, it shall be sufficient that the information listed above is identifiable from the book-entry securities register operated by the Central Depository of Securities.

532. Furthermore, each share shall also include a numerical marking and the signature of the member(s) of the board of directors or the management board. The signatures may be replaced by a signature print, provided that the security features are simultaneously used in the deed in order to protect it against counterfeiting or alteration. For obvious reasons, this requirement is not requested in respect of book-entry shares.

533. Under Czech law, a joint-stock company may issue a share with which the same rights are attached. These shares then form one type of share. The Corporations Act only codifies certain types; hence, it is up to the joint-stock company and its shareholders to set the exact set of rights and obligations that are to be attached to the share. Certain types of shares (e.g., shares to which the right to a certain interest regardless of the company's economic results is attached) are, however, expressly prohibited.

534. Shares of the same nominal value or no-par value shares may carry different rights or different weightings of votes attached to the share. That being said, there are certain ground rules that each share needs to follow. The most important limitation is codified in section 256 paragraph 1 of the Corporations Act, which states that '[a] share is a security or a book-entry security to which the right of the shareholder to participate as a member in managing the company and the profits or

228. In the case of par values, the shares are either to be changed or the new nominal value of the shares is to be marked on each share.

229. Dedič, J. Nenápadné výhody kusových akcií. Online. Patria.cz, 2012. Accessible at: https://www.patria.cz/pravo/2178924/nenapadne-vyhody-kusovych-akcii.html.

liquidation balance in the case of its dissolution with liquidation, in accordance with this Act and the company's articles of association, are attached'. Therefore, each share must always allow its shareholder to participate: (i) in managing the company, (ii) in the company's profit, and (iii) in the liquidation balance in the case of the company's liquidation. None of the above-mentioned rights can be taken away from the share completely.

535. That being said, these requirements are not to be interpreted in a way which would completely prohibit any limitation of the aforesaid rights. For example, a share may be issued without a voting right[230] since the right to participate in managing the company remains despite the lack of voting right incorporated in the share, as such right also includes the right to participate in the company's general meeting, the right to make proposals and counterproposals during the general meeting, the right to request information from the statutory body, etc. However, these non-voting shares may be issued only if the aggregate of their nominal values does not exceed 90% of the share capital.

536. Other limitation criteria (apart from the criteria set above) that always need to be met are set by the general principles of Czech private law. Any change of rights and obligations incorporated in a share is, therefore, subject to the criteria of *bonos mores* (in Czech: dobré mravy), public order (in Czech: veřejný pořádek), or the law concerning the person's status (in Czech: statusové otázky) (*see* section 1 paragraph 2 of the Civil Code).

537. A preference share is one of the special types of shares expressly codified by the Corporations Act. A preference share may only be issued if expressly allowed by the company's articles of association. A preference share comes with priority rights concerning a profit share or a share in the company's other own resources or in the company's liquidation balance. To balance the preference related to the profit, a preference share is issued without voting rights at the joint-stock company's general meeting unless provided otherwise in the articles of association or by the Corporations Act. In this reference, it is key to mention that even the rules specified in the Corporations Act regarding priority shares are not cogent and, therefore, the articles of association may attach different rights and obligations to priority shares.

538. Moreover, the articles of association may provide that a company's employees may acquire its shares or shares of its affiliates under preferential terms. These preferential terms may provide that employees do not have to pay up the entire issue price of the subscribed shares or that they may acquire them under other preferential terms, provided that the difference, if any, between the paid-up part of the issue price and the price, or between the issue price and the price, is covered

---

230. A preference share issued without a voting right is expressly codified by the Corporations Act. Although Czech jurisprudence is not united whether shares without a voting right (other than preference shares) may be issued, the majority of Czech jurisprudence considers such approach a valid option. *See*, e.g., Černá, I. Lze Akcionářům odejmout zákonem přiznaná práva, aneb kdy přestává akcie být akcií?. Bulletin advokacie. 12/2017, p. 17, or Lasák. J. O limitech lidské představivosti: glosa k akciím bez hlasovacího práva (jiným než prioritním). Právní rozhledy 2/2017, p. 58.

from the company's own resources. The rules on employees' shares also apply *mutatis mutandis* to company employees who have retired. Employees' shares are one of the exceptions when it comes to the general rule that a company is to treat all of its shareholders in the same manner under the same circumstances.

539. A common certificate (in Czech: kmenový list) may represent a member's business share in a limited liability company incorporated under Czech law if so provided by the company's memorandum of association. Although the regulation of common certificates partly corresponds to the regulation of shares in a joint-stock company, the regulation itself is not as strict and thorough. The regulation of common certificates corresponds well to the less formal structure of limited liability companies.

540. A common certificate can only be issued for a business share that is not subject to any restrictions or conditions regarding its transferability. A common certificate is an order instrument and cannot be issued as a book-entry security. As a result of less strict regulatory rules, common certificates may also not be subject to public offering or admitted for trading on a European regulated market or other public markets.

541. A common certificate has to include: (a) its designation as a common certificate; (b) an unambiguous identification of the company; (c) the amount of the contribution relating to the business share; (d) an unambiguous identification of the member; (e) the name of the type of share for which the common certificate is issued if the articles of association provide for more than one type of share, and the designation of the share for which the share certificate is issued; (f) the number of the common certificate and the signature of the executive(s). The signature may be replaced by a signature print, provided that security features are simultaneously used in the deed in order to protect it against counterfeiting or alteration.

542. If there is more than one common certificate issued by the same company and owned by the same entity, a global common certificate may be issued to replace them. The global certificate has to include information about the number of common certificates substituted by it as well as identify the business shares substituted by it.

543. An *interim certificate* [231] is a security to which the rights and obligations arising from an outstanding share may be attached. An interim certificate may only be issued if allowed by the company's articles of association. The establishment of a joint-stock company may only be effective in cases where every founder has paid up the share premium if any, and at least 30% in aggregate of the par value (or book

231. Generally on interim certificates, *see*, e.g., Štenglová, I., Havel, B., Cileček, F., Kuhn, P., Šuk, P. Zákon o obchodních korporacích. Komentář. 2. vydání. Praha. C. H. Beck, 2017, pp. 546 et seq., Dědič, J., Štenglová, I., Kříž, R., Čech, P. Akciové společnosti. 7., přepracované vydání. Praha. C. H. Beck, 2012, pp. 119 et seq. or Lasák, J., Dědič, J., Pokorná, J., Čáp, Z. a kol. Zákon o obchodních korporacích. Komentář. 2. vydání. Praha. Wolters Kluwer, 2021, pp. 1410 et seq.

value in the case of no-par value shares) of the subscribed shares within the period set in the articles of association and on the bank account set up by the deposit administrator, but no later than by the date of filing the application for the company's registration in the Companies Register. Hence, Czech law does not require each shareholder to pay the whole par value (or book value) of each share prior to joint-stock company's date of registration. Should that be the case, the joint-stock company may issue an interim certificate that is to be replaced by a share when the par value (or the book value) of the stock is fully paid up.

544. Interim certificates may only be issued as securities to order (ordre). Pursuant to section 285 paragraph 2 of the Corporations Act, each interim certificate must include: (a) an indication of the interim certificate; (b) an unambiguous identification of the company; (c) an unambiguous identification of the interim certificate holder; (d) the par value consisting of the sum of the par values of the outstanding shares; (e) the number of shares substituted by the interim certificate, their form or an indication that it replaces book-entry shares and specification of their type, if different types are to be issued; (f) the paid-up and outstanding part of the issue price of the shares and the maturity dates; and (g) signature of the member(s) of the board of directors or the management board. The signature may be replaced by a signature print, provided that the security features are simultaneously used in the deed in order to protect it against counterfeiting or alteration.

545. Since joint-stock companies are entitled to the rest of the par value (or the book value) of the shares to be paid by the owner of the interim certificate, Czech law establishes a liability of the transferor in cases where the interim certificate is transferred. This concept lowers the risk for an already-registered joint-stock company if the transferee (i.e., the new owner of the interim certificate) cannot pay the rest of the par value (or the book value) of the share in time. The liability of the transferee cannot be contracted away by the agreement entered into between the transferor and the transferee of the respective interim certificate.

546. A bond[232] is a security (or a book-entry security) with the right of the holder to require repayment of the sum owed in the nominal amount from the issuer (*see* section 2 paragraph 2 of the Act on Bonds). Bonds may be due at one time or in several instalments. Other rights codified mainly in the Act on Bonds or arising from the issue conditions (in Czech: emisní podmínky) are also attached to the bonds. Bonds may only be substitutable.

547. Pursuant to section 6 of the Act on Bonds, each bond has to include: (a) the term 'bond' (in Czech: dluhopis) unless it is a covered bond, a treasury bill or a voucher issued by the CNB; (b) an indication of the type of bond, which may be given by reference to the issue conditions, unless it is a bond with no specific right; (c) data identifying the issuer; (d) the nominal value as the amount due; (e) the yield

232. Generally on bonds, *see*, e.g., Bohumil, S. Teorie a praxe dluhopisů I. Praha. Vysoká škola ekonomická v Praze, 2013 or Špička, M. Stahují se nad emisemi korporátních dluhopisů mračna? Právní rádce. 2018, Vol. 24, No. 3, pp. 36 et seq.

of the bond or an indication that the return is determined by the difference between the nominal value of the bond and its issue rate; or, at least, it is clear from the bond that the bond is out of revenue or where it is possible to get acquainted with how it is earned; (f) the date or other time of repayment of the amount due (repayment of the bond) or, where applicable, information on the repayment of the amount due; (g) data identifying the bondholder, unless it is a book-entry bond; (h) the issuer's signature, unless it is a book-entry bond; (i) the numerical designation of the bond, unless it is a book-entry bond; (j) the date of issue; (k) identification of the bond according to the international numbering system for the identification of securities. Should a bond be issued as a book-entry security, all the information required by law (with the exception of the issuer's signature) has to be apparent from the Central Depository for Securities.

548. In the case that the issuer intends to issue bonds, the issue conditions (in Czech: emisní podmínky) of the bonds are to be completed prior to the date of issue. The issue conditions set out in more detail the rights and obligations of the issuer and the bondholders, as well as the bond issue information, including reference to the information contained in the prospectus, if a prospectus is to be completed as well (*see* section 8 of the Act on Bonds). Changes can be made to the issue conditions of the bonds; however, prior approval of the bond owners' meeting is required unless the law explicitly allows otherwise (e.g., in such a case, any change of the relevant legislation has to be reflected in the issue conditions).

549. Pursuant to section 16 of the Act on Bonds, the bond yield may be determined, in particular, as: (a) a fixed interest rate, (b) the difference between the nominal value of the bond and its issue rate, (c) a draw premium or bonus depending on the maturity of the bond, or (d) a floating interest rate derived, for example, from other interest rates or interest income, movements in exchange rates, financial indices or commodity prices. If not excluded by the issue conditions, the right to the bond yield may be separately transferred from the bond and attached to a coupon as a security or book-entry security issued to exercise that right.

550. The Corporations Act acknowledges additional types of bonds, namely convertible and preferential. A joint-stock company may, if so provided by the articles of association, issue convertible bonds with the right to be exchanged for shares or preferential bonds that include a preferential right to subscription of shares. The issue of convertible bonds may be conditional upon an exchange for shares already issued or to a simultaneous decision by the company on a conditional increase of the registered capital. The issue of preferential bonds shall be conditional upon a simultaneous decision by the company on a conditional increase of the registered capital. Although the convertible and preferential bonds are codified in the Corporations Act, they do not form a completely separate category of bonds as the provisions of the Act on Bonds apply to convertible bonds and preferential bonds nevertheless unless explicitly provided otherwise by law. The shareholders have a preferential right to acquire convertible or preferential bonds; such right can be, however, waived.

Bills of Exchange and Promissory Notes[233]

551. A bill of exchange (in Czech: směnka cizí) and a promissory note (in Czech: směnka vlastní) are both primarily governed by Act No. 191/1950 Coll., as amended, Act on Bills of Exchange and Cheque (the 'Bills of Exchange Act'). Although the Bills of Exchange Act was subject to minor changes over the last seventy years, none of the changes was severe (the most important change was related to the complete recodification of the Insolvency Act in 2006). Surprisingly, the Bills of Exchange Act is actually the oldest still effective private law act valid and in force in the Czech Republic. The Act itself is heavily influenced by the Geneva Conventions on the Bills of Exchange and promissory notes from the 1930s. As a result, the Czech law regarding Bills of Exchange and promissory notes is very similar to the legislation that can be found in other states of continental Europe. Moreover, the same Bills of Exchange Act (subject to some minor changes) still remains effective in Slovakia as well.

Differences between a Bill of Exchange and a Promissory Note

552. A promissory note (in Czech: směnka vlastní) is, in essence, an unconditional promise of a drawer (issuer) to pay a determinate sum of money to a creditor (payee). As a rule, a promissory note also needs to contain the expression 'promissory note' (in Czech: 'směnka') in the promise. The promise itself may be, therefore, stated as follows: 'I will pay for this promissory note to the creditor (followed by the name of the creditor) CZK […]. (Signed) Issuer.' As a result, the most basic form of promissory note only includes two participants – the drawer (issuer) and the creditor (payee). Hence, a promissory note forms the drawer's obligation to pay the debt to the creditor.

553. A bill of exchange (in Czech: směnka cizí) is distinguished from a promissory note *inter alia* by the fact that (in its basic form) it includes at least three participants (a drawer (issuer), a creditor, and a drawee). The substance of a bill of exchange is a payment order from a drawer to a drawee to pay a certain financial sum to a creditor. A bill of exchange, therefore, contains the expression 'Pay for this bill of exchange to the creditor (followed by the name of the creditor) CZK […]. (Signed) Issuer.'

554. A bill of exchange is a security to order. When applying rights from a bill of exchange, it is always necessary to present the bill or to hand it over to the obliged person. Usually, the bill is a circulation security, which can be transferred

233. Generally on bills of exchange or promissory notes, *see*, e.g., Kovařík, Z. Zákon směnečný a šekový. Komentář. 6., dopl. vydání. Praha. C. H. Beck, 2014, Kovařík, Z. Směnka a šek v České republice. 6., přeprac. a dopl. vyd. Praha. C. H. Beck, 2011, Bakeš, M. a kol. Finanční právo, 5. vydání. Praha. C. H. Beck, 2009, pp. 411 et seq. or Kovařík, Z. Zákon o omezení plateb v hotovosti ve vztahu ke směnce a šeku. Právní rozhledy. 2005, Vol. 13, No. 7, pp. 234 et seq.

by endorsement. However, the transferability may be excluded by a negative clause. A bill cannot be issued as a bearer security either.[234] The first entitled person always has to be written on the bill.

555. The Bills of Exchange Act allows for the number of participants to be reduced since the drawer, drawee and creditor need not be three different persons. The Bills of Exchange Act enables a bill of exchange drawn on the drawer himself/herself and a bill of exchange payable to his/her order. A bill of exchange with only one participant is invalid. A bill of exchange drawn on the drawer himself/herself is a bill of exchange where the drawer declares himself/herself as the creditor by the words 'to my own order' (in Czech: na svůj vlastní řad).[235] The drawer and payee are the same person in this case.

556. A bill of exchange payable to the drawer's order is a bill of exchange where the drawer orders himself/herself to pay to the payee. The drawer and drawee are the same person in this case. To get a direct debtor, the bill of exchange has to bear an acceptance by the drawee.

Participants

557. A person becomes liable on a bill only after his/her signature is put on it. Debtors (drawers) may sign a bill of exchange in the position of a direct or indirect (regress) debtor. A direct debtor is the one against whom it is possible to claim directly and without so-called preserving (maintaining) acts (presentation and protest). Putting forward the claim is, in fact, not bound with presumptions other than the due presentation of a bill of exchange.

558. On the other hand, a regress debtor is a secondary debtor. The main role of a regress debtor is to secure the debt arising from the bill of exchange in the case that the direct debtor fails to fulfil its obligations. It includes cases when either a bill of exchange is not accepted or the debt is not paid duly or on time.

559. Czech law recognizes the following participants with respect to a bill of exchange.

560. Drawer (Issuer): an issuer as an author of the promise or order to pay is the key person of the bill relationship (*see* section 9 paragraph 1 of the Bills of Exchange Act). The issuer must always sign the bill of exchange or the promissory note since the lack of the drawer's signature causes it to be invalid (*see* section 1 point 8 of the Bills of Exchange Act). The issuer may be either a direct or an indirect debtor. The issuer of a promissory note promises to pay the creditor by the due date; therefore, he/she is the direct debtor. The drawer of a bill of exchange is an indirect debtor (*see* section 9 paragraph 1 of the Bills of Exchange Act). The drawer

234. Judgment of the Supreme Court of the Czech Republic dated 22 Aug. 2007, File No. 29 Odo 574/2006.
235. Such a declaration is expressively allowed by s. 3 para. 1 of the Bills of Exchange Act.

guarantees both acceptance and payment and may be approached if either the bill of exchange was not accepted or the debt arising from the bill of exchange was not paid duly and on time. However, pursuant to section 9 paragraph 2 of the Bills of Exchange Act, a drawer may exclude itself from guaranteeing acceptance with the special stipulation 'without recourse for acceptance'.

561. Creditor (Payee): A payee is a person named on the front page of a bill of exchange or a promissory note to receive the respective payment. The payee is the first creditor and beneficiary from a bill.

562. Drawee: A drawee of a bill of exchange is the addressee of the drawer's payment promise. He/she is the person who is to make the payment to the creditor. However, he/she only becomes a debtor if he/she accepts the bill of exchange (*see* section 28 paragraph 1 of the Bills of Exchange Act). A drawee may only be a participant to a bill of exchange, as the issuer of the promissory note is always the person who is to promise to make the payment.

563. Acceptor: As mentioned above, a drawee is only obliged to make the payment if it accepts the drawer's order. Acceptance of the bill of exchange benefits the creditor; hence, a bill of exchange is likely to be accepted (provided that the drawer and the drawee cooperate during the whole process) before the bill is passed on to the creditor. Only the person stated as the drawee can accept the bill. An acceptor is a direct debtor of a bill of exchange (in an analogical position to the issuer of a promissory note).

564. Surety: The Bills of Exchange Act stipulates a special guarantee for payment of a bill (also called aval). The surety is a person giving a guarantee and secures the payment arising from the bill of exchange or promissory note to be duly and timely made. The surety is bound in the same manner as the person for whom he has become a guarantor. A simple signature constitutes a surety (aval) relationship unless the person who signed the bill of exchange or the promissory note is either a drawee or an issuer (*see* section 31 paragraph 3 of the Bills of Exchange Act).

565. Endorser and Endorsee: Unless expressly specified on the bill of exchange or the promissory note, each promissory note or bill of exchange may be transferred by means of an endorsement. The parties of endorsement are the endorser and endorsee. The endorser, by means of the endorsement, endorses the rights arising from the bill to the other party, the endorsee. The first endorser is always the payee. The endorser would become an indirect (regress) debtor unless it excluded itself from the guarantee by a special stipulation.[236]

566. Domicile: A bill of exchange may be payable at the domicile of a third person either in the place where the drawee has his/her domicile or in another place (*see* section 4 of the Bills of Exchange Act). In such a case, the person stated on the

236. Such exclusion is allowed by s. 15 of the Bills of Exchange Act.

bill of exchange as the domicile does not benefit nor is obliged from the respective bill of exchange or the promissory note as the name of the person is only used to state the place where the bill of exchange or the promissory note is to be due. Such a place may also be stated by different means (commonly by stating an address).

Forms

567. A bill of exchange or a promissory note must always be in writing. Writing includes handwriting, typing or printing (with the exception of signatures, which is always to be in handwriting). A book-entry bill of exchange is not allowed by Czech law.

568. A blank bill of exchange or a promissory note is intentionally issued as incomplete. Commonly, a blank bill of exchange or a promissory note is used as a security provided for the debtor. The due date and the bill sum are usually left blank for the creditor to complete in the case that a debt has not been duly and timely paid. An agreement on the right to fill a promissory note (or the bill of exchange) specifying the rights and obligations of the debtor is likely to be executed in relation to the issuance of a blank promissory note as it provides a certain level of security for the debtor(s).

Principle of Independence of Bill Statements

569. The Bills of Exchange Act states that if a bill of exchange bears signatures of persons incapable of binding themselves by a bill of exchange, or forged signatures, or signatures of fictitious persons, or signatures which for any other reason cannot bind the person who signed the bill of exchange or on whose behalf it was signed, the validity of the obligations of the other persons who have signed is not prejudiced (*see* section 7 of the Bills of Exchange Act). Furthermore, the High Court in Prague has stated that an internal reservation in the execution of a legal act has no effect on the legal relationship established by that act. Even the assertion of the issuer of a promissory note that he/she intended to secure only part of the debt by a promissory note, although he/she issued the promissory note to the remitter's proposal to secure the entire debt, could not change their relationship.[237] Hence, it is apparent that even Czech courts approach the questions regarding promissory notes and Bills of Exchange rather formally.

237. Judgment of the High Court in Prague dated 8 Jan. 2001, File No. 9 Cmo 471/2001 stated that 'an internal reservation in the execution of a legal act has no effect on the legal relationship established by that act. Even the assertion of the issuer of a promissory note that he intended to secure only part of the debt by promissory note, although he issued the promissory note to the remitter's proposal to secure the entire debt, could not change their relationship'.

Chapter 8. Commercial Contracts

§1. General Principles of Contract Law

570. Since 2014, Czech contract law – including basic contract types and their essential elements – has been regulated mainly in the Civil Code. Before the Civil Code came into effect, Czech contract law regulation was scattered between the former Civil Code (Act No. 40/1964 Coll., the Civil Code) and the Commercial Code (Act No. 513/1991 Coll., the Commercial Code), whereas a number of contract types were regulated in both regulations (e.g., contracts for work). While the Commercial Code was applied for relationships between entrepreneurs, the former Civil Code governed the other contractual relationships.

571. Since the new Civil Code repealed both the former Civil Code and the Commercial Code, the dichotomy of Czech contract law was removed. Therefore, contractual relationships are no longer governed by two different legal codes and are, on the contrary, subject solely to the Civil Code. As a consequence, any special rules applicable to businesses are only dealt with separately for each type of contract. Nevertheless, certain special acts obviously still apply to some special types of contracts (such as employment contracts, which are subject to and governed by the Labour Code (Act No. 262/2006 Coll., the Labour Code)).

572. According to Czech legal doctrine, a contract[238] is a bilateral or multilateral legal act that leads to the creation of an obligation.[239] The fundamental principle upon which Czech contract law is based is the autonomy of will, which reflects the general requirement of human freedom and the possibility of free decision-making and acting in accordance with such decision. It can be briefly described as a broad possibility for private entities to form relationships according to their free will, which is protected by private and constitutional law.[240] The Czech Constitution[241] and related case law of the Czech Constitutional Court[242] understand the autonomy of will as the possibility of acting in a way that is not prohibited by law and concurrently as a prohibition against forcing anyone to do what the law does not impose. In this light, we can deduce that autonomy of will can be restricted by law in certain cases. Typical examples are the corrections thereof connected to *bonos mores*, public order, protection of weaker party and principles of fairness and good faith.

238. Please note that Czech law does not differentiate between contracts and agreements. Certain types of obligations are usually used with the term 'contract' while others with the term 'agreement'. Nonetheless, such difference is merely an expression of a language convention.
239. Hulmák, M. In Hulmák, M. a kol.: Občanský zákoník V. Závazkové právo. Obecná část (§ 1721–2054). 1. edition. Prague: C. H. Beck, 2014, p. 18.
240. Lavický, P. In Lavický, P. a kol.: Občanský zákoník I. Obecná část (§ 1-654). Komentář. 1. edition, Prague: C. H. Beck, 2014, pp. 51–65.
241. *See* Art. 2(4) of the Czech Constitution or Art. 2(3) of the Czech CHRF.
242. Decision of the Czech Constitutional Court from 12 May 2004, File No. I. ÚS 167/04, decision of the Czech Constitutional Court from 6 Nov. 2007, File No. II. ÚS 3/06, or decision of the Czech Constitutional Court from 13 Sep. 2019, File No. II. ÚS 4235/18.

573. Specifically, in contract law autonomy of will is an expression of the possibility: (i) to choose whether to enter into a contract or not, (ii) to determine the second contracting party (e.g., the recipient of a legal offer), and (iii) to determine the content of the respective contract. The above-mentioned restrictions apply in respect of determining the content of a contract, whereas the choice of the contracting party is restricted by anti-discrimination regulation (e.g., Act No. 198/2009 Coll., the anti-discrimination law).

574. In addition to the above, Czech Commercial contract law is – within the framework of the Civil Code – governed mainly by the following principles.

I. *Pacta Sunt Servanda*

575. The requirement for contracts to be respected is another historical fundamental principle common to legal systems across the world, which basically means that the creditor cannot be forced to accept against its will anything other than what corresponds to its claim and that the debtor cannot be forced to provide anything against its will other than what is owed in the place, time and manner agreed by the parties in the contract (*see* section 1910 of the Civil Code). Also, according to the Czech Constitutional Court, Czech private law is based on – besides autonomy of will – the principle of *pacta sunt servanda*, which is even considered the highest principle of law, or the highest natural rule from which all law is derived.[243]

576. A contract is binding for the parties even if the performance thereof becomes more onerous for one of them (*see* section 1764 of the Civil Code). Nevertheless, this rule shall not apply in the case of a substantial change of circumstances that creates a gross disproportion in the rights and duties of the parties by disadvantaging one of them, either by disproportionately increasing the cost of the performance or disproportionately reducing the value of the subject of performance. In such a case, the affected party has the right to request renegotiating the contract with the other party, provided that it is proved that the affected party could not have anticipated or influenced the change and that the change occurred only after the contract was concluded or the party became aware thereof only after the contract was concluded (*see* section 1765(1) of the Civil Code). Upon failure to renegotiate the contract within a reasonable time limit, the court may, at the request of either party, issue a decision to change the contractual obligation by restoring the balance of the parties' rights and duties or cancelling it as of the date and under the conditions specified in the respective court decision (*see* section 1766(1) of the Civil Code).

243. *See* the decision of the Czech Constitutional Court from 13 Sep. 2019, File No. II. ÚS 4235/18.

577. Additionally, any party can demand termination of a contract that has been concluded for a definite period (without a serious reason) binding an individual for his/her entire life, or binding anyone for more than ten years[244] (*see* section 2000(1) of the Civil Code).

II. Principle of Fairness

578. One of the next general principles of Czech private law is everyone's obligation to act fairly in legal transactions (*see* section 6(1) of the Civil Code).

579. The general nature of section 6 of the Civil Code implies that the principle of fairness always applies, i.e., even if no specific provision expressly invokes it. Any private relationship can thus be measured by the standard of fair behaviour, not only during the duration of the relationship but also at the stage of its establishment.[245]

580. With respect to contract law, Czech legal doctrine deduced that the principle of fairness serves, in particular, an interpretative, complementary and corrective function.[246]

581. The second subsection of the respective provision is a literal manifestation of the *nemo turpitudinem suam allegare potest* principle, which prohibits anyone from benefiting from its own unfair or unlawful act. The same rule applies to benefiting from an unlawful situation which the person caused or which it has control over. In this context, the Czech Supreme Administrative Court, for instance, held that if a claimant had brought an action before a regional court with no local jurisdiction and such court still dealt with the case, the claimant could not later invoke such lack of jurisdiction in the proceeding before the Czech Supreme Administrative Court.[247]

582. One of the specific expressions of the mentioned principle included in the Civil Code is the rule according to which a person who has caused a legal act (e.g., a contract) to be invalid does not have the right to invoke its invalidity or claim for itself any benefit arising therefrom (*see* section 579 of the Civil Code).

583. In addition, the principle of fairness is amplified and complemented by section 8 of the Civil Code pursuant to which an evident abuse of a right does not enjoy legal protection.

---

244. Right to demand can be claimed after the expiry of a ten-year period.
245. Lavický, P. In Lavický, P. a kol.: Občanský zákoník I. Obecná část (§ 1-654). Komentář. 1. edition, Prague: C. H. Beck, 2014, p. 77.
246. *Ibid.*, pp. 77–80.
247. Decision of the Czech Supreme Administrative Court from 22 Mar. 2007, File No. 8 Azs 118/ 2006-81.

III. The Priority of Relative Invalidity of Contracts

584. Generally, the Civil Code favours the validity of a legal act before its invalidity. Therefore, in the new Czech private law, the *in favorem negotii* (*in favorem contractus*) principle applies (*see* section 574 of the Civil Code).

585. As concerns the invalidity of legal acts or contracts, in contrast with the old regulation, the Civil Code set absolute invalidity to be trimmed down as much as possible (absolute invalidity of legal acts nevertheless remained in cases of an apparent conflict with the public order, *bonos mores*, or the impossibility to perform). In addition, it is now possible to waive particular objections against a contract's (in)validity; nevertheless, such waiver cannot be made on a general basis. Moreover, the Civil Code has introduced the opportunity to subsequently remedy vague or incomprehensible legal acts with *ex ante* effects.

IV. Explicit Pre-contract Liability

586. Even though pre-contract liability (liability for abandoning the contracting process for no obvious reason) was under specific circumstances promulgated by case law even under the former Civil Code, the new Civil Code's explicit provisions governing pre-contract liability have made it even more important for contract negotiations to be conducted properly.[248]

587. Pre-contract liability is not in conflict with the principle of autonomy of will (*see* above). According to the Civil Code, everyone is entitled to conduct contract negotiations freely and is not liable for failure to conclude the contract unless it commences or continues the negotiations of a contract without the intention to conclude it (*see* section 1728(1) of the Civil Code). On the other hand, should the negotiations between parties reach a point where the conclusion of the contract seems highly probable, the party which terminates the negotiations without a just cause despite reasonable expectations of the other party to enter into the contract acts unfairly. In such a case, the unfairly acting party shall compensate the other party for the damage caused, but only to the extent of the loss from failing to conclude a contract in similar cases (*see* section 1729 of the Civil Code).

588. According to the case law of the Czech Supreme Court,[249] a just cause for terminating contract negotiations in the final stage cannot be determined, in general, but rather regarded ad hoc. It will always depend on the circumstances of the

248. On the pre-contract liability under Czech law, *see*, e.g., Matula, Z. Culpa in contrahendo. Praha. Wolters Kluwer ČR, 2012, Hrádek, J. Předsmluvní odpovědnost: Culpa in contrahendo. Praha. Auditorium, 2009, Pelikán, M. K některým otázkám předsmluvní odpovědnosti v praxi. Obchodněprávní revue. 2017, Vol. 9, No. 5, pp. 129 et seq., Janoušková, A. Rozsah a limitace odpovědnosti za ukončení vyjednávání o smlouvě bez spravedlivého důvodu. Právní rozhledy. 2016, Vol. 24, Nos 23–24, pp. 807 et seq. or Linhart, A. Meze předsmluvní odpovědnosti podle o. z. a výkladová praxe soudů. Bulletin advokacie. 2017, Vol. 2017, No. 3, pp. 29 et seq.
249. Decision of the Czech Supreme Court from 30 Oct. 2018, File No. 25 Cdo 856/2018.

particular case. The occurrence of any liability for damage resulting from negotiations terminated without a just cause is intended to be the exception rather than the rule, and the assessment of the reason's fairness, and hence the honesty or dishonesty of the conduct, must not be too strict. Any rational reasoning of the acting party, based on objective facts but also on a defensible subjective belief based on the particular circumstances at the given place and time, should be considered as a fair reason (i.e., just cause). It is, therefore, apparent that the provisions of the Civil Code concerning pre-contract liability shall be interpreted rather restrictively.

V. Freedom to Choose the Form of Legal Acts and to Determine Specifics of the Contracting Process

589. Generally, the parties are free to choose the form of contract, i.e., oral or written. In certain cases, however, the Civil Code requires the written form.[250] For example, certain types of contracts (e.g., exclusive licence agreements) or contracts relating to certain objects (e.g., contracts that establish, transfer, alter or extinguish a right in rem to any immovable thing) have to be in writing. An even stricter form, that being a notarial deed, is required, for example, in the following cases: a pledge contract to an enterprise, trust by-laws or an inheritance contract.

590. Moreover, the Civil Code has brought the opportunity to set and adjust the contracting process at the parties' discretion, as compared to the previous, mostly mandatory, provisions of the old Civil Code.

591. In this context, it is worth mentioning that the Civil Code has partially abandoned the principle of full consent. The Civil Code provides for several opportunities that a commitment may be established between the parties in a wording different than what was agreed. First, it is possible to accept an offer with a minor alteration of the terms and conditions thereof (a major alteration would be considered a counterproposal), and such acceptance leads directly to the execution of the contract with such alterations, unless the proposing party explicitly refuses the alterations without undue delay (*see* section 1740(3) of the Civil Code). Moreover, the Civil Code sets forth that if a commercial contract that need not be concluded in writing is, in fact, confirmed in writing by one of the parties in good faith that the confirmation provides a true picture of the contract's contents, the text of the written confirmation shall prevail even if the verbal agreement was different (*see* section 1757 of the Civil Code).

250. Please note that ever since the Civil Code came into effect, oral form is sufficient for a contractual penalty arrangement.

VI. Surprising Covenants in General Terms and Conditions

592. The Civil Code further puts a strong emphasis on protecting weaker parties by setting forth that surprising covenants (in terms of their contents) in sales terms and conditions may be deemed ineffective unless the weaker party has acceded thereto explicitly.[251]

593. For instance, both the Czech Supreme Court[252] and the Czech Constitutional Court[253] have ruled that a contractual penalty arrangement may not be included in general terms and conditions.

§2. Sale of Goods

I. International Sale of Goods

594. In terms of international trade, as of 1 September 1980, the Czech Republic is a signatory to the United Nations Convention on Contracts for the International Sale of Goods (CISG) that came into effect with respect to the Czech Republic on 1 April 1991. The main goal of the CISG was to unify the rules regarding international trade (i.e., sales contracts with an international element). Therefore, the CISG currently applies to all sales contracts entered into by a Czech entity and another party from a different contracting state.[254]

595. Once again, the basic pillar of the CISG is the autonomy of will (contractual autonomy). Thus, the rules of the Convention do not apply if the parties or commercial practices determine otherwise. The measure of applicability of non-contractual rules is governed by the applicable national law, which assesses the permissible degree of deviation in terms of its fundamental principles.[255]

II. Domestic Sale of Goods

596. As concerns Czech national law, sales contracts are governed primarily by the relevant provision in the Civil Code (*see* especially sections 2079 et seq. of the

251. On surprising covenants, *see*, e.g., Příkazská, M. Překvapivá ujednání v obchodních podmínkách a jejich důsledky. Právní rozhledy. 2017, Vol. 25, No. 12, pp. 419 et seq., Hulmák, M. a kol. Občanský zákoník V. Závazkové právo. Obecná část (§ 1721–2054). Komentář. Praha. C. H. Beck, 2014, pp. 168 et seq. or Bejček, J. Některá úskalí racionality obchodních podmínek. Právní rozhledy. 2015, Vol. 23, No. 18, pp. 611 et seq.
252. Decision of the Czech Supreme Court from 28 Feb. 2017, File No. 32 ICdo 86/2015.
253. Decision of the Czech Constitutional Court from 12 Nov. 2013, File No. I. ÚS 3512/11.
254. More than ninety states are signatories to the CISG.
255. Tichý, L., Pipková P. J., Balarin, J.: Kupní smlouva v novém občanském zákoníku. Komentář. 1. edition. Prague: C. H. Beck, 2014, p. 8.

Civil Code).[256] The regulation of sales contracts in the Civil Code is a great example of the unification of previously separately codified regulations in the old Civil Code and the Commercial Code (as mentioned above).

Basic concept of sales contracts

597. Seller's obligation under a sales contract: the seller is obliged to allow the buyer to acquire ownership and possession of the object of sale (*see* section 2079(1) of the Civil Code). The sales contract thus has effects both in rem and in personam. Generally, the seller is obliged to deliver the object of sale without any legal or factual defects, which means that the object of sale: (i) should exhibit the quality stipulated by law or directly in the contract (*see* section 2095 of the Civil Code), and (ii) should not be encumbered by the rights of third parties.

598. Buyer's obligation under a sales contract: the buyer is obliged to pay the seller the purchase price and to take over the object of sale.

599. Unless otherwise stipulated in the contract or by commercial practices, the seller and the buyer shall fulfil the above-mentioned obligations simultaneously (*see* section 2079(2) of the Civil Code).

600. As follows, a sales contract is a synallagmatic bilateral legal act. Synallagma is mutual performance: the transferred thing on one side and money on the other. The purchase price constitutes the consideration in the form of the general equivalent, i.e., in the form of money, which represents the main difference from the exchange (contract type) from which the purchase originally developed.[257]

Object of sale

601. According to section 2079(1) of the Civil Code, an object of sale transferred on the basis of a sales contract is a thing, whereas it is irrelevant whether it is an already-existing thing or a thing that is to be created in the future. Nevertheless, if the dominant part of the supplier's performance consists in the performance of an activity or the 'buyer' undertakes to hand over to the other party a substantial part of what is needed to produce the thing, the provision relating to the sales contract shall not apply (*see* section 2086 of the Civil Code). Such performance would constitute, for instance, a contract for work (*see* sections 2586 et seq. of the Civil Code).

---

256. Generally on the (domestic) sale of goods, *see*, e.g., Selucká, M. a kol. Koupě a prodej: nový občanský zákoník, společná evropská právní úprava prodeje. Praha. C. H. Beck, 2013 or Tichý, L., Pipková P. J., Balarin, J. Kupní smlouva v novém občanském zákoníku. Komentář. Praha. C. H. Beck, 2014.

257. Tichý, L., Pipková P. J., Balarin, J.: Kupní smlouva v novém občanském zákoníku. Komentář. 1. edition. Prague: C. H. Beck, 2014, p. 2.

602. From the same point of view, it is also irrelevant whether the ownership right to the sold thing already belongs to the seller at the moment the sales contract is concluded or whether it will be acquired in the future.[258]

603. A thing is, according to section 498 of the Civil Code, defined as everything that is different from a person and serves the needs of people. Please note that according to Czech law, living animals are not considered things (*see* section 494 of the Civil Code). Nevertheless, the Civil Code shall apply to them to the extent which is not contrary to their nature.

604. Further, please take into account the following exemptions from the above, i.e., objects that cannot be objects of a sale:[259]

(a) values that cannot be disposed of according to Czech private law (personality rights under sections 81 et seq. of the Civil Code, parts of the human body[260] under section 112 of the Civil Code);
(b) granted rights of public law (e.g., driving or trade licence);
(c) parts of a thing (e.g., a building that forms a part of a land plot).

Purchase price

605. The sales contract is a contract for consideration, i.e., a conceptual sign of a purchase is a consideration in money. If the parties intend to conclude a sales contract without determining the purchase price, the purchase price at which the same or a comparable thing is usually sold at the time the contract is concluded and under similar contractual terms is presumed conclusively to be the stipulated purchase price (*see* section 2085(2) of the Civil Code).

Transfer of ownership

606. In general, the right of ownership to a thing specified individually is transferred by the contract itself upon its effectiveness, unless otherwise stipulated or provided by a statute (*see* section 1099 of the Civil Code). As concerns movable things determined by kind, ownership is acquired not earlier than at the time when the thing can be determined by sufficiently distinguishing it from other things of the same kind (*see* section 1101 of the Civil Code).

---

258. Bednář, V. and Kasík P. In Hulmák, M. a kol.: Občanský zákoník VI. Závazkové právo. Zvláštní část (§ 2055–3014). Komentář. 1. edition. Prague: C. H. Beck, 2014, p. 32.
259. Tichý, L., Pipková P. J., Balarin, J.: Kupní smlouva v novém občanském zákoníku. Komentář. 1. edition. Prague: C. H. Beck, 2014, pp. 25–26.
260. Please note that s. 112 of the Civil Code sets forth that one can dispose of hair or similar parts of the human body which can be painlessly removed without anaesthesia and which are naturally restored without limitation.

607. Provided that the ownership of a movable thing is registered in a public register (e.g., cadastral register, trademark register, etc.), the ownership right is transferred upon registration in the register unless otherwise provided by another legal regulation (*see* section 1102 of the Civil Code). The same principle applies to immovable things registered in a public register (cadastral register).

Transfer of risk

608. Generally, the risk of damage to the object of sale passes to the buyer upon takeover. The same consequences shall occur if a buyer fails to take over the transferred thing even though it is allowed by the seller to dispose of it (*see* section 2121 of the Civil Code).

609. Provided that the seller hands over the object of sale to a carrier for delivery to the buyer at the place stipulated by the sales contract, the risk of damage passes to the buyer upon handover to the carrier at that place and if no such place has been agreed, upon handover to the first carrier to the destination (*see* section 2123 of the Civil Code).

610. Within this context, it is worth mentioning that damage to a thing that was incurred after the risk of damage passed to the buyer does not affect the buyer's duty to pay the purchase price unless the seller caused the damage by being in breach of its duties. However, this rule shall not apply if the buyer has asserted the right to request a replacement thing or has withdrawn from the contract (*see* section 2125 of the Civil Code).

611. In addition, the buyer is obliged to inspect the object of sale as soon as possible after the risk of damage to the thing passes and to verify its properties and quantity (*see* section 2104 of the Civil Code). Failure to do so affects the buyer's right to claim apparent defects.

Liability for defects

612. Defective performance establishes the buyer's right to removal of the defect (by having it repaired) or a reasonable reduction of the purchase price, provided that the defect constitutes merely a non-material breach of the contract (*see* section 2107 of the Civil Code), and if the defect constitutes a material breach, additionally the right to be supplied a new defect-free thing or to withdraw from the contract (*see* section 2106 of the Civil Code). The choice between the listed rights belongs to the buyer. Nevertheless, once the buyer makes its choice, it can change it only with the seller's consent.

613. The buyer loses its right from the defective performance if it fails to notify the defect without undue delay after it could have discovered it during a timely inspection and by exercising adequate care, and in the case of latent defects, no later than two years after delivery. However, the court shall take a late notification of the defect into account only if invoked by the seller. Additionally, the seller is not entitled to assert a defence if the defect is due to a fact which the seller was or must have been aware of at the time the thing was delivered (*see* section 2112 of the Civil Code).

614. Until a defect is removed, the buyer is not obliged to pay the part of the purchase price which is estimated as reasonably corresponding to its right to a price reduction (*see* section 2108 of the Civil Code).

615. The right from defective performance does not exclude the right to damages. However, what can be achieved by asserting the right from defective performance may not be claimed for any other legal cause (*see* section 1925 of the Civil Code).

Quality guarantee

616. Beyond the liability for defective performance, the seller may take over a quality guarantee (*see* sections 2113 et seq. of the Civil Code), i.e., undertake that a thing will be fit for use for the usual purpose for a certain period of time or that it will retain its usual properties. An indication of a guarantee period or a 'use by' date on the packaging or in advertising of the thing has the same effect. A guarantee may also be granted for a single component part of a thing. Where a contract and declaration of guarantee determine different guarantee periods, the longer period shall apply.

Form of sales contract

617. Entering into a sales contract does not require a specific form (i.e., it may be concluded even orally). A stricter form may, however, be required by law. For instance, the sale of an immovable thing needs to be realized in writing (even an alteration thereof). An additional requirement may be provided by a special law. For example, the Corporations Act (Act No. 90/2012 Coll., on business corporations) requires officially verified signatures on a sales contract where a share in a limited liability company is being transferred (*see* section 209(2) of the Corporations Act).

Ancillary stipulations to the sales contract

618. Apart from the essentials of the sales contract, the parties are allowed to agree on certain subsidiary arrangements to the contract. The list of such stipulations is not limited (only by general principles such as public order, *bonos mores,* etc.) and the Civil Code lists demonstratively the following:

(a) reservation of the right of ownership (acquisition of ownership upon full payment of the purchase price) (*see* sections 2132 et seq. of the Civil Code);
(b) reservation of repurchase (the buyer's obligation to transfer the object of sale back to the seller for consideration at the seller's request) (*see* sections 2135 et seq. of the Civil Code);

(c) reservation of resale (the seller's obligation to buy the object of sale back from the buyer for consideration at the buyer's request) (*see* sections 2139 et seq. of the Civil Code);
(d) pre-emptive right (*see* sections 2140 et seq. of the Civil Code);
(e) trial purchase (*see* sections 2150 et seq. of the Civil Code);
(f) reservation of a better buyer (*see* section 2152 et seq. of the Civil Code);
(g) price clause (adjustments to the purchase price with respect to the costs of production) (*see* sections 2154 et seq. of the Civil Code).

§3. Commercial Services

I. Distribution

A. Distribution Agreement

619. Czech law does not regulate a distribution agreement as a specific type of contract.[261] Therefore, distribution agreements are concluded as innominate contracts and are governed by the general provisions of contract law contained primarily in the Civil Code. The old Commercial Code contained a specific contract type called 'exclusive sales contract', under which the supplier undertook not to deliver the goods specified in the contract to any person other than the customer (distributor) in a certain area (*see* sections 745 et seq. of the Commercial Code). The Civil Code did not adopt a similar piece of legislation. However, this does not prevent the parties from negotiating a similar arrangement themselves.

620. Distribution agreements are usually defined as contracts setting framework conditions for the future conclusion of sales contracts between the parties. These framework contracts usually contain pre-agreed content of future individual sales contracts, as well as a liability clause, payment method, the above-mentioned ancillary stipulations or other business terms and conditions. The goal of such contracts is usually long-term cooperation between the parties that is presumed to ensure the entry of goods to the market where the producer (supplier) of the goods does not have sufficient means (e.g., resources, licences, contacts, etc.) to ensure access to the market itself.

621. It is usual for framework contracts to simplify the contracting process, especially with respect to the conclusion of the individual contracts. To accept such individual contracts, it is often sufficient to confirm the order placed by the distributor which includes the necessary specification of the goods to be delivered (e.g., quantity, time of delivery, type of goods, etc.). The rest of the contractual relationship based on the individual contract is governed by the framework contract. Therefore, there is a certain similarity with general terms and conditions. In contrast to

261. Generally on distribution contracts under Czech law, *see*, e.g., Bejček, J. Praktické problémy distribučních dohod. Právní rozhledy. 2011, Vol. 19, No. 18, pp. 643 et seq. or Kindl, J. Kartelové a distribuční dohody: teorie a praxe. Praha. C. H. Beck, 2009.

those, however, the framework contract does not have to be attached to the individual contract. Moreover, the framework contract need not be referred to in the individual contracts in order to apply.[262]

622. According to the case law of the Czech Supreme Court,[263] a framework contract does not establish a contractual relationship between entrepreneurs and, therefore, the parties' claims and obligations do not arise therefrom. It is only upon the conclusion of the individual sales contract that, unless the parties have agreed otherwise, the terms and conditions contained in the framework agreement become part of the contractual agreement, thereby forming (co-creating) the content of the individual sales contract.

623. In addition to and partially different from the aforementioned decision-making practice of the Czech Supreme Court, Czech legal doctrine has come to the conclusion that a framework contract obviously contains rights and obligations, i.e., it establishes a contractual relationship. Such contractual relationship encompasses the reciprocal right and obligation of the contracting parties to comply with the framework contract when concluding and performing a particular individual sales contract without having to refer to and renegotiate the conditions determined by the framework contract. Nevertheless, the purchase of the object of sale is realized only upon entering into the individual sales contract.

624. Special attention should be paid to distribution agreements from the perspective of competition law. Both Czech[264] and European[265] regulation regarding competition law declare agreements whose objective or effect is to distort competition to be null and void provided that no exemption is set by either Czech or European law or the supervisory authority in the area of competition law (the Commission or the Czech Competition Authority). Suppliers and distributors should, therefore, avoid entering into agreements with said potential, especially since the invalidity of the contract may not be the only consequence: considerable sanctions may also be imposed.

B. Franchising

625. As the title of this subchapter (distribution) implies, franchising is more of an economic term that describes a distribution method rather than a legal institute.[266] Franchising can be defined as a system of marketing goods, services and/or

---

262. Hulmák, M. In Hulmák, M. a kol.: Občanský zákoník V. Závazkové právo. Obecná část (§ 1721–2054). 1. edition. Prague: C. H. Beck, 2014, p. 152.
263. *See*, for instance, the decision of the Czech Supreme Court from 22 Sep. 2009, File No. 23 Cdo 1888/2007 or the decision of the Czech Supreme Court from 28 Jun. 2011, File No. 32 Cdo 24/2010.
264. Mainly Act No. 143/2001 Coll., on the protection of competition.
265. Mainly, the TFEU (Art. 101).
266. Generally on franchising contracts, *see*, e.g., Ctibor, J., Horáčková, I. Franchising. Praha. Wolters Kluwer, 2017, Řezníčková, M. Franchising: podnikání pod cizím jménem. 3. vyd. Praha. C.H.

technology which is based upon a close and ongoing collaboration between legally and financially separate and independent entities, namely the franchisor and its individual franchisees.

626. Under a franchise agreement, the franchisor grants the franchisee the right, and imposes the obligation, to conduct business in accordance with the franchisor's concept. In other words, the franchisee is entitled and concurrently compelled, in exchange for direct or indirect financial consideration, to use the franchisor's trade name, trademark and/or service mark, know-how, business and technical methods, procedural system, and other industrial and/or intellectual property rights, supported by the continuous provision of commercial and technical assistance, within the framework and for the term of the franchise agreement concluded between the parties for this purpose.

627. It is thus clear that the franchisor especially has an eminent interest in ensuring that no information about its know-how is leaked to the public. Therefore, franchise agreements are usually accompanied by some form of a non-disclosure arrangement.

628. As regards the legal basis, there is no special legal regulation concerning franchise agreements in the Czech Republic. Franchise agreements are a type of innominate contract, which may consist in elements from various contract types, in particular, licence agreements, lease agreements, sales contracts (in the case of supplies of goods), and/or service provision agreements. There are no specific formal requirements for a franchise agreement under Czech law. In certain cases, however, the franchise agreement must be concluded in written form. For instance, when the franchise agreement includes an exclusive licence arrangement or licence that needs to be registered in a public register (e.g., trademark licence).

629. With respect to the absence of a legal definition of a franchise agreement, the High Court in Prague has qualified this type of agreement as a long-term vertical contract that brings profit and balanced advantages to both contractual parties.[267] As further follows from the court's decision, a franchisee usually operates a business under the franchisor's business name, which is already well established on the market and is provided assistance by the franchisor. The franchisor grants the franchisee the right to use its trademark, image, and experience. The granted licence entitles the franchisee to operate its own business on the basis of a proven entrepreneurial concept and the franchisor's know-how.

Beck, 2009, Zima, P. K možnosti analogické aplikace ustanovení o obchodním zastoupení na frans˘ízové smlouvy. Obchodněprávní revue. 2017, Vol. 9, No. 10, pp. 289 et seq., Marek, T. Franchisingová smlouva perspektivou některých institutů práva duševního vlastnictví. Právní fórum. 2012, Vol. 9, No. 8, pp. 377 et seq. or Ctibor, J., Zelená, I. Kdy se z franšízanta stává zaměstnanec. Právní rádce. 2020, Vol. 28, No. 1, pp. 46 et seq.

267. Decision of the High Court in Prague from 28 Apr. 1998, File No. 7A 170/1995.

630. The aspects of competition law mentioned above with regard to distribution agreements (framework contracts) are fully applicable to franchise agreements, as well.

II. Contracts with Middlemen

631. The Civil Code regulates obligations arising from mandate-type contracts, i.e., contracts whose subject is arranging matters for another, in sections 2430–2520.

A. *Mandate*

632. The subject of a mandate contract is the activity of the mandatary, which aims to arrange a certain matter for the principal (mandator), but not the result of such activity (*see* sections 2430 and 2438 of the Civil Code).[268,269] The result pursued by the mandate is indeed the ultimate objective of the mandatary, but not the subject of the mandate.[270]

633. The mandatary acts as the mandator's direct representative, i.e., on behalf of the mandator and on its account. Furthermore, the mandatary fulfils its mandate personally, fairly and diligently according to its abilities (*see* sections 2432 and 2434 of the Civil Code). By engaging another person to perform the mandate, the mandatary assumes the same liability as if it performed the mandate on its own. However, if the mandator allowed the mandatary to appoint a substitute or if a substitute was necessary, the mandatary shall be responsible only for the choice of substitute (*culpa in eligendo*) and, as the case may be, shall compensate the damage caused by its wrong choice (*see* section 2434 of the Civil Code).

634. In general, the mandatary is bound by the mandator's instructions. Nevertheless, the mandatary is obliged to comply with the instructions only provided that they do not go beyond the scope of the mandate, i.e., provided they relate to the manner in which the mandate is to be executed.[271] Even so, the mandatary may derogate from the mandator's instructions if they are in conflict with the latter's

268. Generally on mandate contracts, *see*, e.g., Pilík, V. Příkazní smlouva. Praha. Wolters Kluwer, 2017, Hulmák, M. a kol. Občanský zákoník VI. Závazkové právo. Obecná část (§ 1721–2054). Komentář. Praha. C. H. Beck, 2014, pp. 779 et seq., Pilík, V. Ke vztahu úplaty a náhrady nákladů za obstarání podle smluv příkazního typu. Obchodněprávní revue. 2019, Vol. 11, No. 5, pp. 121 et seq. or Marek, K. K některým smlouvám příkazního typu. Bulletin Stavební právo. 2019, Vol. 22, No. 2, pp. 35 et seq.

269. *See also* the decision of the Czech Constitutional Court from 14 Aug. 2001, File No. II. ÚS 474/2000.

270. Simon, P. In Hulmák, M. a kol.: Občanský zákoník VI. Závazkové právo. Zvláštní část (§ 2055–3014). Komentář. 1. edition. Prague: C. H. Beck, 2014, p. 781.

271. *Ibid.*, p. 791.

interest (provided that the mandator's consent cannot be obtained in time) (*see* section 2432 of the Civil Code). Moreover, the mandatary is obliged to notify the mandator of an obviously incorrect instruction and shall comply with the instruction only if the mandator insists on it (*see* section 2433 of the Civil Code).

635. It is a common practice for the mandatary to receive remuneration for arranging the matters of the mandator. Should the parties not agree on remuneration, the mandatary is entitled to it if remuneration is usual, in particular, with regard to the mandator's business activities (*see* section 2438(1) of the Civil Code). The mandator shall provide remuneration even in the case that the mandatary fails to achieve the desired result unless the failure was caused by a breach of the mandatary's duties or the result was frustrated by accident attributable to the mandatary (*see* section 2438(2) of the Civil Code).

636. If the situation regarding the procured matter requires the mandator to be represented, the mandator shall appoint the mandatary as its proxy and for that purpose draft a power of attorney.

637. Finally, it is important to bear in mind that the provisions regarding mandate contracts also apply, with necessary modifications, to cases where a person has a duty arising from a contract or other statutory provisions to arrange a matter on account of another (e.g., commercial agency, commission, brokerage but also escrow agreement or letter of credit).

B. Commercial Agency

638. Under a commercial agency contract, the commercial agent (proxy) undertakes to pursue long-term activities for the principal which are aimed at facilitating the conclusion of a certain type of business transaction by the principal or negotiating business transactions on behalf of the principal and on its account (*see* section 2483 of the Civil Code).[272,273] On the other hand, the principal is to pay the commercial agent a commission (otherwise, the provisions on commercial agency shall not apply – *see* section 2520 of the Civil Code).

639. Further, please note that the commercial agent carries out said activities as an independent entrepreneur (*see* section 420 of the Civil Code). In addition, the Civil Code emphasizes the agent's independence from other entrepreneurs and,

---

272. Generally on commercial agency, *see*, e.g., Hulmák, M. a kol. Občanský zákoník VI. Závazkové právo. Obecná část (§ 1721–2054). Komentář. Praha. C. H. Beck, 2014, pp. 877 et seq., Marek, K. Ke smlouvě o obchodním zastoupení. Daně a právo v praxi. 2016, Vol. 2016, No. 2, pp. 40 et seq. Or Rejmont, V. Další závazky ze smluv příkazního typu (komise, obchodní zastoupení). Účetnictví. 2016, Vol. 2016, No. 1, pp. 49 et seq.
273. *See also* the decision of the Czech Supreme Court from 4 Aug. 2009, File No. 23 Cdo 2093/2009.

apart from the limits of the commercial agency contract, also the principal.[274] The status of an agent as an entrepreneur distinguishes commercial agency as a private law obligation from an employment relationship.[275] Additionally, the parties may agree on a non-compete clause that will survive after the commercial agency has terminated (maximum two years).

640. As indicated above, a commercial agency differs from a mandate contract in the duration of the carried-out activity. Whereas the mandate is usually agreed for procuring a specific matter for the mandator, the commercial agency anticipates longer-lasting cooperation. Moreover, the commercial agent is not entitled to conclude business transactions on behalf of the principal or to accept any performance in its stead. If the contrary is stipulated, the related rights and duties of the parties are governed by the provisions regulating mandate contracts (*see* section 2486 of the Civil Code).

641. Commercial agency may be agreed as exclusive or non-exclusive. In the case of business transactions covered by an exclusive commercial agency that are concluded by the principal without the participation of the commercial agent, the commercial agent is entitled to a commission as if these business transactions were concluded with its participation (*see* section 2487(2) of the Civil Code).

642. If the amount of commission has not been stipulated in the commercial agency contract, the commercial agent is entitled to a commission in the amount according to the usages at the place of the agent's activity with regard to the kind of goods or services which constitute the subject of the respective transactions. In the absence of such usages, the commercial agent is entitled to a commission in a reasonable amount, taking into account the substantial circumstances of the activity performed (*see* section 2499(1) of the Civil Code). The commission is presumed to also include costs associated with the commercial agency (*see* section 2500 of the Civil Code).

643. In terms of the commercial agent's provision, the Civil Code further differentiates between situations when the commercial agency was agreed as the commercial agent's obligation to only arrange for the principal an opportunity to conclude a business transaction and when not. If so, the right to payment of the commission arises immediately upon arranging such opportunity (*see* section 2503 of the Civil Code). Otherwise, the agent becomes entitled to a commission when the principal has fulfilled its obligation or was obliged to fulfil its obligation arising from the contract concluded with the third person, or where the third person has fulfilled the obligation arising from such a contract (*see* section 2504(1) of the Civil Code). In addition, the commercial agent is entitled to special remuneration after the commercial agency is terminated in cases where the commercial agent acquired new

274. Such conflict could result in extinction of the right to commission (*see* s. 2508 of the Civil Code).
275. Horák, P. In Hulmák, M. a kol.: Občanský zákoník VI. Závazkové právo. Zvláštní část (§ 2055–3014). Komentář. 1. edition. Prague: C. H. Beck, 2014, p. 880.

customers or significantly developed the principal's business with its existing customers, the principal still enjoys substantial benefits from this business and also provided the amount of special remuneration is fair with regard to all the circumstances of the case (*see* section 2514 of the Civil Code).

644. Last but not least, as concerns the required form of commercial agency contracts, section 2483(2) of the Civil Code requires them to be in writing.

C. Commission

645. Under a commission contract (contract of undisclosed agency), the mandatary undertakes to arrange, on its own behalf, a particular matter for the mandator on the mandator's account (usually to buy or sell something).[276] Therefore, legal acts made by the mandatary with respect to a third person do not oblige or entitle the mandator, but rather establish obligations and rights for the mandatary itself. In contrast with a mandate, commercial agency, and brokerage, commission is a typical example of indirect representation.

646. In general, third parties to whom a mandatary's legal action is addressed need not be informed that the mandatary is not acting on its own but rather on the mandator's account. In some cases, however, it is necessarily obvious to third parties that the mandatary is acting on behalf of another person (the mandator). This is particularly the case regarding trading with investment instruments when an investment firm is required to record the instruments in the customer accounts separately from its assets in the customer accounts.[277]

647. However, this does not affect the mandatary's obligation to follow the mandator's instructions. As a consequence of not observing the instructions, the mandator may, without undue delay, refuse to recognize the act performed on its account (*see* section 2457 of the Civil Code).

648. In the Czech legal environment, commission contracts, generally, allow taking advantage of the mandatary's better opportunities to access different markets, its experience and knowledge or reputation. The mandatary is usually a professional entrepreneur, which is why commission has always been the domain of commercial law. From an economic point of view, currently, its use in the area of investment services can be considered the most important (for more details, *see* Act

---

276. Generally on commission contracts, *see*, e.g., Hulmák, M. a kol. Občanský zákoník VI. Závazkové právo. Obecná část (§ 1721–2054). Komentář. Praha. C. H. Beck, 2014, pp. 834 et seq., Marek, K. Problémy realizace nové úpravy smlouvy o zprostředkování a smlouvy komisionářské. Bulletin advokacie. 2014, Vol. 2014, No. 6, pp. 17 et seq., Pilík, V. Komisionářská smlouva. Bulletin Stavební právo. 2018, Vol. 21, No. 1, pp. 7 et seq. or Rejmont, V. Další závazky ze smluv příkazního typu (komise, obchodní zastoupení). Účetnictví. 2016, Vol. 2016, No. 1, pp. 49 et seq.

277. Pihera, V. In Hulmák, M. a kol.: Občanský zákoník VI. Závazkové právo. Zvláštní část (§ 2055–3014). Komentář. 1. edition. Prague: C. H. Beck, 2014, p. 836.

No. 256/2004 Coll., on capital market business). In particular, commission contracts are concluded between investors and investment firms for the purpose of buying or selling investment instruments or between issuers of investment instruments and investment firms for the placement of those instruments on the market.[278]

649. Reciprocally to the mandatary's obligations, the mandator undertakes by entering into the commission contract to pay remuneration to the mandatary. Where no amount of remuneration has been stipulated, the mandatary is entitled to remuneration appropriate to the activity performed and the result achieved (*see* section 2468 of the Civil Code). Should the commission be agreed as gratuitous, the contract shall be considered merely a mandate.[279]

650. The mandator may require the third person to provide it with the performance which was arranged for it by the mandatary if the mandatary, for reasons attributable to it, is unable to arrange the performance to be provided by the third person to the mandator (*see* section 2467 of the Civil Code). Further, the mandatary acquires ownership of the assets bought on the basis of an individual contract (concluded between the mandatary and a third person). These assets are then transferred (in the case of rights – assigned) to the mandator.[280]

651. In terms of terminating the commission, the mandator is entitled to revoke the mandate only prior to an obligation's having been established between the mandatary and a third person (*see* section 2470 of the Civil Code).

D. Brokerage

652. The subject matter of a brokerage contract is the obligation of a broker to arrange conclusion of a contract between the client and a third person (*see* section 2445 of the Civil Code). In other words, brokerage involves searching for persons who might be interested in concluding a brokered contract with the client, evaluating and identifying their specific intention to conclude such a contract and then conveying such information to the client.[281]

653. Brokerage may be agreed as: (i) arranging the conclusion of a brokered contract itself, or (ii) arranging for the client the opportunity to conclude such contract. In any case, it is advisable to specify the content of the brokered contract directly in the brokerage contract, thus avoiding any future disputes in respect of the broker's claim to remuneration. On top of that, parties may agree that the remuneration shall be due only upon the third party's fulfilment of its obligations arising

278. *Ibid.*, p. 835.
279. *Ibid.*, p. 836.
280. *Ibid.*, p. 837.
281. Handlar, J. In Hulmák, M. a kol.: Občanský zákoník VI. Závazkové právo. Zvláštní část (§ 2055–3014). Komentář. 1. edition. Prague: C. H. Beck, 2014, p. 816.

from the arranged contract (not applicable if not fulfilled for reasons attributable to the client) (*see* section 2448 of the Civil Code).

654. Within the framework of brokerage, the broker is not a client's representative, i.e., it neither acts on its behalf nor on its account. In any case, the broker must not propose concluding a contract with a person about whom the broker has or, given the circumstances, should have a reasonable doubt as to whether such person will fulfil the duties under the arranged contract properly and in due time (*see* section 2452 of the Civil Code).

655. For arranging the conclusion of a contract (or the opportunity to conclude a contract), the client is obliged to pay the broker remuneration. Similar to the commission, if the brokerage is agreed without remuneration, it shall be governed only by the provisions regulating the mandate. Exceptions prove the rule and the Civil Code sets a rebuttable legal presumption that if at the conclusion of a (brokerage) contract, it is evident from the circumstances that remuneration will be required for arranging the conclusion of the brokered contract, it is presumed that a brokerage contract has been concluded (*see* section 2445(2) of the Civil Code). This will be the case, in particular if the broker is an entrepreneur acting in the course of its business but may also arise from the course of the (brokerage) contract negotiations or from the previous practice of the contracting parties.[282]

III. Insurance

656. Private law regulation of insurance is comprehensively regulated in the Civil Code, specifically by sections 2758–2872. Generally, under an insurance contract, an insurer undertakes to provide the policyholder or a third person with insurance indemnity in the case of a random event covered by insurance (an insured event), and the policyholder undertakes to pay a premium to the insurer (*see* section 2758(1) of the Civil Code).[283] In setting the premium, it is prohibited to take into consideration nationality, racial or ethnic origin, pregnancy or maternity, or any other consideration contrary to the principle of equal treatment (especially considerations prohibited under Act No. 198/2009 Coll., the anti-discrimination law).

657. An insurance contract stipulating insurance for more than one year must be in writing. As concerns the specifics of the contracting process, the written form is required, and timely payment of the premium suffices for accepting the offer (*see* section 2758(2) of the Civil Code).

282. *Ibid.*, p. 817.

283. Generally on insurance contracts, *see*, e.g., Přikryl, V., Čechová, J. Pojistná smlouva a její základní znaky. Právní rozhledy. 2018, Vol. 26, No. 10, pp. 364 et seq., Jankanič, D. Předložení pojistné smlouvy jako podmínka pro uzavření smlouvy na plnění veřejné zakázky. Veřejné zakázky. 2018, Vol. 2018, No. 1, pp. 46 et seq., Hulmák, M. a kol. Občanský zákoník VI. Závazkové právo. Obecná část (§ 1721–2054). Komentář. Praha. C. H. Beck, 2014, pp. 1292 et seq. or Jandová, L., Šlauf, P., Svejkovský, J. Pojištění v novém občanském zákoníku. Komentář. Praha. C. H. Beck, 2014, pp. 4 et seq.

658. Pursuant to section 2764 of the Civil Code, the validity of the insurance contract requires an insurable interest of the policyholder, i.e., a legitimate need for protection against the consequences of an insured event. If an insurable interest is extinguished during the duration of insurance, so will the insurance (*see* section 2765 of the Civil Code).

659. The Civil Code specifically regulates the following types of insurance:

(a) insurance against loss and damage (*see* sections 2811–2820 of the Civil Code);
(b) fixed-amount insurance (*see* sections 2821–2823 of the Civil Code);
(c) life insurance (*see* sections 2833–2843 of the Civil Code);
(d) accident insurance (*see* sections 2844–2846 of the Civil Code);
(e) sickness insurance (*see* sections 2847–2848 of the Civil Code);
(f) property insurance (*see* sections 2849–2855 of the Civil Code);
(g) legal expenses insurance (*see* sections 2856–2860 of the Civil Code);
(h) third-party liability insurance (*see* sections 2861–2867 of the Civil Code);
(i) credit insurance or guaranty insurance (*see* sections 2868–2870 of the Civil Code);
(j) insurance of financial losses (*see* sections 2871–2872 of the Civil Code).

IV. Financial Services

A. Banking Services

660. Account contracts, lump sum deposit contracts, letter of credit contracts and collection contracts are traditionally referred to as banking contracts, in particular, because the former legislation made the bank (or similar financial institution) an obligatory party to such contracts.[284]

661. The current legislation (especially the Civil Code) no longer explicitly provides for such condition, meaning that banking contracts may be concluded by anyone unless they do so for business purposes. In such a case, i.e., for the continuous conclusion of banking contracts for profit, public law requires obtaining appropriate authorization (e.g., a banking licence).[285]

662. Other common features of banking contracts are that part of the contract is usually determined by reference to business terms and conditions (*see* section 1751 of the Civil Code) and that they are concluded in an adhesive manner (i.e., without

284. Generally on banking services contracts, *see*, e.g., Liška, P., Elek, Š., Marek, K. Bankovní obchody. Praha. Wolters Kluwer, 2014, Hulmák, M. a kol. Občanský zákoník VI. Závazkové právo. Obecná část (§ 1721–2054). Komentář. Praha. C. H. Beck, 2014, pp. 690 et seq. or Liška, P. Nad institutem bankovní záruky. Právní rozhledy. 2007, Vol. 15, No. 18, pp. 651 et seq.

285. Liška, P. In Černá, S., Štenglová, I., Pelikánová, I., Dědič, J. a kolektiv. Obchodní právo – podnikatel, podnikání, závazky s účastí podnikatele. 1. edition. Prague: Wolters Kluwer ČR, 2016, p. 562.

the weaker party having any real opportunity to affect the contents of the essential terms of the contract – *see* sections 1798 et seq. of the Civil Code).[286]

663. According to the Czech Bank Act (Act No. 21/1992 Coll., on banks), banks are further entitled (subject to the authorization in the granted banking licence) to carry out the following activities:

(a) providing loans and credits;
(b) investing in securities on its own account;
(c) financial leasing;
(d) payment services and electronic money issuance;
(e) the issuance and administration of payment instruments, except in the case of the provision of payment services or the issuance of electronic money under point 0;
(f) providing guarantees;
(g) providing investment services;
(h) financial brokerage;
(i) acting as a depositary;
(j) exchange activities;
(k) providing banking information;
(l) trading on its own account or on behalf of a client with foreign exchange values other than investment instruments and gold;
(m) rent of safety deposit boxes;
(n) administration of investment funds and foreign investment funds;
(o) activity of an accredited person according to the act regulating business on the capital market (*see* Act No. 256/2004 Coll., on capital market business);
(p) providing data reporting service under the act regulating business on the capital market (*see* Act No. 256/2004 Coll., on capital market business).

B. Credit

664. As indicated above, credit is usually provided by banks or similar financial institutions. Under a credit contract, a credit provider (usually a bank) undertakes to provide a credit recipient with funds[287,288] up to a specific amount (credit limit) at the credit recipient's request and for the credit recipient's benefit, and the credit recipient undertakes to return the funds provided and to pay interest (*see* section 2395 of the Civil Code).

665. If the credit contract stipulates that funds are to be used only for a specific purpose and the credit recipient uses them for a different purpose, the credit provider may withdraw from the respective contract and demand the credit recipient to

---

286. *Ibid.*
287. Generally on credit type agreements, *see*, e.g., Hulmák, M. a kol. Občanský zákoník VI. Závazkové právo. Obecná část (§ 1721–2054). Komentář. Praha. C. H. Beck, 2014, pp. 690 et seq.
288. Subject of a credit may not be things other than money.

repay all received funds plus interest without undue delay. This also applies if using the funds for the agreed purpose is or becomes impossible (*see* section 2400 of the Civil Code).

666. In practice, it is quite common to provide so-called syndicated credit, i.e., credit provided by multiple banks, which is used mainly in cases of higher borrowed amounts. Further, it is usual to secure the receivables from the credit contract by a pledge (*see* sections 1309 et seq. of the Civil Code) or by suretyship (guarantee) (*see* sections 2018–2028 of the Civil Code).

667. For some legal entities, the conclusion of a credit contract is subject to specific internal approval procedures. For instance, the municipal authority decides on the conclusion of a contract on the acceptance or provision of credit by the municipality (*see* section 85(j) of Act No. 128/2000 Coll., on municipalities). Similar regulation applies to the regional authority of all Czech regions[289] (*see* section 36(i) of Act No. 129/2000 Coll., on regions).[290]

668. A loan agreement (loan for consumption) is similar to a credit contract (*see* sections 2390–2394 of the Civil Code). While a credit contract may only cover the lending of funds and the credit always bears interest, under a loan agreement not only funds (cash) may be provided but also any other substitutable items, and the monetary loan may be agreed as being either interest-free and interest-bearing. The fundamental difference between a credit and a loan for consumption is the fact that a loan for consumption is a real contract, i.e., it arises only by the provision of the borrowed items (e.g., funds) to the borrower (loan beneficiary), while a credit contract is a consensual contract which does not require the provision of funds to the credit recipient for it to be concluded. As a rule, the credited funds are provided only after the credit contract is concluded and on the basis of the credit recipient's request.[291]

C. Leasing

669. Leasing contracts are not regulated as a specific type of contract by Czech law.[292] Therefore, leasing can be understood as a contractual relationship emerging

289. Please note that for the capital city of Prague its own act was adopted (Act No. 131/2000 Coll., on the capital city of Prague) according to which conclusion of such contracts is approved by the municipal authority or municipal council depending on the borrowed/lent amount or potentially by authorities of individual city districts.
290. Elek, Š. In Hulmák, M. a kol.: Občanský zákoník VI. Závazkové právo. Zvláštní část (§ 2055–3014). Komentář. 1. edition. Prague: C. H. Beck, 2014, p. 696.
291. *Ibid.*, p. 704.
292. Generally on leasing contracts, *see*, e.g., Valouch, P. Leasing v praxi, 5. aktualizované vydání. Praha. GRADA Publishing, a.s., 2012, Marek, K. Leasingová smlouva, smlouva o koupi najaté věci. Komorní listy. 2012, Vol. 4, No. 2, pp. 28 et seq., Zbránek, M. Leasing a zásada poctivého obchodního styku. Bulletin advokacie. 2010, Vol. 2010, No. 5, pp. 33 et seq. or Marek, K. Leasingová smlouva. Právní rádce. 2009, Vol. 17, No. 4, pp. 16 et seq.

from an innominate contract.[293] Even though leasing is close in design to an ordinary lease relationship, it usually combines several different and mutually interdependent contractual relationships. Depending on the circumstances and leasing type (*see* below), in addition to the lease, leasing may include, in particular, a mandate, a future sales contract and/or a credit relationship.[294]

670. Generally, practice identifies two types of leasing contracts: financial and operating.

Financial leasing

671. Financial leasing contracts are often constructed as a combination of sales and lease contracts.[295] The ultimate objective of financial leasing is for the lessee to acquire ownership of the leased item, whilst the lessee is, for the duration of the leasing relationship, obliged to pay leasing instalments. According to the case law of the Czech Supreme Court,[296] leasing instalments should not be confused with rent. Pursuant to the mentioned decision, lease instalments are of a different nature than rent because they are not primarily a consideration for using the leased item but are, in fact, instalments of the price at which the leased item was acquired by the lessor, plus any additional components (e.g., insurance, etc.) and include the lessor's reasonable profit.

672. For the duration of the leasing relationship, the lessee bears the risk of damage to the leased item and other risks associated with its use and is obliged to pay the costs of maintenance, insurance, taxes, etc.[297]

673. In conclusion, under financial leasing, the lessor provides financing for the lessee's purchase of the leased item and concurrently secures its receivable by ownership thereof. From a material point of view, therefore, financial leasing is closest to a transfer of a right as security under sections 2040 et seq. of the Civil Code.[298]

293. *See* the decision of the Czech Supreme Court from 13 Jan. 2010, File No. 31 Cdo 4356/2008.
294. Černá, S. In Černá, S., Štenglová, I., Pelikánová, I., Dědič, J. a kolektiv. Obchodní právo – podnikatel, podnikání, závazky s účastí podnikatele. 1. edition. Prague: Wolters Kluwer ČR, 2016, p. 531.
295. Tichý, L., Pipková P. J., Balarin, J.: Kupní smlouva v novém občanském zákoníku. Komentář. 1. edition. Praha: C. H. Beck, 2014, p. 14.
296. *See* the decision of the Czech Supreme Court from 11 May 2010, File No. 32 Cdo 568/2009.
297. Černá, S. In Černá, S., Štenglová, I., Pelikánová, I., Dědič, J. a kolektiv. Obchodní právo – podnikatel, podnikání, závazky s účastí podnikatele. 1. edition. Prague: Wolters Kluwer ČR, 2016, p. 533.
298. Tichý, L., Pipková P. J., Balarin, J.: Kupní smlouva v novém občanském zákoníku. Komentář. 1. edition. Praha: C. H. Beck, 2014, p. 15.

Operating leasing

674. On the contrary, operating leasing is not aimed at acquiring the title to the leased item, and the lessee is obliged to return the item to the lessor after termination thereof. In contrast to financial leasing, the lessor usually carries out maintenance and repairs on the subject of the leasing.

675. In light of the above, it is apparent that operating leasing overlaps in content with a lease relationship.

D. Factoring

676. Similar to leasing, factoring is not specifically regulated by Czech law.[299] In general, factoring consists of the assignment of a receivable to a factor (bank), for which the bank will credit the client with consideration and monetize the receivable upon maturity. As a rule, the client undertakes to offer the factor all its receivables from supplier relations. The factor, on the other hand, undertakes to accept these receivables and to pay the client consideration after deducting its costs. In other words, factoring represents a framework contract which establishes a long-term contractual relationship.[300]

677. In summary, factoring represents an alternative way of financing by selling (assigning) short-term receivables to the factor for consideration, whereas the factor usually undertakes to ensure administration (management) of the respective receivables.

V. Carriage by Land, Sea and Air

678. General regulation relating to the carriage of things is included in the Civil Code under contracts for carriage of a thing (*see* sections 2555 et seq. of the Civil Code).[301]

---

299. Generally on factoring, *see*, e.g., Blümelová, K. Nový občanský zákoník rozšíří možnosti factoringu (rozhovor s Tomášem Morávkem). Právní rádce. 2013, Vol. 21, No. 10, pp. 74 et seq. or Uminský, P. Účetní a daňové souvislosti faktoringu. Daně a právo v praxi. 2012, Vol. 2012, No. 12, pp. 25 et seq.

300. Tichý, L., Pipková P. J., Balarin, J.: Kupní smlouva v novém občanském zákoníku. Komentář. 1. edition. Praha: C. H. Beck, 2014, p. 6.

301. Generally on carriage contracts, *see*, e.g., Frinta, O. Smlouva o přepravě osoby v novém soukromém právu. Praha. Wolters Kluwer, 2018, Hrádek, J. Smlouvy o přepravě v občanském zákoníku. Komentář. Praha. C. H. Beck, 2017, Hrádek, J. Vymezení smluvních typů přepravních smluv po rekodifikaci. Obchodněprávní revue. 2017, Vol. 9, Nos 7–8, pp. 198 et seq. or Lojda, J. Rozsah a způsob použití Úmluvy CMR. Obchodněprávní revue. 2014, Vol. 6, No. 4, pp. 121 et seq.

679. Pursuant to a contract for carriage of a thing, a carrier undertakes to carry a consignor's thing (consignment) from the point of dispatch to a certain destination, and a consignor undertakes to pay freight (remuneration) to the carrier (*see* section 2555 of the Civil Code).

680. At the other party's request, the consignor shall confirm the order of the carriage and the carrier shall confirm takeover of the consignment.[302] The confirmations must be in writing (*see* section 2556 of the Civil Code).

681. Generally, the carrier shall compensate the damage caused to a consignment between its receipt by the carrier and its surrender to the consignee (final recipient), whereas stipulations limiting the carrier's liability shall be disregarded (*see* section 2566 of the Civil Code). This does not apply, i.e., the carrier is released from its duty to compensate for the damage, in the following cases:

(a) if the carrier proves that the damage could not have been prevented even by exercising professional care;
(b) if the carrier proves that the damage was caused by the consignor, consignee or owner of the consignment;
(c) if the carrier proves that the damage was caused by a defect or inherent nature of the consignment, including usual loss;
(d) where damage is caused by the consignment's defective packaging and the carrier proves that it notified the consignor of the defect upon takeover of the consignment for carriage (provided that the defect could have been discovered).

682. In addition, section 2569 of the Civil Code provides for a special limitation period with respect to the right to claim damages. If such right is not asserted against the carrier within six months from the date of the takeover of the consignment, or if the consignment was not taken over within six months from the date on which it should have been delivered, it shall become time-barred.

683. As regards the carrier's right under a carriage contract, the carrier is entitled to sell the consignment on account of the consignor if there is an imminent threat of substantial damage to the consignment, if there is no time to obtain instructions from the consignor, or if the consignor is in delay with providing such instructions (*see* section 2570 of the Civil Code). Furthermore, the carrier has a pledge in respect of the consignment to secure its contractual debts as long as the carrier can dispose of them (*see* section 2571 of the Civil Code).

684. The Civil Code envisages more detailed regulation of carriage by another legal regulation, especially the regulations providing for rules of carriage, unless provided by a directly applicable regulation of the European Communities (*see* section 2578 of the Civil Code).

---

302. Confirmation of takeover of the consignment can be substituted with a bill of lading (*see* s. 2572 of the Civil Code).

685. Currently, only the following rules of carriage (in the form of regulation) are applicable in the Czech Republic: rules of carriage for public rail and road passenger transport (*see* Regulation No. 175/2000 Coll.) and rules of carriage for public rail freight transport (*see* Regulation No. 1/2000 Coll.).[303]

686. As concerns directly applicable European regulation, *inter alia*, the following is of relevance:[304]

(a) Regulation EU No. 181/2011 of the European Parliament and of the Council of 16 February 2011 concerning the rights of passengers in bus and coach transport and amending Regulation (EC) No. 2006/2004.
(b) Regulation (EC) No. 1371/2007 of the European Parliament and of the Council of 23 October 2007 on rail passengers' rights and obligations.
(c) Regulation (EC) No. 261/2004 of the European Parliament and of the Council of 11 February 2004 establishing common rules on compensation and assistance to passengers in the event of denied boarding and of cancellation or long delay of flights, and repealing Regulation (EEC) No. 295/91.
(d) Regulation (EC) No. 889/2002 of the European Parliament and of the Council of 13 May 2002 amending Council Regulation (EC) No. 2027/97 on air carrier liability in the event of accidents and the Montreal Convention on air carrier liability.
(e) Regulation (EC) No. 1107/2006 of the European Parliament and of the Council of 5 July 2006 concerning the rights of disabled persons and persons with reduced mobility when travelling by air.
(f) Regulation (EU) No. 1177/2010 of the European Parliament and of the Council of 24 November 2010 concerning the rights of passengers when travelling by sea and inland waterway and amending Regulation (EC) No. 2006/2004.
(g) Regulation (EC) No. 392/2009 of the European Parliament and of the Council of 23 April 2009 on the liability of carriers of passengers by sea in the event of accidents.

A. *Carriage of Goods by Road*

687. As concerns the International Carriage of goods by road, the Czech Republic is bound by the Convention on the Contract for the International Carriage of Goods by Road (CMR) from 19 May 1956 (Geneva).[305]

688. The CMR applies to any contract for the carriage of goods by road (for remuneration) if the place of receipt of the consignment and the intended place of delivery as specified in the contract are situated in two different states, at least one

303. Hrádek, J. Smlouvy o přepravě v občanském zákoníku. Komentář. 1. edition. Prague: C. H. Beck, 2017, p. 186.
304. *Ibid.*, pp. 187–188.
305. Including protocol to CMR from 5 Jul. 1978 and protocol to CMR from 20 Feb. 2008.

of which is a contracting state to the CMR. The CMR has a mandatory character and does not allow the contracting parties to derogate from it.[306]

689. National road transport is further regulated by the Road Transport Act (Act No. 111/1994 Coll., on road transport) and related regulation adopted on its basis. On top of that, since 1 January 2019, the Road Transport Act extends the applicability of the CMR concerning the conclusion and implementation of a contract of carriage, liability of the carrier, complaints and actions and the carriage carried out gradually by several carriers even to national road freight transport (*see* section 9a of the Road Transport Act).[307]

B. Carriage of Goods by Rail

690. In terms of the International Carriage of goods by rail, the Czech Republic adopted the Convention concerning International Carriage by Rail (COTIF). In addition to the Civil Code, national regulation of rail transport is encompassed, in particular, in the Railways Act (Act No. 266/1994 Coll., on railways) (*see* especially sections 24–42 of the Railways Act) and the rules of carriage for public rail freight transport (*see* Regulation No. 1/2000 Coll.).

C. Carriage of Goods by Air

691. Regarding the International Carriage of goods by air, the Czech Republic is a signatory to the Montreal Convention on air carrier liability (1999) and the Convention for the Unification of Certain Rules Relating to International Carriage by Air (Warsaw, 1929). Whereas the former is directly applicable as both the Czech Republic and the European Union are contracting parties thereto, the Warsaw Convention is only relevant in relation to those states that are not a party to the Montreal Convention.[308]

692. Domestic regulation is contained especially in the Civil Aviation Act (Act No. 49/1997 Coll., on civil aviation) and related regulation adopted on its basis.

D. Carriage of Goods by Sea and Inland Waterways

693. Concerning international carriage of goods by sea, the United Nations Convention on the Carriage of Goods by Sea is binding for the Czech Republic as of 1

306. Hrádek, J. Smlouvy o přepravě v občanském zákoníku. Komentář. 1. edition. Prague: C. H. Beck, 2017, p. 81.
307. Please note that the application of the CMR to national road freight transport shall apply only to contracts concluded after 31 Dec. 2018.
308. Hrádek, J. Smlouvy o přepravě v občanském zákoníku. Komentář. 1. edition. Prague: C. H. Beck, 2017, p. 83.

July 1996. Other conditions of maritime navigation under the national flag of the Czech Republic and the rights and obligations of legal and natural persons associated therewith are determined by the Maritime Navigation Act (Act No. 61/2000 Coll., on maritime navigation).

694. In terms of international transport of goods by inland waterways, as of 1 March 2006, the Czech Republic is bound by the Budapest Convention on the Contract for the Carriage of Goods by Inland Waterways (CMNI).

695. As regards domestic transport, additional conditions for operating CMNI are set forth by the Inland Navigation Act (Act No. 114/1995 Coll., on inland navigation).

Part II. Economic Law

Chapter 1. General Principles

§1. Institutional Framework

696. After the Velvet Revolution in 1989 (consequently followed by the split of Czechoslovakia into the Czech Republic and Slovakia), the country underwent a process of privatization, which replaced state ownership with private ownership by private persons (natural and legal). The principles on which the former legal regulation was based have fundamentally changed, as the Czech Republic became a Member State of the European Union in 2004, and consequently, Czech legislation is now significantly influenced by EU law. Thus, the Czech legal regulation of economic law is affected by national legislation, legislative acts adopted at the EU level and international treaties. The Czech Constitution states[309] that promulgated treaties which the Parliament has given its consent to ratifying and by which the Czech Republic is bound to form a part of the Czech legal order. If a treaty provides something which a national statute does not, the treaty shall apply. The Czech Republic is also a member of the European Convention on Human Rights. The case law of the CJEU and of the European Court of Human Rights provides, next to the case law of national courts, important guidance for interpreting particular regulatory provisions.

697. The most important public institution bodies involved in setting the regulatory framework are as follows:

(a) the government, which plays a vital role in the legislative process and is entitled to issue regulations, coordinates executive power and policy, and is authorized to issue orders to implement statutory acts while remaining within the bounds thereof;
(b) the ministries (currently fourteen), which govern particular areas and which, if empowered by a statutory act, may issue regulations on the basis of and within the bounds of those statutory acts;
(c) central administrative government-controlled authorities, which perform tasks set in individual statutory acts within their respective sphere of competence

309. Act No. 1/1993 Coll., on the Constitution of the Czech Republic, as amended.

(e.g., the Competition Authority, IPO, Energy Regulatory Office, Czech Telecommunication Office, etc.[310]) and which may also be empowered by a statutory act to issue regulations on the basis of and within the bounds of a statutory act;

(d) central administrative ministry-controlled authorities, which are not entitled to issue regulations (e.g., the Czech Trade Inspection Authority, Czech Environmental Inspection Agency or State Labour Inspection Office, etc.);

(e) other public bodies, such as local administration (regional and district) and specialized administrative offices (e.g., Financial Offices, Cadastral Registers, Customs Administration Offices, etc.).

698. The CNB, which is enshrined directly in the Czech Constitution, holds a special position within the system. The CNB Act[311] governs the competences of the CNB, which consists mainly of instruments to secure economic and financial stability. The CNB also supervises the financial sector and its participants and issues authorizations for certain activities within the financial sector and markets.

§2. State Intervention in Economic Activities

699. The fundamental principles of economic law come from the CHRF,[312,313] which forms a part of the Czech Constitution order and contains, *inter alia*, economic and social human rights. One of the institutional imperatives is contained in Article 2 of the CHRF, pursuant to which *'[s]tate authority may be asserted only in cases and within the bounds provided for by law and only in the manner prescribed by law'* [314] and which provides that *'[e]veryone may do that which is not prohibited by law; and nobody may be compelled to do that which is not imposed upon him/her by law'.* [315] Individual rights and obligations are set in statutory acts and other regulations. The statutory acts also empower public bodies to exercise their authority and competence and provide instruments (procedural or substantive) to achieve their set tasks.

700. Article 26 of the CHRF provides everyone with the right to freely choose their profession, to engage in conducting business and to pursue other economic activities. However, Article 26 of the CHRF must be read together with Article 41 of the CHRF, which sets that Article 26 of the CHRF may be claimed only within the confines of the statutory acts which implement Article 26.

---

310. For details *see* Act No. 2/1969 Coll., on the establishment of ministries and other central bodies of the state administration of the Czech Socialist Republic, as amended.
311. Act No. 6/1993 Coll., on the Czech National Bank, as amended.
312. The following text does not cover the legislative process. The Authors' opinion is that it is not necessary to describe that the regulation framework sets the boundaries of legal economic activity.
313. Resolution of the Presidium of the Czech National Council of 16 Dec. 1992 on the Declaration of the CHRF as a Part of the Constitutional Order of the Czech Republic.
314. Article 2(2) of the CHRF.
315. Article 2(3) of the CHRF.

701. The Czech Constitutional Court in recent years rendered several decisions related to the area of economic law, in particular, on the freedom of entrepreneurship and the boundaries of admissible regulation. For example, the court analysed whether electronic records of sales regulation comply with the Czech Constitution (including the CHRF's provisions).[316] In another case, the admissibility of the prohibition of smoking inside restaurants was assessed.[317] In both cases, the Constitutional Court permitted the regulation. However, both findings contain several dissenting opinions.

702. Regulation and supervision of competition (generally) and of certain regulated sectors could also be comprehended as 'State Intervention in Economic Activities'. The state sets the basic boundaries for the conduct of market participants in order to steer the general development of the market while taking into account the interests of various stakeholders. The regulated sectors encompass, for example, the energy sector, telecommunications, healthcare industry, capital markets and financial services. The sector regulation shall comply with the regulation adopted at the EU level and is often closely tied with it. The aim is to ensure continuous stability, functionality, development and security of the specific sectors.

§3. Basic Principles of Economic Law

I. Free Movement

703. According to Article 14(1) of the CHRF, the freedom of movement (and residence) is guaranteed. The second paragraph of this article provides that everyone who is legitimately staying within the territory of the Czech Republic has the right to freely leave this territory. These freedoms may be limited by law if doing so is unavoidable for state security, to maintain the public order, and to protect the rights and freedoms of others or, in demarcated areas, for the purpose of protecting nature. Every Czech citizen has the right to freely enter the territory of the Czech Republic and may not be forced to leave it.

704. Article 20(1) of the Treaty on the Functioning of the European Union (TFEU) provides that 'every person holding the nationality of a Member State shall be a citizen of the Union'[318] which, *inter alia*, encompasses the right to move and reside freely within the territory of the Member States[319] subject to the limitations and conditions laid down in the Treaties and by the measures adopted to give them effect.[320]

---

316. Constitutional Court Plenum Finding File No. Pl. ÚS 26/16.
317. Constitutional Court Plenum Finding File No. Pl. ÚS 7/17.
318. Article 20(1) of the TFEU.
319. Article 20(2)(a) of the TFEU.
320. Article 21(1)(a) of the TFEU.

II. Equality

705. CHFR provides that fundamental human rights and freedoms must be guaranteed to everyone regardless of sex, race, skin colour, language, faith, religion, political or other conviction, ethics or social origin, membership in a national or ethnic minority, property, birth, or other statuses (Article 3 of the CHFR).

706. Along with the CHFR, Act No. 198/2009 Coll., on equal treatment and on the legal means of protection against discrimination and amending some laws, Anti-discrimination Act (ADA) has established the basic legal framework of Czech anti-discrimination law. The ADA prohibits discrimination in the Czech legal order and defines the means of protection for victims of discrimination.

III. Free Competition

707. Czech competition law is governed by Act No. 143/2001 Coll., on the Protection of Competition. This Act regulates the protection of competition in the market of products and services against the elimination, restriction, other distortion, or imperilment thereof (section 1 of the Act on the Protection of Competition).

708. The Competition Authority may prohibit agreements or procedures which constrain competition, and it may also fine a company which has breached competition law. The protection against unfair competition is provided by the Civil Code. Further information on competition law can be found in the following chapters.

IV. State Planning

709. Before the fall of the communist regime, the economy of Czechoslovakia was centrally planned. This economic system was applied by the communists through their authorities, such as the state planning office, whose role was subsequently taken over by the state planning commission, which was established in 1959 and abolished with the transition to a market economy. One of the main tasks of the state planning commission was to prepare proposals for the development plan of the national economy and then submit these proposals to the government.

710. Over the past thirty years, the Czech economy has become a standard market economy, and the purchasing power of people has increased two and a half times. According to data from the Czech Statistical Office and calculations of analysts, since November 1989, the gross domestic product (GDP) has increased nominally by around 700%.[321]

---

321. https://www.irozhlas.cz/ekonomika/ekonomika-hdp-cesko-hruby-domaci-produkt-trzni-ekonomika_1908040847_dok.

§4. STATE SHAREHOLDING

711. The Czech Republic has shareholdings in several companies, some of which have the legal form of a state corporation and are essentially 'owned' by the state (through the particular ministry responsible for the sector). These include Česká pošta, s.p. (Czech post), whose annual turnover is approximately CZK 19 billion, and Lesy České republiky, s.p. (Czech Forest Service), whose annual turnover is approximately CZK 12 billion.[322] The Czech Republic also owns Budějovický Budvar, národní podnik, which has a historic legal form similar to a state corporation;[323] its annual turnover in recent years amounted to approximately CZK 3 billion.

712. The Czech Republic also owns shares in several joint-stock companies. The biggest is Central Europe energy giant ČEZ, a.s., in which the Czech Republic owns approx. 70%, and whose annual turnover amounts to approximately CZK 210 billion. The Czech Republic also owns Letiště Praha, a.s. (Prague's airport and services), whose annual turnover in 2019 was approximately CZK 89.2 billion and in 2020 was approximately CZK 3 billion, and petroleum products company ČEPRO, a.s., whose annual turnover is approximately CZK 54 billion.

322. The annual turnovers correspond with years 2020 or 2019.
323. One of the reasons that Budějovický Budvar has maintained its legal form is historical international trademark disputes.

Chapter 2. Law of Establishment and Supervision of Economic Activities

§1. Freedom to Conduct a Business and Law of Establishment

I. Freedom to Conduct a Business

713. In accordance with Article 26(1) of the European Convention on Human Rights (the 'ECHR'), everybody (including foreign nationals) has the right to freely choose his/her profession and the training for that profession, as well as the right to engage in conducting business and pursuing other economic activities. However, conditions and limitations may be set by the statutory acts for conducting certain professions or activities.[324] Such conditions and limitations are adopted in order to achieve security and to protect customers and the general public.

Regulated and unregulated business activities

714. Generally, businesses can be divided into businesses further regulated by law and businesses unregulated by law. The latter is not very common in the Czech Republic. Activities which fulfil the definition of a business stated in Article 420 of the Civil Code[325] but which are not governed by the Trade Licensing Act[326] ('TLA') or any other statutory act which would regulate the conditions for the specific activity are understood as an unregulated business. Examples include the leasing of property, including residential and non-residential property, and the sale of unprocessed plant and animal products by natural persons who operate their own small-scale cultivation and breeding business.

Business activities regulated by the TLA and by other specific regulation

715. Regulated business activities can be divided into business activities regulated by the TLA and specific business activities which are excluded from the scope of the TLA[327] and are regulated by other statutory acts.[328] These specific business activities typically require specialized skills, knowledge and technological and/or financial capacities. In order to conduct them, it is necessary to obtain an authorization in accordance with the conditions set in the specific regulation and to comply with the regulation.

324. This is in accordance with Art. 26(2) of the ECHR. In addition, all right listed in the Art. 26 of the ECHR may be claimed only within the confines of the laws implementing these provisions.
325. Act No. 89/2012 Coll., the Civil Code, as amended.
326. Act No. 455/1991 Coll., on licensed trade (the Trade Licensing Act), as amended.
327. *See* an exhaustive list of the activities which are not considered as a trade under s. 3 of the TLA.
328. Examples of such specific sectors are the financial sector, energy sector, telecommunication sector, etc. Other fields include liberal professions such as healthcare services, legal services, etc.

716. Most of the general activities are considered trades and are regulated by the TLA. According to section 2 of the TLA, 'a trade shall mean a systematic activity carried out independently under the conditions laid down in this Act, under a person's own name and liability, with a view to making a profit'. The trades regulated by the TLA are classified as:

(a) notifiable trades, which may be carried out once they have been notified to the Trade Office and provided that the conditions stated in the TLA are met; and
(b) permitted trades, which may be carried out pursuant to a concession issued by the Trade Office.[329]

717. Notifiable trades are further divided into:

(a) vocational trades, which are listed in Annex 1 to the TLA, where a condition for carrying out the trade is professional competence documented by proof of a certain level of education and/or experience in the field;
(b) professional trades, where a condition for carrying out the trade is professional competence as referred to in Annex 2 to the TLA; and
(c) unqualified trades, where no professional competence is set as a condition for carrying out the trade.

718. In order to carry on a trade, natural persons must always fulfil general conditions set by Article 6 of the TLA. In order to carry on a trade, a natural person shall have:

(a) full legal capacity; and
(b) good character; a person fails to be of good character if he/she was convicted of an intentional criminal offence which was committed in connection with conducting a business or with the line of business for which such person is applying.

719. Section 8 of the TLA provides impediments to carrying on a trade. A natural or legal person cannot carry on a trade:

(a) if he/she is (or was in the previous three years) subject to qualified bankruptcy;
(b) if, due to a prohibition, the scope of trade involves activities which the applying person cannot perform for the duration of such prohibition;
(c) if the Trade Office revoked its authorization.

329. Permitted trades include the production of alcohol.

II. Law of Establishment (Conducting Business by Foreigners)

Legal personality and capacity to carry out legal acts

720. According to section 26 of the Act on PIL,[330] a foreigner is understood to be a natural person who is not a citizen of the Czech Republic, while a foreign legal person is understood to be a legal person whose registered office is located outside the territory of the Czech Republic. In the matter of natural persons, the legal personality and capacity to carry out legal acts shall be governed by the law of the state in which such person has his/her habitual residence. As for legal persons, the PIL is based on incorporation theory, according to which legal personality and legal capacity to carry out legal acts shall be governed by the law of the state under which it was established (incorporated).

Distinguishing between the freedom of establishment and providing services

721. The Czech Republic is a Member State of the European Union and party to the TFEU, which in its Article 26(2) provides the right of free movement of goods, persons, services and capital. The freedom of establishment (and providing services) belongs among one of the EU's four core freedoms (the others are: free movement of goods, free movement of capital, and free movement of persons). The freedom of establishment and freedom of providing services are distinguished in the length of the activity performed. The CJEU analysed the difference in the *Gebhard* case. While providing a service is understood to be an activity pursued in a Member State on a temporary basis,[331] *'the concept of establishment allows a national of a Member State to participate, on a stable and continuous basis, in the economic life of a Member State other than his/her State of origin and to profit therefrom'.* [332] The CJEU also described the basic elements which should be taken into account when considering the temporary nature. '*The temporary nature of the activities in question has to be determined in the light, not only of the duration of the provision of the service, but also of its regularity, periodicity or continuity.'* [333]

722. Therefore, the law of establishment should be distinguished from the offering of services, which is only temporary. This implies that there are two different regimes for offering services. One is for EU citizens and legal persons whose internal relations are governed by the law of a Member State of the European Union and who have their registered office, headquarters or principal place of business activities in a Member State of the European Union. Those persons are entitled to offer services temporarily in the Czech Republic if they are entitled to conduct business

330. Act No. 91/2012 Coll., on Private International Law, as amended.
331. Case C-55/94 *Gebhard v. Consiglio dell'Ordine degli Avvocati e Procuratori di Milano* [1995] ECR I-04165, para. 26.
332. *Ibid.*, para. 25.
333. *Ibid.*, para. 27.

activities in another Member State of the European Union. Citizens of other Member States that are parties to the European Economic Area Agreement, citizens of the Swiss Confederation, and legal persons whose registered office is in such states shall be regarded as persons from another Member State of the European Union.

723. The second regime applies to other foreign persons (non-EU), who have to comply with the general provisions of the TLA even in cases where they pursue offering services temporarily. The definition of foreign persons in the TLA corresponds to the definition stated in section 26 of the PIL.

Freedom of establishment (business activities conducted by foreigners)

724. Foreign persons may carry on a trade in the Czech Republic under the same conditions and to the same extent as Czech nationals (*see* point 715). Natural persons who are not EU citizens must submit a document proving they have been granted a visa for residence for more than ninety days or a long-term residence permit, together with the trade notification or the application for a concession.[334] A foreign legal person who does not want to relocate its registered office to the Czech Republic (and thus become a Czech legal person) typically conducts its business activities in the Czech Republic by establishing a branch, which it must register in the Czech Companies Register.

725. It should be noted that the Czech regulation must comply with Directive 2006/123/EC on services in the internal market,[335] which aims to remove *'overly burdensome authorisation schemes, procedures and formalities that hinder the freedom of establishment and the creation of new service undertakings therefrom'* [336] and forbids discriminatory requirements within the authorization process. Directive 2006/123/EC was transposed to the Czech law by Act No. 222/2009 Coll., on the free movement of services, which entered into force on 28 December 2009.

Financial requirements for prudential control

726. Certain sectors of the economy are regulated more strictly because of potential harm which could be caused in the case of mismanagement or other kinds of failure.[337] Those who intend to conduct business in such fields must usually obtain a licence from supervising public bodies and comply with the conditions set

---

334. *See* s. 5(5) of the TLA in connection with s. 46 of the TLA. However, it should be emphasized that according to the last sentence of the provision in question this obligation 'shall not apply to a foreign natural person who intends to carry on a trade in the Czech Republic by means of a branch'.

335. Directive 2006/123/EC of the European Parliament and of the Council of 12 Dec. 2006 on services in the internal market which aims to remove existing barriers and facilitate the free movement of services within the EU internal market.

336. *Ibid.*, recital 42.

337. Examples of such sectors are mentioned in footnote No. 326.

in a particular regulation. Those conditions include financial requirements for prudential control which are required from banks and other similar institutions, insurance companies and also providers of investment services (especially security brokers) in accordance with EU Regulation 575/2013 on prudential requirements for credit institutions and investment firms.

727. Under the Czech regulation, banks must take the form of a joint-stock company;[338] moreover, their minimum registered capital shall amount to CZK 500,000,000, which must be composed of pecuniary contributions that must be paid up in full. In order to obtain a licence, the bank's capital and other funds must be of transparent and unexceptionable origin, sufficient amount and appropriate structure.[339] Banks which have obtained a banking licence in another Member State of the European Union can establish a branch in the Czech Republic, but they must maintain the capital of at least 8% of their total volume of capital risk exposure.[340] There are currently forty-nine banks and foreign branches in the Czech Republic.[341] Foreign financial or credit institutions and branches of foreign financial or credit institutions can provide cross-border services in the Czech Republic on the basis of the EU single passport principle if they notify their home state's supervising authority, which then notifies the CNB. Currently, there are 448 subjects providing such services.[342]

338. Section 1(1) of Act No. 21/1992 Coll., on banks, as amended.
339. Section 4 of Act No. 21/1992 Coll., on banks, as amended.
340. Section 12a(1) of Act No. 21/1992 Coll., on banks, as amended.
341. The Czech National Bank's statistics as of 12 Jul. 2019.
342. *Ibid.*

Chapter 3. State Incentives for Economic Activities

§1. Introduction

728. State incentives are one of the tools for attracting foreign investment.[343] The amount and the structure of the investment incentives is an important factor that affects investors' decisions on where to invest. It also motivates investors to place their projects in less developed areas.

729. The Investment and Business Development Agency (CzechInvest) as a state contributory organization subordinate to the Ministry of Industry and Trade of the Czech Republic promotes the Czech Republic abroad as a suitable destination for investments. It arranges both domestic and foreign investments for the Czech Republic in the areas of manufacturing, business support services and technology centres. It also supports small, medium-sized and innovative start-up companies, the country's business infrastructure, and innovation. It is the exclusive organization that may submit applications for investment incentives to the governing bodies. CzechInvest also supports Czech companies that are interested in becoming involved in the supply chains of multinational companies. Through its services and development programmes, CzechInvest contributes to the development of domestic firms, Czech and foreign investors and the business environment as a whole.[344]

730. In arranging investments, CzechInvest focuses on key sectors of the Czech economy, both in the manufacturing industry (production) and in research, development and services (technology centres and business support services). With its regional and foreign offices, CzechInvest operates in all regional capitals in the Czech Republic and in key destinations around the world. All of CzechInvest's services are provided free of charge.

§2. Basic Legal Framework

731. The Incentives Act provides a basic legal framework for investment incentives and conditions under which investment incentives can be provided.

732. An investment incentive is legally defined as state aid in the form of:[345]

---

343. Generally on public subsidies, *see*, e.g., Kincl, M. Veřejná podpora v příkladech a poznámkách. Praha. Wolters Kluwer, 2017, Neubauer, J. Veřejná podpora bankám ve světle směrnice o ozdravných postupech a řešení krize na finančním trhu. Obchodněprávní revue. 2018, Vol. 10, No. 3, pp. 73 et seq., Hamerník, P. Regulace veřejné podpory profesionálnímu sportu jako příklad vyvažování zájmů na periferii práva EU. Právník. 2017, Vol. 156, No. 8, pp. 686 et seq. or Hálová, M. Právní povaha kontrolních činností při kontrole veřejné účelové podpory poskytované na řešení projektů výzkumu, experimentálního vývoje a inovací. Právník. 2015, Vol. 154, No. 11, pp. 895 et seq.

344. Czechinvest.org: Business and Investment Development Agency. Available at: https://www.czechinvest.org/en/About-CzechInvest/About-Us.

345. Section 1a(1)(a) Incentives Act.

- income tax relief;
- transfer of land, including related infrastructure, at a preferential price;
- material support for the creation of new jobs;
- material support for retraining or training of employees;
- material support for the acquisition of tangible and intangible fixed assets for a strategic investment operation; and
- exemption from real estate tax in favoured industrial zones.

733. The Incentives Act further defines three categories of investment projects that can be supported by investment incentives and that are realized in:[346]

(1) *the manufacturing industry*, in order to introduce production, increase production capacity, expand the product range with new products and/or fundamentally change the overall production process;
(2) *technology centres*, in order to build them, increase capacity or expand output by new products; technology centres are focused on applied research, development and innovation of technically or otherwise advanced products, technologies and production processes, including creation and innovation of their software;
(3) *centres of strategic services* that can be realized in the form of:
   - a software creation centre focused on creating new software or innovation of an existing one;
   - a data centre focused on data storage, sorting and management;
   - a repair centre focusing on the repair of high-tech equipment; or
   - a shared services centre focusing on taking over the management, operation and administration of internal activities from the controlling or controlled person or from contractual partners for which these activities are not the subject of their business.

734. On 6 September 2019, an amendment to the Incentives Act came into effect. The main change concerned the preferential treatment of projects with higher added value, especially technology centres, which will consequently be able to receive material support for new jobs and training and retraining of new employees in all districts of the Czech Republic except Prague.[347]

735. The amendment to the Investment Incentives Act will also contribute to greater support for Czech companies. For SMEs, which are the domain of domestic entrepreneurs, incentives should be made more accessible by easing investment entry requirements compared to those of large enterprises. Smaller enterprises are also granted a higher rate of public support.

346. Section 1c(1) Incentives Act.
347. *See* web pages of the Ministry of Industry and Trade of the Czech Republic. Available at: https://www.mpo.cz/cz/podnikani/dotace-a-podpora-podnikani/investicni-pobidky-a-prumyslove-zony/investicni-pobidky/novela-zakona-c--72-2000-sb---o-investicnich-pobidkach--ve-zneni-zakona-c--210-2019-sb---250247/.

736. The system of investment incentives has been redistributed between the law and government regulations, which will increase the flexibility of the whole support system and improve its link with the economic situation in the country and the state and labour market. The amendment also strengthens the role of the Government of the Czech Republic. The government will newly approve every application for an investment incentive, and without this approval, it will not be possible to provide investment incentives. This takes into account, in particular, the benefits of the project for the region and the state.

737. In practice, this means that all applicants for investment incentives must quantify in their applications in detail the anticipated contributions to public budgets or the impact of the investment on the labour market. In addition, they must describe how they want to incorporate research and development into their activities and collaborate with research institutions or schools, or how to tap the potential of local suppliers or contribute to the development of local infrastructure.

§3. EU Law Regulating State Aid

738. The Incentives Act follows the law of the European Union that governs state aid and must be in line with it, especially with Commission Regulation (EU) No. 651/2014 declaring certain categories of aid compatible with the common market (General Block Exemption Regulation) pursuant to Articles 107 and 108 of the TFEU. Thus, Articles 107 and 108 of the TFEU provide the fundamental legal framework for granting state aid.

739. Under Article 107 section (1) of the TFEU, aid granted in any form by the state or through state resources which distorts or threatens to distort competition by favouring certain undertakings or the production of certain goods is, provided it is liable to affect trade between the Member States, incompatible with the internal market unless the TFEU provides otherwise. State aid is, therefore, generally prohibited. It may be granted if a legal title (exception) for the provision can be found. Such exceptions may include, for example, *de minimis* aid, regional aid or public service compensation in accordance with the relevant rules.

740. Under Article 107 section (2) of the TFEU, the following shall be compatible with the internal market:

- aid having a social character, granted to individual consumers, provided that such aid is granted without discrimination related to the origin of the products concerned;
- aid to make good the damage caused by natural disasters or exceptional occurrences.

741. Under Article 107 section (3) of the TFEU, the following may be considered to be compatible with the internal market:

- aid to promote the economic development of areas where the standard of living is abnormally low or where there is serious underemployment, and of the regions referred to in Article 349 of the TFEU, in view of their structural, economic and social situation;
- aid to promote the execution of an important project of common European interest or to remedy a serious disturbance in the economy of a Member State;
- aid to facilitate the development of certain economic activities or of certain economic areas, where such aid does not adversely affect trading conditions to an extent contrary to the common interest;
- aid to promote culture and heritage conservation where such aid does not affect trading conditions and competition in the European Union to the extent that is contrary to the common interest;
- such other categories of aid as may be specified by a decision of the Council on a proposal from the European Commission.

742. Reckless granting of state aid can lead to competition threats. For this reason, it is strictly regulated in the European Union. If state aid is found incompatible with the internal market, both its provider and the beneficiary are exposed to the risk of recovery. If a negative decision is issued by the European Commission in the case of unlawful aid, the provider is obliged to recover the state aid. The beneficiary shall recover the aid, including interest. Moreover, the granting of illegal state aid may also lead to invalidity of the concluded contracts.

743. On the basis of the above-mentioned definition under Article 107 section (1) of the TFEU, the four basic criteria must be examined to conclude whether state aid is incompatible with the internal market:

(a) the aid is granted by the state or through public funds;
(b) the aid favours certain undertakings or business sectors and is selective;
(c) trade between the Member States is affected; and
(d) the competition is distorted or threatened to distort.

I. The Notion of State Aid

744. The notion of state aid covers any directly or indirectly granted advantage financed by state resources, granted by the state as such or by an intermediary body acting under conferred powers. Influencing the public budget is the basic prerequisite for fulfilling this definition, but it is not decisive whether the public budget is influenced directly (by issuing funds) or indirectly (by not expanding the revenue side, which would normally occur). Funds controlled by public authorities are also considered public funds. For instance, the Commission in this context concluded:

745. 'According to settled case-law, the definition of aid is more general than that of a subsidy, because it includes not only positive benefits, such as subsidies themselves, but also measures which, in various forms, mitigate the charges which are normally included in the budget of an undertaking and which thus, without being subsidies in the strict sense of the word, are similar in character and have the same effect (see, inter alia, Case C-143/99 Adria-Wien Pipeline and Wietersdorfer & Peggauer Zementwerke [2001] ECR I-8365, paragraph 38, and Case C-501/00 Spain v Commission [2004] ECR I-6717, paragraph 90 and the case-law cited there).'[348]

746. 'It follows that a measure by which the public authorities grant to certain undertakings a tax exemption which, although not involving a transfer of State resources, places the persons to whom the tax exemption applies in a more favourable financial situation than other taxpayers constitutes State aid within the meaning of Article 87(1) EC (see Case C-387/92 Banco Exterior de Espana [1994] ECR I-877, paragraph 14). Similarly, a measure which grants to certain undertakings a tax reduction or a deferral of liability to tax that would otherwise be payable may constitute State aid.'[349]

747. The interpretation of the meaning of state aid brought by the Court of First Instance in *Germany v. Commission* [350] should also be added:

> 38. Aid, within the meaning of that provision, necessarily refers to advantages granted directly or indirectly through State resources or constituting an additional charge for the State or for bodies designated or established by the State for that purpose (see, in particular, Joined Cases C-52/97 to C-54/97 Viscido and Others [1998] ECR I-2629, paragraph 13, and Case C-53/00 Ferring [2001] ECR I-9067, paragraph 16).
> 39. The Court has held, in particular, that in order to determine whether a State measure constitutes aid it is necessary to establish whether the recipient undertaking receives an economic advantage which it would not have obtained under normal market conditions (Case C-39/94 SFEI and Others [1996] ECR I-3547, paragraph 60, and Case C-342/96 Spain v Commission [1999] ECR I-2459, paragraph 41).
> 40. Finally, it must be noted that aid, as defined in the Treaty, is a legal concept which must be interpreted on the basis of objective factors. For that reason, the Community courts must in principle, having regard both to the specific features of the case before them and to the technical or complex nature of the Commission's assessments, carry out a comprehensive review as to whether a measure falls within the scope of Article 87(1) EC.

748. The definition of state aid implies that aid can be implemented in various forms. The most common forms of state aid include direct subsidies, state guarantees, tax relief, privatization at a special price, capital increase, loans, loans and waivers of social and health insurance payments.

---

348. Judgment of the Court, C-66/02 *Italy v. Commission* [2005], ¶ 77.
349. *Ibid.*, ¶ 78.
350. Judgment of the Court, C-98/00 *Germany v. Commission* [2002], ¶ ¶ 38–40.

II. The Aid Favours Certain Undertakings or Business Sectors and Is Selective

749. Also, the notion of an undertaking is defined according to the settled case law of the European Union. In the context of competition law, 'undertaking' or 'enterprise' means any entity engaged in economic activity, regardless of its legal status and the way in which it is financed.[351] Any activity consisting in offering goods or services on a given market constitutes an economic activity.[352]

750. As stated above, an enterprise is any entity that carries out an economic activity, regardless of its legal status or the way in which it is financed. Thus, in the Czech legal environment, an enterprise is any natural or legal person, any association or group of persons without legal personality, as well as any public authority, either with a separate legal personality or falling under a public authority having such separate legal personality. What is important is the business activity of the company, whether it can be considered economic or not. Based on decision-making practice, 'economic activity' means the offering of goods and/or services on the market. Not even profitability plays a crucial role in a particular case.

751. An advantage is a situation which would not occur under normal market conditions. There is already an advantage when the aid reduces the costs that the beneficiary would normally have to bear from its budget in the normal course of its operation. A selective measure is one which is not applied equally to all undertakings on the market and cannot, therefore, be described as a general measure.

III. The Competition Is Distorted or Threatened to Distort

752. The distortion of competition, as well as other criteria affecting trade between the Member States is rather anticipated by the European Commission. Competition is distorted if the measure strengthens the position of the beneficiary over its competitors.

IV. Trade Between Member States Is Affected

753. There is no threshold where a specific measure already affects trade between the Member States. However, it is clear from the case law that even a small amount, or small-sized recipient, of state aid can affect the market between the

351. Judgment of the Court, C-41/90 *Höfner and Elser v. Macrotron* [1991], ¶ 21; Judgment of the Court, Joint Cases C-264/01, C-306/01, C-354/01 a C-355/01, *AOK Bundesverband and Others* [2004], ¶ 46.
352. Judgment of the Court, C-35/96 *Italy v. Commission* [1998], ¶ 36; Judgment of the Court, Joint Cases C-180/98–C-184/98 *Pavel Pavlov and Others* [2000], ¶ 75.

Member States. As a rule, trade is not affected if the measure in question operates only locally (regionally) or the recipients of the services supported come from only one Member State.

754. A well-known case is the public funding of the pool in Dorsten.[353] Here, the local authorities attempted to resolve the dilapidated state of the swimming pool by transferring it to a private entity (resulting from a selection procedure), which would modernize the site and ensure its use for the local population, schools and various swimming associations. Among other things, the municipality of Dorsten undertook to pay the entity an annual contribution (subsidy) for thirty-five years, which was the main reason why the case was submitted to the Commission for consideration.

755. Here, the Commission concluded that the subsidy does not constitute state aid, precisely because of the absence of any sign of possible effect on trade between EU countries. The Commission's reflections depended on the nature of the services offered by the pool. In this respect, it concluded that pool services could not be exported abroad. However, trade could be affected if the demand for the services came from abroad, that is if foreign visitors would come to Dorsten to use the pool. In this case too, the Commission concluded that this was not the case, as it was not a specific pool, i.e., a famous attraction. Its services were capable of addressing only residents of the city and the surrounding organizations, not foreigners who would go to Dorsten specifically to 'bathe'. On this issue, however, it was stressed that a different conclusion would have been reached if public funding concerned aqua parks, other amusement parks or spas whose services are advertised at a national or transnational level. In such a case, an effect on trade between EU countries would almost certainly be found.

756. Another example addressing the issue of fulfilling the above-mentioned criterion may be the Commission's decision concerning the Municipal House in Přerov.[354] In this case, the European Commission assessed the granting of a subsidy by the City of Přerov to the company IMIT s.r.o. for the second half of 2006 and 2007 for the purpose of organizing cultural events in the Municipal House in Přerov. On the basis of a selection procedure, the company was hired with the obligation to implement certain cultural events in this cultural facility (Municipal House in Přerov). The City of Přerov then decided to provide IMIT s.r.o. a subsidy in order to partially cover the costs of these cultural performances. Here, the Commission also analysed the possible impact of the proposed subsidy on trade between the EU Member States and concluded that the activities and cultural events offered by the Municipal House were of limited regional importance, clearly not intended to 'attract foreign audiences'. The Commission supported this view by the fact that the cultural facility's website was only in Czech. The performances were also performed in Czech. These were facts which clearly showed that the cultural programme was intended only for the local Czech population, so the advantage was not

353. Commission Decision in Case N 258/00 – Germany – Dorsten Swimming Pool.
354. Commission Decision in Case N 497/2006 – Czech Republic – Municipal House in Přerov.

capable of affecting trade between the Member States. In this context, it should be noted that the Commission also addressed whether the subsidy will not be 'spilled over' by IMIT s.r.o. Here it concluded that it would not because the City of Přerov guaranteed that the company would keep separate accounts.

757. Also, *de minimis* aid does not affect trade between the Member States or distort competition. The Supreme Administrative Court has held in this context:[355]

> 'De minimis aid within the meaning of Act No. 215/2004 Coll., on the regulation of certain relations in the field of state aid, does not fulfil all the defining features of state aid within the meaning of Article 107 of the TFEU, because it is not liable to affect trade between Member States or distort competition. However, small-scale aid must fulfil the definition of being granted by the State or through State resources to certain undertakings within the meaning of Article 107 of the TFEU.'

758. On a national level, the Competition Authority is the body responsible for state aid control. The powers of the Competition Authority, as a coordinating body in the field of state aid, are defined by Act No. 215/2004 Coll., regulating certain relations in the field of state aid and amending the Act on Support of Research and Development, as amended. These powers of coordination, advisory, consultancy and monitoring activities are exercised by the Competition Authority in all areas, with the exception of agriculture and fisheries, in particular, in relation to state aid providers.

355. Judgment of the Supreme Administrative Court of the Czech Republic dated on 21 Jan. 2016, No. 7 as 286/2015-21.

Chapter 4. Competition Law

§1. Introduction

759. Competition law aims to secure a fair environment on the market. In its broadest extent, the notion of competition law encompasses antitrust law (also designated as competition law in a narrow sense) and the law of unfair competition and trade practices. Within the European legal culture, including the Czech Republic, antitrust law has been perceived as mainly public law regulation enforced by competition authorities. The law of unfair competition is considered a private law instrument that is enforced *inter partes* (between individual private parties). However, one can see that some aspects of both branches of competition law[356] tend to slightly deviate from their traditional course and converge in order to stimulate a competitive environment.

760. For example, in cases of unfair competition, a claim against the violator to refrain from competing unfairly may be, in certain cases, asserted not only by the injured party but also by a legal person entitled to defend the interests of competitors or customers.[357] This implicates that there might be entities (legal persons) acting for the benefit of others or (consequently) for the public good (fair competitive environment). This partially reassembles certain aspects of the goals and competencies of antitrust authorities.

761. Another example is the development of private enforcement of competition (antitrust) law within the EU, which is encouraged by the CJEU case law and also by legislative development, such as the Damages Directive.[358] Although in some EU Member States, it is possible to consider private enforcement as already established within the particular's state legal culture,[359] in the Czech Republic, it is still developing.

§2. Antitrust

762. Antitrust law in the Czech Republic is generally in compliance with European competition law and follows the same principles and grounds. As such, the general principles and concepts are in alliance with the CJEU's interpretation of competition law rules and the Commission's practice. Because the development and interpretation of the competition law rules are, by definition, quite dynamic and

356. Broadly speaking.
357. *See* s. 2989 of the Civil Code, which implements EU Directive 2009/22/EC of the European Parliament and of the Council of 23 Apr. 2009 on injunctions for the protection of consumers' interests.
358. Directive 2014/104/EU of the European Parliament and of the Council of 26 Nov. 2014 on certain rules governing actions for damages under national law for infringements of the competition law provisions.
359. For example, the United Kingdom, Germany or the Netherlands.

depend vastly on case law, it might take a certain period of time before new interpretations are implemented into practice. However, Czech competition law certainly belongs in the European competition law culture.

763. Czech competition law is built on three pillars which all have the common goals of protecting competition and contributing to consumer welfare. Two of those pillars investigate the competition behaviour *ex post*: regulation of anticompetitive agreements and regulation of abuse of dominance. The third is the regulation of mergers and merger clearance.

764. The basic statute is the Protection of Competition Act[360] (PCA). However, there are also other important rules in the field of competition environment, such as the Act on Significant Market Power in the Sale of Agricultural and Food Products and Abuse Thereof[361] and the Public Procurement Act.[362] Because Czech competition law enforcement is closely tied within the EU system, the regulation at the EU level must also be taken into account. Those regulations include, for instance, Regulation 1/2003,[363] Merger Regulation,[364] and Regulation 330/2010.[365] It should also be noted that a number of guidelines and notices have been issued by antitrust authorities. Soft law is an important instrument in antitrust law as it strengthens the legitimate expectations of the addressees of the regulation. There are specific regulations adopted for certain sectors of the economy.[366] However, this chapter focuses only on the basics of the three pillars of competition law and does not encompass public procurement or particularities of certain sectors.

765. It should be noted that pursuant to Article 5 of Regulation 1/2003, the Czech Competition Authority (in Czech: *Úřad pro ochranu hospodářské soutěže*) is empowered to apply Articles 101 and 102 of the TFEU in individual cases. However, the initiation by the Commission of proceedings shall relieve the Competition Authority of its competence to apply Articles 101 and 102 of the TFEU. If the Competition Authority is already acting on a case, the Commission shall only initiate proceedings after consulting with the Competition Authority.[367] When acting under Article 101 or Article 102 of the TFEU, the Competition Authority has the duty to

---

360. Act No. 143/2001 Coll., on the Protection of Competition and on amendment of Certain Acts (Protection of Competition Act), as amended.
361. Act No. 395/2009 Coll., on Significant Market Power in the Sale of Agricultural and Food Products and Abuse Thereof, as amended.
362. Act. No. 134/2016 Coll., on Public Procurement, as amended.
363. Council Regulation (EC) No. 1/2003 of 16 Dec. 2002 on the implementation of the rules on competition laid down in Arts 81 and 82 of the Treaty.
364. Council Regulation (EC) No. 139/2004 of 20 Jan. 2004 on the control of concentrations between undertakings (the EC Merger Regulation).
365. Commission Regulation (EU) No. 330/2010 of 20 Apr. 2010 on the application of Art. 101(3) of the TFEU to categories of vertical agreements and concerted practices.
366. For instance, Commission Regulation (EU) No. 461/2010 of 27 May 2010 on the application of Art. 101(3) of the TFEU to categories of vertical agreements and concerted practices in the motor vehicle sector or already mentioned Act No. 395/2009 Coll., on Significant Market Power in the Sale of Agricultural and Food Products and Abuse Thereof, as amended.
367. *See* Art. 11(6) of Regulation 1/2003.

inform the Commission before, or without delay after, commencing the first formal investigative measure. It also has the duty to inform the Commission thirty days before a decision is adopted.[368]

766. For the Czech antitrust law's coherence with EU competition law, the decisions in the *Česká rafinérská* case were important.[369] Czech competition law uses the term 'competitor' instead of 'undertaking', which in the past was the subject of quite a broad jurisprudence discussion. Although there might be some particularities to be questioned, the main discussion was ended by the Czech Supreme Administrative Court's decision in a case in which it stated that *'the interpretation of the term "competitor" used in Act No. 143/2001 Coll., shall correspond with the term "undertaking" in the* [TFEU]*'*. The argumentation in the decision suggests that the core institutes of antitrust law should be interpreted by the Czech courts in accordance with the EU law.[370]

I. Anticompetitive Agreements

767. The regulation of anticompetitive agreements generally corresponds with EU law, except that the presence of an influence on trade between Member States as required under Article 101 of the TFEU is not required. According to section 3(1) of the PCA, *'all agreements between undertakings, decisions by associations of undertakings and concerted practices which have as their object or effect the distortion of competition shall be prohibited and null and void'.*

On the term 'agreement'

768. The interpretation of the notion of 'agreement' (in connotation with antitrust law) is usually rather broad. The basic objective is to ensure that each undertaking in the market determines its behaviour independently.

769. Czech jurisprudence distinguishes between three forms of anticompetitive agreements: (i) anticompetitive agreements in a narrow sense; (ii) concerted practices; and (iii) decisions by an association of undertakings. This formal distinction originates from the wording of section 3(1) of the PCA. The distinction should be respected in antitrust enforcement practice in order to comply with the requirement of legal certainty and precise qualification of an administrative offence, which is required by general Czech administrative law.[371]

---

368. *See* Art. 11(3) and 11(4) of Regulation 1/2003.
369. The Czech Supreme Administrative Court's decision, File No. 5 as 61/2005-183, Česká rafinérská.
370. The decision by the Czech Supreme Administrative Court stated that '[i]t is clear from the above that the applied provision of the Act is indeed the result of the harmonization of Czech law and that the application of EC case law and administrative practice interpreting the provisions in question is perfectly appropriate'.
371. Munková, J., Kindl, J., Svoboda, P., Soutěžní právo. 2. vydání. Praha: C. H. Beck, 2012. p. 128.

770. Although EU law does not distinguish between the individual forms of anticompetitive agreements, essentially when there is a question of whether a particular behaviour is prohibited or not, the outcomes should be the same. This conclusion was partially confirmed in a decision by the Czech Supreme Administrative Court in connection with 'complex and long-lasting conduct'.[372] However, the current general perception is that the Competition Authority should distinguish between the individual forms when commencing an investigation and during the proceedings.

771. An 'anticompetitive agreement in a narrow sense' shall not be interpreted as under general contract law, but it should encompass *'any agreement (consensual act) which implies a concerted manifestation of the will of the competitors concerned to act in a certain way in the future and thus restricts their own competitive decision-making and freedom of action'.* [373] In this decision, the Czech Supreme Administrative Court also revealed its general interpretation of decisions by an association of undertakings and of concerted practices. The Czech Supreme Administrative Court stated that *'a decision by an association of competitors shall be understood as an act by an association of competitors towards its members which implies at least indirectly an effort to unify the behaviour of a particular class of competitors, without, however, implying its binding effect. Concerted practice of competitors, preceded by direct or indirect mutual contacts between them, which results in their independent competitive behaviour being replaced by practical cooperation in order to prevent any doubt as to the future behaviour of competitors, is considered to be concerted practice'.* [374]

772. In the following text, the term 'agreement' is used for agreements in a narrow sense, concerted practices, and decisions by an association of undertakings.

Horizontal and vertical agreements

773. Competition law generally distinguishes between horizontal and vertical agreements. The distinction is important, particularly in connection with the *de minimis* doctrine.

774. According to section 5(1) of the PCA *'agreements between undertakings operating on the same product market level shall be deemed horizontal agreements'.* However, contrary to a pure linguistic interpretation, the Competition Authority's Notification on Agreements whose Impact on Competition Is Negligible ('Notification')[375] provides that 'horizontal agreements are considered

372. Czech Supreme Administrative Court's decision, File No. 5 Afs 40/2007-204.
373. Czech Supreme Administrative Court's decision, File No. 1 Afs 78/2008-721.
374. *Ibid.* Please note that the Czech terminology uses term 'competitor' instead of 'undertaking'. However, the notion of competitor corresponds with the notion of undertaking as confirmed by the Czech Supreme Administrative Court in the *Česká rafinérská* case.
375. Oznámení Úřadu pro ochranu hospodářské soutěže o dohodách, jejichž dopad na hospodářskou soutěž je zanedbatelný; available (only in Czech): http://www.uohs.cz/download/Legislativa/HS/SoftLaw/oznameni_deminimis_2018_04.pdf.

agreements concluded between actual competitors or *potential competitors* on any of the relevant markets affected by the agreement', [376] which corresponds with EU competition law.

775. Section 5(2) of the PCA provides that 'agreements between undertakings operating on different product market levels shall be deemed vertical agreements'. For the purposes of the *de minimis* doctrine, the Competition Authority's Notification states that 'vertical agreements are agreements concluded between competitors operating at different market levels which are not actual or potential competitors in any of the relevant markets affected by the agreement'. In addition, the Notification adds that in cases where there is doubt about whether an agreement is horizontal or vertical, it should be considered to be horizontal. This is in accord with section 5(3) of the PCA, according to which 'mixed agreements between undertakings operating on the same horizontal level as well as on different vertical levels of the product market shall be deemed to constitute horizontal agreements. In the case of doubts, any such agreement shall be deemed a horizontal agreement'.

776. Competition law considers horizontal agreements to be potentially more harmful to competition than vertical agreements.[377] However, *'they can, nevertheless, in some cases, also have a particularly significant restrictive potential'.* [378] This is, *inter alia*, expressed in the threshold values as provided by the *de minimis* Notices.

Exceptions

777. Section 3(1) of the PCA, in addition to the prohibition regulation, contains a *de minimis* clause which states that *'agreements with insignificant impact on competition shall not be prohibited'.* The Competition Authority's Notification conceptually corresponds with the *de minimis* Notice from the European Commission.[379], [380] According to the Competition Authority's Notification, section 3(1) of the PCA shall not apply to agreements if their object is not to distort competition and if:

(a) the aggregated market share of the competitors participating in the horizontal agreement does not exceed 10% on any of the relevant markets affected by the agreement;[381] and
(b) the market share of any of the competitors participating in the vertical agreement does not exceed 15% on any of the relevant affected markets.[382]

376. *Ibid.*, para. 2.2.
377. Case C-32/11 *Allianz Hungária* [2013] EU:C:2013:160, para. 43.
378. *Ibid.*
379. Communication from the Commission – Notice on agreements of minor importance which do not appreciably restrict competition under Art. 101(1) of the TFEU (*de minimis* Notice).
380. Petr, M. Vztah českého a unijního soutěžního práva. 1st edition. Prague: C. H. Beck, 2018, p. 116.
381. The provision corresponds with the Commission's *de minimis* Notice, para. 8(a).
382. *Ibid.*, para. 8(b).

778. Section 3(4) of the PCA correlates with Article 101(3) of the TFEU and provides a possible exemption for agreements which restrict competition by their object or effect. The prohibition of certain agreements pursuant to section 3(1) of the PCA shall not apply to agreements which:

(a) contribute to improving the production or distribution of goods or to promoting technical or economic progress while allowing consumers a fair share of the resulting benefit;
(b) do not impose on the undertakings' restrictions which are not indispensable to attaining the objectives pursuant to point 0;
(c) do not afford the undertakings the possibility of eliminating competition with respect to a substantial part of the market of goods, the supply or purchase of which constitutes the objective of the agreement.

779. It is also important to note that according to section 4(1) of the PCA the block exemptions which implement Article 101(3) of the TFEU shall also be applied in relation to the prohibition under section 3(1) of the PCA. Thus, the block exemptions adopted at the EU level also apply to conduct which does not have an impact on trade between the Member States. In other words, the EU block exemptions legislation should also be applied in antitrust cases which do not affect the European Single Market. It is thus very likely that the Competition Authority's practices should correspond with the Commission's practice and development of the CJEU's case law.

II. Monopolies and Abuse of Dominance

780. Abuse of a dominant position is addressed only by two provisions in the PCA. Section 10 of the PCA contains a definition of 'dominant position', and section 11 PCA regulates the prohibition against abuse of a dominant position. The latter consists of a general clause which is followed by a demonstrative list of merits that are particularly assessed as abuse of dominance.

Definition of dominant position (section 10 PCA)

781. According to section 10(1) of the PCA, 'one or more undertakings collectively (collective dominance) shall be deemed to have a dominant position in the relevant market if their market power enables them to behave independently to a significant extent of other undertakings or consumers'. The definition is clearly inspired by the CJEU's famous decision in the *United Brands* case,[383] according to which 'the dominant position [...] relates to a position of economic strength enjoyed by an undertaking which enables it to prevent effective competition being

383. Case C-27/76 *United Brands* [1978] ECLI:EU:C:1978:22.

maintained on the relevant market by giving it the power to behave to an appreciable extent independently of its competitors, customers and ultimately of its consumers'.[384] Although the definition under Czech law might seem slightly different because it does not mention the criterion of preventing effective competition, it seems that there should not be significant practical consequences caused by omitting this criterion.[385]

782. The provision encompasses not only the definition of a single dominant undertaking but also of 'collective dominance' by more undertakings. Collective dominance might be relevant, especially in oligopoly markets. The traditional concept of collective dominance under European competition law was expressed in the *Airtours* case[386] (so-called *Airtours criteria*), which set three conditions for assessing the conduct of undertakings on the (oligopoly) market as collective dominance.[387] The Competition Authority applies the *Airtours criteria* in practices which can be documented, for instance, in its assessment in the case of banking charges in 2005.[388] The *Airtours criteria* can be summarized as follows.

First, each member of the dominant oligopoly must have the ability to know how the other members behave in order to monitor whether they are adopting a common policy. There must be sufficient market transparency for all members of the dominant oligopoly to be aware, sufficiently precisely and quickly, of the way in which the other members' market conduct is evolving.
Second, the situation of tacit coordination must be sustainable over time, meaning that there must be an incentive not to depart from the common policy on the market but rather to maintain the parallel conduct from which the involved undertakings can benefit. The notion of retaliation in respect of conduct which deviates from the undertakings' common policy is inherent to this condition.
Third, it is necessary to establish that the foreseeable reaction of current and future competitors, as well as of consumers, would not jeopardize the results expected from the common policy adopted by the undertakings.

783. The position of dominance should always be based on the actual market situation within which the dominant undertaking enjoys a level of economic strength[389] that allows it to behave independently regardless of the market's response. In other words, there is a lack of competitive constraints which would

384. *Ibid.*, para. 65.
385. *See,* for example, Petr, M. Vztah českého a unijního soutěžního práva. 1st edition. Prague: C. H. Beck, 2018, p. 131; or explanatory memorandum to the original s. 9 of the PCA according to which 'the proposed regulation is in compliance with the concept of dominance in EC competition law, which is settled in decisions of the European Commission and judgments of the Court of Justice'.
386. Case T-342/99 *Airtours* [2004] ECLI:EU:T:2004:192. Although this case was related to merger control, the conclusions were upheld by the General Court in Case T-193/02 *Piau* [2005] ECLI-:EU:T:2005:22, para. 111.
387. *Ibid.*, para. 62.
388. *See* the Competition Authority's decision File No. OK/S016/05-177/05-SOHS II.
389. Although that the definition under the PCA uses the term 'market power', the criterion should be understood as synonymous.

force the concerned undertaking to adjust its conduct. As provided in section 10(2) of the PCA, the Competition Authority shall assess the market power on the basis of the amount of the ascertained volume of sales or purchases in the relevant market for the goods in question (market share) which was achieved by the relevant undertaking or undertakings in a collective dominant position during the examined period and on the basis of other indices, in particular, the economic and financial power of the undertakings, legal or other obstacles for other undertakings to enter the market, the level of vertical integration of the undertakings, market structure, and size of the market shares of the immediate competitors. Therefore, multiple factors should be taken into account when assessing whether an undertaking (or undertakings collectively) holds a dominant position in the relevant market.

784. However, as suggested by the wording of section 10(2) of the PCA, one of the most significant factors is market share. In addition, section 10(3) of the PCA provides a rebuttable presumption that an undertaking or undertakings in joint dominance shall be deemed not to be in a dominant position if its/their share in the relevant market achieved during the examined period does not exceed 40%.

Abuse of dominant position (section 11 PCA)

785. It should be emphasized that the position of dominance does not on its own violate any legal regulation. However, as expressed in the CJEU case law, which was projected into the Commission's Guidance on abusive exclusionary conduct by dominant undertakings,[390] *'holding a dominant position confers a special responsibility on the undertaking concerned'.* [391] Abuse of a dominant position was developed through case law. In the often-cited case *Hoffman-La Roche,* the CJEU stated that *'the concept of abuse is an objective concept relating to the behaviour of an undertaking in a dominant position which is such as to influence the structure of a market where, as a result of the very presence of the undertaking in question, the degree of competition is weakened and which, through recourse to methods different from those which condition normal competition in products or services on the basis of the transactions of commercial operators, has the effect of hindering the maintenance of the degree of competition still existing in the market or the growth of that competition'.* [392] However, the aim of the abuse of dominant position regulation is to protect the competitive process, not the competitors, which are not on the merits as efficient as the dominant undertaking.[393] The conclusions mentioned above are generally accepted by the Czech courts.[394]

390. Communication from the Commission – Guidance on the Commission's enforcement priorities in applying Art. 82 of the EC Treaty to abusive exclusionary conduct by dominant undertakings, OJ C 45, 24.2.2009 ('Guidance on Abusive Conduct').
391. *Ibid.*, paras 9 and 23.
392. Case 85/76 *Hoffman-La Roche* [1979] ECLI:EU:C:1979:36, para. 91.
393. *See* Guidance on Abusive Conduct, para. 6.
394. *See* Petr, M. Vztah českého a unijního soutěžního práva. 1st edition. Prague: C. H. Beck, 2018, p. 135 and the case law cited.

786. As stated in section 11(1) of the PCA 'abuse of a dominant position to the detriment of other undertakings or consumers shall be prohibited'. As the Constitutional Court clarified: 'the occurrence of harm is one of the necessary elements of an administrative offense [...] the harm must be proven as existing, it cannot be satisfactory that the injury is merely threatening or threatened in the past'.[395] In a recent decision, the Constitutional Court further commented on the condition of harm and emphasized that 'harm includes all harmful consequences that are causally related to the conduct of the dominant undertaking, and taking into account that harm must be caused, not merely threatened, it must be interpreted broadly. In addition to direct material damage, harm cannot be considered to be also loss of customers, loss of market position, the need to overcome barriers to enter the market, but also the need of the competitor whose harm is being investigated to respond immediately to the dominant's conduct in way which otherwise would not be necessary [...] There is no need to quantify precisely the harm in relation to individual market participants (as it would be in the case of "damage" – that is to say, material harm expressed in money), but it is necessary to specify what such harm is'.[396] Therefore, the notion of harm should be interpreted rather broadly.

787. Section 11(1) of the PCA also includes a demonstrative list of merits of abuse of a dominant position, which include:

(a) direct or indirect enforcement of unfair conditions in agreements with other market participants, especially enforcement of performance, which is at the time the contract is concluded conspicuously inadequate to the counter-performance provided;
(b) making the conclusion of contracts subject to the other party's acceptance of the supplementary performance, which by its nature or according to commercial usage has no connection with the object of such contracts;
(c) application of dissimilar conditions to identical or equivalent transactions with other market participants, thereby placing them at a competitive disadvantage;
(d) termination or limitation of production, sales or research and development to the detriment of consumers;
(e) consistent offer and sale of goods for unfairly low prices, which results or may result in distortion of competition;
(f) refusal to grant other undertakings access for a reasonable reimbursement to transmission grids or similar distribution networks or other infrastructure facilities which are owned or used on other legal grounds by the undertaking in a dominant position, provided the other undertakings are unable for legal or other reasons to operate in the same market as the dominant undertakings without being able to jointly use such facilities, and such dominant undertaking fails to prove that such joint use is unfeasible for operational or other reasons or that it cannot be reasonably requested to enable such use. This also applies in due proportion to any refusal to grant other undertakings access for a reasonable reimbursement to the use of the intellectual property or access to networks owned or

395. Decision of the Constitutional Court File No. II. ÚS 192/05-2.
396. Decision of the Constitutional Court File No. II. ÚS 1867/14.

used on other legal grounds by the undertaking in a dominant position, provided such use is necessary for participating in competition in the same market as the dominant undertaking or in any other market.

III. Mergers and Acquisitions

788. Competition law is aimed not only at investigating and punishing violations of competition *ex post* but also at a priori preventing situations which could be harmful. Thus, national competition authorities are entitled to assess mergers between undertakings before they are completed. However, not every merger or other form of concentration must be assessed. The merging parties are obliged to notify the national Competition Authority only if the sizes of their businesses exceed certain turnover thresholds. The mergers of undertakings whose turnovers are below the threshold criteria do not have to be notified and assessed. However, if the thresholds are met, the merging undertakings are obliged to notify the relevant Competition Authority. If they fail to do so and complete the merger anyway (referred to as 'gun jumping'), they could be handed quite hefty fines.[397]

789. A 'one-stop-shop' system stems from the Merger EU Regulation. The system is built to 'permit effective control of all concentrations in terms of their effect on the structure of competition in the Community and to be the only instrument applicable to such concentrations'. [398] Significant structural changes to the market whose impact goes beyond the national borders of a Member State should be generally reviewed exclusively at the EU level.[399] A concentration which does not have a significant impact on the common market but which is significant enough for a respective geographical market should be assessed within the jurisdiction of the respective Member State.

790. According to Article 21(3) of the Merger Regulation, *'[n]o Member State shall apply its national legislation on competition to any concentration that has a Community dimension'*. Therefore, only the Commission has the authority to assess concentrations which have an EU dimension. This is supposed to decrease the amount of cases in which a transaction has to be notified to multiple competition authorities, which *'increases legal uncertainty, effort and cost for undertakings and*

397. For instance, in June 2019, the Commission handed Canon a EUR 28 million fine for its acquisition of Toshiba Medical Systems Corporation. Commissioner Margrethe Vestager stated that 'Companies have to respect our competition rules and procedures. They are obliged to notify and wait for our approval before a merger can go ahead. […] Our merger assessment and decision-making depends on the Commission being sure that companies are not jumping the gun and implementing mergers without our approval', *see* the press release available at: https://ec.europa.eu/commission/presscorner/detail/en/IP_19_3429.

398. Recital 6 of the Merger Regulation.

399. *See* Recital 8 of the Merger Regulation.

may lead to conflicting assessments'.[400] However, in cases which involve a transaction among business(es) in multiple Member States and where the EU turnover thresholds are not met, it might be necessary to notify the transaction to multiple national competition authorities.[401]

791. The turnover thresholds of concentrations with an EU dimension are set in Article 1 of the Merger Regulation. A concentration has an EU dimension, i.e., it should be notified to the Commission, if:

(a) the combined aggregate worldwide turnover of all the undertakings concerned is more than EUR 5,000 million, and the aggregate community-wide turnover of each of at least two of the undertakings concerned is more than EUR 250 million unless each of the undertakings concerned achieves more than two-thirds of its aggregate community-wide turnover within one and the same Member State;[402] or
(b) the combined aggregate worldwide turnover of all the undertakings concerned is more than EUR 2,500 million, while in each of at least three Member States the combined aggregate turnover of all the undertakings concerned is more than EUR 100 million, and in each of at least three Member States, the aggregate turnover of each of at least two of the undertakings concerned is more than EUR 25 million, and the aggregate community-wide turnover of each of at least two of the undertakings concerned is more than EUR 100 million unless each of the undertakings concerned achieves more than two-thirds of its aggregate community-wide turnover within one and the same Member State.

792. The calculation of the turnover, for instance, its attribution or geographical allocation, plays, of course, a vital role and is described in detail in section C.IV of the Jurisdiction Notice issued by the Commission.[403] The calculations of aggregate turnover comprise *'the amounts derived by the undertakings concerned in the preceding financial year from the sale of products and the provision of services falling within the undertakings' ordinary activities after deduction of sales rebates and of value added tax and other taxes directly related to turnover'.*[404]

793. It is not unusual that the merging undertakings at the EU level consist of holding groups. Thus, it is important to note that Article 5(4) of the Merger Regulation sets specific rules governing which entities' turnovers shall be taken into consideration for calculating the aggregated turnover. However, at the same time, *'the*

400. Recital 12 of the Merger Regulation.
401. However, it should be noted that if the concentration is capable of being reviewed under the national competition laws of at least three Member States, the merging parties can ask to have the concentration examined the Commission. For details, *see* Art. 4(5) of the Merger Regulation.
402. Article 1(2) of the Merger Regulation.
403. Commission Consolidated Jurisdictional Notice under Council Regulation (EC) No. 139/2004 on the control of concentrations between undertakings, OJ C 95/1, 16. 4. 2008 ('Jurisdictional Notice').
404. Article 5(1) of the Merger Regulation.

aggregate turnover of an undertaking concerned shall not include the sale of products or the provision of services between any of the undertakings referred to in [Article 5(4), i.e., the group to which the undertaking concerned belongs]*'.* [405]

794. As already briefly described above, the concentration might exceed 'only' national thresholds and not the thresholds set by Merger Regulation. In such a case, the concerned undertakings are obliged to notify the Competition Authority of the respective Member State.[406] Section 6 of the PCA sets the rules on concentrations of undertakings in the Czech Republic.

795. According to section 13 of the PCA, a concentration is subject to the approval of the Competition Authority if:

(a) the total net turnover of all undertakings concerned achieved in the last accounting period in the market of the Czech Republic exceeds CZK 1.5 billion, and each of at least two of the undertakings concerned achieved in the market of the Czech Republic in the last accounting period a net turnover exceeding CZK 250 million; or
(b) the net turnover of the target undertaking or at least of one of the undertakings concerned achieved in the last accounting period in the market of the Czech Republic exceeds CZK 1.5 billion, and at the same time, the worldwide net turnover achieved in the last accounting period by another undertaking concerned exceeds CZK 1.5 billion.

796. Section 14 of the PCA provides rules for calculating turnovers, which generally follow the Jurisdictional Notice. The assessment of a holding group's turnover is contained in section 14(2) of the PCA, according to which *'aggregate net turnover shall include net turnovers achieved by: (a) all the undertakings concerned; (b) persons who will control the undertakings concerned after the implementation of the given concentration, and persons who are controlled by the undertakings concerned; (c) persons controlled by the person who will control the undertakings concerned after implementation of the given concentration; and (d) persons controlled jointly by two or more persons referred to in (a) to (c) above'.*

797. However, the aggregate net turnover shall not include the turnover achieved by the sale of goods between the undertakings concerned and the entities listed in letters (b) to (d) above.[407] If only a part of an undertaking is subject to the concentration, only the portion of turnover achieved by such part shall be included in the net turnover.[408] In order to prevent circumvention of the notification obligation, if

405. *Ibid.*
406. In the case of a merger of undertakings operating in multiple Member States, the concerned undertakings are obliged to notify the competition authorities of the respective Member States.
407. Section 14(3) of the PCA.
408. Section 14(4) of the PCA.

two or more concentrations take place between the same undertakings within a two-year period, such concentrations shall be assessed as one concentration.[409]

The notion of concentration

798. The notion of a concentration of undertakings is contained in section 12 of the PCA and generally follows the notion of concertation under Article 3 of the Merger Regulation. A concentration of undertakings shall occur in the case of a merger of two or more previously independent competitors.[410] A concentration of undertakings also encompasses the situation when one or more entrepreneurs[411] acquire the possibility to directly or indirectly control another undertaking or part thereof.[412] Pursuant to section 12(3) of the PCA, a part of an undertaking shall also be understood as the assets of the undertaking which are used for its activities and to which the turnover achieved by the sale of goods in the relevant market may be unequivocally assigned.[413]

799. The criterion of control is vital for the notion of concentration. Section 12(4) of the PCA provides that: 'control shall mean the possibility, based on a matter of law or fact, to exercise decisive influence over the activity of another undertaking or part thereof, particularly on the basis of a) ownership or right to use the controlled undertaking's enterprise or a part of the controlled undertaking; or b) right or other matter of law which provides a decisive influence on the composition, voting and decision-making of the controlled undertaking's bodies'.

800. To qualify parties' conduct as a concentration, it is sufficient to be in the position to exercise a decisive influence and not to actually exercise it,[414] which is recognized by the Competition Authority.[415] However, the internal restructuring of an undertaking should not be considered as a concertation.[416] The Jurisdictional Notice distinguishes between sole control (which can be positive or negative) and

409. Section 14(5) of the PCA. A similar regulation is contained in Art. 5(2) of the Merger Regulation.
410. Section 12(1) of the PCA.
411. Or one or more persons who are not entrepreneurs but control at least one undertaking (*see* s. 12(2) of the PCA).
412. Section 12(2) of the PCA, which also provides a demonstrative list of cases where control is acquired: acquisition of equity shares, business or membership interests or by a contract or by other means which allow exercise of control over an undertaking or part thereof.
413. Section 12(3) of the PCA adds that the fact that the question whether a part of an undertaking forms an independent organizational unit of the enterprise is not relevant.
414. For instance, regarding the notion of undertaking in connection with subsidiaries, it is necessary that a parent company actually exercises the decisive influence over the subsidiary (except the cases of wholly or nearly wholly owned subsidiaries, on the topic, *see*, for example, Case C-440/11 *P Stichting Administratiekantoor Portielje* [2013] ECLI:EU:C:2013:514, paras 36 et seq.).
415. Notice on the concept of concentration of competitors within the meaning of the Act on the Protection of Competition issued by the Competition Authority, para. 17.
416. For instance, *see* the Competition Authority's decision File No. S 9/03-802/03, available at: https://www.uohs.cz/download/sbirky_rozhodnuti/dokumenty/pis10727.pdf.

joint control.[417] The Competition Authority, in general, accepts this. The same applies to changes in the quality of control and joint ventures.[418]

Notification proceedings

801. Concentration approval proceedings shall be initiated on the basis of a notification[419] and must contain a justification and documents certifying the facts decisive for the concentration.[420] The Competition Authority is empowered to issue a legal regulation to set the details of the justification and documents certifying the facts which are decisive for the concentration.[421] Based on this provision, the Competition Authority issued implementing Decree No. 294/2016 Coll. ('Implementing Decree'). The Implementing Decree sets the documents which must be submitted together with the formal notification. The most important of those documents is the Questionnaire, which is similar to Form CO as provided under Regulation 802/2004.[422] The alternative for simplified proceedings is the Simplified Questionnaire, which corresponds with Short Form CO. The other documents to be submitted are: (i) extracts from the Companies Register; (ii) the documents on the basis of which the concentration should take place; (iii) annual reports; (iv) consolidated financial statements; (v) schemes and methods of turnover calculation; and (vi) other relevant documents, such as expert reports, studies, etc. The proceedings are commenced once the complete notification (including the appropriate Questionnaire and all other documents) is submitted.

802. It should also be noted that the Competition Authority is open to pre-notification contacts, which is a rather informal process that is supposed to facilitate the course of the proceedings.[423]

803. The concentration can be notified in ordinary proceedings[424] or, under certain conditions, in simplified proceedings.[425] Ordinary proceedings can be divided into two stages. In the first stage, the Competition Authority assesses whether the concentration is subject to its approval. If it is not, the Competition Authority issues the relevant decision within thirty days. If the concentration is subject to approval but will not result in a substantial distortion of competition, the Competition Authority shall issue a decision approving the concentration within thirty days.[426] However, if the Competition Authority *'finds that the concentration raises serious concerns as to a significant impediment to competition, primarily due to the fact that*

417. *See* ss B.II.2-3 of the Jurisdictional Notice.
418. *See* ss B.III-IV of the Jurisdictional Notice.
419. Section 15(1) of the PCA.
420. Section 15(3)(b) of the PCA.
421. Section 26(1) of the PCA.
422. Commission Regulation (EC) No. 802/2004 of 21 Apr. 2004 implementing Council Regulation (EC) No. 139/2004 on the control of concentrations between undertakings.
423. Please note that the Competition Authority issued Notice on pre-notification contacts with merging competitors.
424. Section 16 of the PCA.
425. Section 16a of the PCA.
426. Section 16(2) of the PCA.

it would create or strengthen a dominant position of the undertakings concerned or any of them, the Competition Authority shall inform the parties to the proceedings in writing of this fact within the stipulated deadline and inform them that it is continuing the proceedings'. [427] In such an event, the proceedings enter the second stage, and the Competition Authority has five months to issue a decision.[428] It also should be noted that pursuant to section 16(6) of the PCA, the Competition Authority may request the parties in writing for further information or evidence. The Competition Authority's deadlines for issuing a decision are suspended during the period between the day when the relevant party receives the request and the day on which the obligation is fulfilled. Therefore, if the proceedings enter the second stage, in practice, it could take more than five months.

804. The notification for simplified proceedings can be submitted if:

(a) none of the undertakings concerned is operating in the same relevant market, or their combined share in such market does not exceed 15%, and at the same time, none of the undertakings concerned is operating in the market vertically connected to the relevant market in which another undertaking concerned operates, or their share in every such market does not exceed 25%; or
(b) the undertaking acquires sole control over another undertaking or part thereof in which it has participated in joint control so far.[429]

The Competition Authority again first assesses whether the concentration is subject to its approval. If it is not, it issues the relevant decision within twenty days. If the concentration is subject to its approval but will not result in a substantial distortion of competition, the Competition Authority shall issue a decision approving the concentration within twenty days. If it concludes that the concentration could raise serious concerns about a substantial distortion of competition, it shall request the parties within twenty days to file a complete concentration notification.[430]

Law of unfair competition and trade practices

Introduction

805. The law on unfair competition and trade practices[431] has by its very nature private characteristics and, unlike antitrust law, is not enforced by public authorities. The provisions governing unfair competition are laid down mainly in Division 2, Chapter 2, Title III of the Civil Code. However, the case law is also quite important because it identifies the boundaries of the abstract (normative) provisions in

427. *Ibid.*
428. Section 16(5) of the PCA.
429. Section 16a(1) of the PCA.
430. Section 16a(3) of the PCA.
431. In the following text, the term 'unfair competition' will be used for both unfair competition and unfair trade practices.

specific cases. Such case law consequently provides guidelines for the application of the relevant provisions in future cases.[432]

806. 'Unfair competition means behaviour that falsifies competition, thus affecting elements other than the quality level and quantity of economic performance.'[433] According to section 2972 of the Civil Code, 'a person who engages in competition (a competitor) may, in competitive activities or in associating for the purpose of pursuing competitive activities, neither abuse his/her own engagement in the competition by competing unfairly, nor restrict others in their engagement in the competition'. Logically, this behaviour is deemed harmful from both an individual and objective perspective and is prohibited.

807. It should be emphasized that the definition of 'competitor' is completely different from the definition of 'undertaking' in antitrust law[434] and encompasses natural and legal persons (from the perspective of private law). A competitor under unfair competition law does not have to be in a strictly competitive position to infringe unfair competition law, *'but it can also be a third person who, through its actions, interferes unfairly in the competition process. However, it is necessary to deduce the specific interest of the person acting unfairly in the success of one competitor to the detriment of the other, i.e., the outcome of the competition of two competitors'.* [435]

808. The regulation of unfair competition contained in the Civil Code is applicable to the extent to which the acts have effect in the Czech Republic unless otherwise provided by international treaties by which the Czech Republic is bound and which were published in the Collection of International Treaties.[436]

The General Clause

809. The behaviour of entities participating in the competition (i.e., competitors) can be envisaged only to a limited extent. The legislation reflects this fact with the following structure of the Civil Code provisions. The keystone of the regulation is set in section 2976(1) of the Civil Code – the so-called general clause.[437] The general clause contains three conditions which must be met cumulatively in order to assess an act as unfair competition. The conditions are as follows:

---

432. However, it is crucial to keep in mind that the Czech legal system belongs to civil law culture, not common law.
433. Pelikánová I. in Černá a kolektiv. Obchodní právo – podnikatel, podnikání, závazky s účasté podnikatele. 1st edition. Prague: Wolters Kluwer ČR, 2016, p. 280.
434. Please note that there was a significant debate whether the definition of an 'undertaking' under Czech antitrust law, which also uses the term 'competitor', complies with the definition under EU law. This debate was settled by the decision of the Czech Supreme Administrative Court, File No. 5 as 61/2005-183, Česká rafinérská, which stated that the interpretation of the term 'competitor' under Czech antitrust law must be interpreted in conformity with EU law.
435. Decision of the Czech Supreme Court, File No. 32 Odo 1464/2006.
436. Section 2973 of the Civil Code.
437. The wording of s. 2976(1) of the Civil Code is as follows: 'If, in business relations, a person gets into conflict with good morals of competition as a result of his/her conduct which is capable of

(a) the act is conducted in a business relationship;
(b) the act conflicts with good morals of competition; and
(c) the act is capable of causing harm to other competitors or customers.

810. Any conduct which fulfils all the conditions stated above is regarded as unfair competition. The first condition of acting in a business relationship should be interpreted rather broadly and should encompass not only direct competitors but also all affected entities which act in similar or *inter alia* substitutable fields or economic activities.[438]

811. With regard to the second condition, it is important to emphasize that there is a difference between general 'good morals'[439] and 'good morals of competition'.[440] A higher level of aggressivity is tolerated for the latter due to the competitive nature and clash of the participants on the market over the customers. The assessment of whether certain conduct is in compliance with good morals of competition is a legal question, which is solved by the courts. It can evolve over time as society's standards and values change. Conduct, which is contrary to the law or other regulations, should always be considered as a violation of good morals of competition.[441]

812. The third condition should be interpreted in a way that even a threat of harm is sufficient to cause unfair competition. Therefore, it is not necessary to prove that actual harm was caused to competitors or customers. The harm might be caused to an asset or be non-pecuniary. It should also be noted that the last condition mentions competitors and customers. The current regulation is broader than the previous one, which was aimed at consumers instead of customers. However, even the previous case law and jurisprudence developed a model of 'average consumer', and it is from this view that the conduct of a potential perpetrator should be assessed. Although there is a difference between a consumer and a customer, the conclusions arising from the model of an average consumer as interpreted under the previous regulation should also be applied to customers.

---

causing harm to other competitors or customers, such a person has competed unfairly. Unfair competition is prohibited.' The Czech legislation follows the concept of the general clause as was already included in Art. 10bis (2) of the Paris Convention for the Protection of Industrial Property by which the Czech Republic is bound.

438. Ondrejová D. in Hulmák, M. a kol.: Občanský zákoník VI. Závazkové právo. Zvláštní část (§ 2055–3014). Commentary. 1st edition. Prague: C. H. Beck, 2014.

439. The term of general 'good morals' is used, for example, in s. 2(3) of the Civil Code which states that '[t]he interpretation and application of a legal regulation must not be contrary to good morals and must not lead to cruelty or inconsiderate behaviour offensive to ordinary human feelings'.

440. The difference was spotted even nearly a hundred years ago. *See*, for example, the decision of the Supreme Court of the Czechoslovak Republic, File No. Rv I 1625/31.

441. Ondrejová D. in Hulmák, M. a kol.: Občanský zákoník VI. Závazkové právo. Zvláštní část (§ 2055–3014). Commentary. 1st edition. Prague: C. H. Beck, 2014.

813. The Czech model of an average consumer is well developed and follows the case law of the CJEU.[442] The Czech Supreme Court has stated that the average consumer is sufficiently attentive, responsive and circumspect[443] and has sufficient information and is reasonably attentive and cautious, taking into account social, cultural and linguistic factors.[444]

Demonstrative list of merits of unfair competition

814. Section 2976(2) of the Civil Code contains the following demonstrative list of merits of unfair competition: (i) misleading advertising; (ii) misleading identification of goods and services; (iii) creating a likelihood of confusion; (iv) freeriding on the reputation of an enterprise, product or services of another competitor; (v) bribery; (vi) disparaging a competitor; (vii) comparative advertising, unless allowed as admissible; (viii) breach of trade secrets; (ix) unsolicited advertising; and (x) threat to health and the environment. The merits mentioned in section 2976(2) are described in the subsequent paragraphs.

815. Section 2977 of the Civil Code covers misleading advertising. Misleading advertising is advertising which relates to business activities or a profession, aims to promote the sales of movable or immovable things or the provision of services, including rights and duties, which misleads or is capable of misleading the persons to whom it is addressed or whom it reaches by its presentation or in any other way, and is thus evidently capable of affecting the economic behaviour of such persons. In determining whether advertising is misleading, the account is taken of all its distinctive features. Particular account is taken of the information which the advertising contains regarding: (i) the availability, nature, design, composition, production method, date of production or provision, fitness for the intended purpose, usability, quantity, geographical or commercial origin, as well as a more detailed definition and other features of the goods or services, including the expected results of their use or the results and essential features of the tests and checks performed; (ii) the price or the method of determining the price; (iii) the terms under which the goods are supplied or services provided; and (iv) the nature, characteristics and rights of an advertiser, including, but not limited to, its identity, property, professional competence, its intellectual property rights or its awards and honours.

816. Section 2978 of the Civil Code covers misleading identification of goods and services. Misleading identification of goods and services is the identification which, in economic transactions, is capable of causing a misleading assumption that the goods or services so identified come from a particular region or place, or from a specific producer, or that they have a particular characteristic feature or a particular quality. It is irrelevant whether the identification was placed directly on the

442. *See*, for example, C-210/96 *Gut Springenheide a Tusky v. Oberkreisdirektor des Kreises Steinfurt* [1998] I-04657.
443. Decision of the Czech Supreme Court File No. 23 Cdo 2000/2013.
444. Decision of the Czech Supreme Court File No. 32 Odo 229/2006.

goods, on the packaging, in a commercial document or elsewhere. It is also irrelevant whether the misleading identification was direct or indirect, and what means were used for such identification. An indication generally established in economic transactions to designate kind or quality is also misleading if it is accompanied by additions capable of misleading, including, without limitation, by using the term *'pravý'* (genuine), *'skutečný'* (real), or *'původní'* (original). Those provisions do not affect other legal regulations on the protection of industrial or other intellectual property.

817. Section 2979 of the Civil Code covers common provisions on misleading advertising and misleading identification of goods and services. An indication which is correct in itself may also be capable of misleading if it can mislead because of the circumstances and context in which it was provided. In assessing the misleading nature, the account is also taken of additions, including, but not limited to, the use of terms such as *'druh'* (kind), *'typ'* (type), *'způsob'* (manner), as well as of omissions, abbreviations and overall external presentation.

818. Section 2980 of the Civil Code covers comparative advertising. Comparative advertising directly or indirectly identifies another competitor or its goods or services. Comparative advertising is permitted in terms of making comparisons in the following cases: (i) if it is not misleading; (ii) if it only compares goods or services which satisfy the same need or which are intended for the same purpose; (iii) if it objectively compares one or several relevant, important, verifiable and typical properties of goods or services, including price; (iv) if it compares goods with a designation of origin only to goods of the same designation; (v) if it does not disparage a competitor, its position, its activities or its results, or their identification, or unfairly benefits therefrom; and (vi) if it does not offer goods or services as an imitation or copy of goods or services identified by a trademark of a competitor or by the competitor's name. All six conditions must be fulfilled simultaneously.

819. Section 2981 of the Civil Code covers creating a likelihood of confusion. A person who uses the name or a special designation of an enterprise which is already lawfully used by another competitor shall cause a likelihood of confusion. Likelihood of confusion is also caused by a person who uses a special designation of an enterprise or a special designation or presentation of a product, performance or business material of an enterprise which customers consider to be typical for the particular enterprise. Likelihood of confusion is also caused by a person who imitates another's product, its packaging or performance unless it is an imitation of elements which are functionally, technically or aesthetically predetermined given the nature of the product and the imitator took all measures which could have been required to exclude or at least substantially reduce the likelihood of confusion if such acts are capable of causing the likelihood of confusion or a false impression of being associated with the competitor, its enterprise, name, special designation, or with a product or performance of another competitor.

820. Section 2982 of the Civil Code covers freeriding on another's reputation, which consists in the abuse of the reputation of an enterprise, product or service of another competitor which allows a benefit to be gained for the results of one's own or another's business activities, where the competitor would not have gained such a benefit otherwise.

821. Section 2983 of the Civil Code covers bribery, which is constituted by an act whereby a competitor directly or indirectly offers, promises or provides any benefit to a person who is the member of a governing body or some other body of another competitor, or is employed by another competitor, in order to obtain, through that person's unfair conduct, priority or some other undue advantage in the competition for himself/herself or for some other competitor at the expense of other competitors, or whereby such person directly or indirectly requests or accepts any benefit, or has such a benefit promised to him/her, for the same purpose.

822. Section 2984 of the Civil Code covers disparagement of a competitor, which is constituted by an act whereby a competitor states or spreads a false statement about the situation, performance or product of another competitor, where such a statement is capable of causing harm to that competitor. Disparagement is also constituted by stating and spreading a true statement about the situation, performance or product of another competitor if it is capable of causing harm to the competitor. However, if the competitor was forced to perform such acts by the circumstances, it shall not constitute unfair competition (legitimate defence).

823. Section 2985 of the Civil Code covers breach of trade secrets, which is constituted by an act whereby the person who acts unlawfully discloses or makes available to another person, or uses for himself/herself or for another person, trade secrets which can be used in competition and of which the person learned: (i) as a result of having been entrusted with the secrets or as a result of the secrets having been made available to him/her otherwise under his/her employment relationship with a competitor, or under another relationship with the competitor, or, where applicable, in the discharge of the office to which he/she was selected by a court or another body; or (ii) by the person's own act or the act of another which is in breach of a statute.

824. Section 2986 of the Civil Code covers unsolicited advertising. Unsolicited advertising consists in disclosing information about a competitor, goods or services, as well as in offering goods or services using the telephone, fax, electronic mail or similar means where the recipient clearly wishes to be subject to no such activity, or in the communication of advertising in which its originator conceals or disguises information which allows for its identification, and does not specify where the recipient can have the advertising ended without incurring extraordinary costs. Where advertising is sent to an electronic address which an entrepreneur acquired in connection with the sale of goods or provision of services, this does not constitute unsolicited advertising if the entrepreneur uses the address for direct advertising of its own goods or services, and the other party has not prohibited such advertising despite having been clearly informed by the entrepreneur in acquiring the address and each time it was used it notified the recipient of its right to have the advertising ended without any additional costs.

825. Section 2987 of the Civil Code covers threats to health or the environment, which is constituted by an act whereby a competitor distorts the conditions of competition by operating production, marketing a product, or carrying out performance threatening an interest in the protection of health or the environment protected by a statute in order to obtain a benefit for himself/herself or another person at the expense of another competitor or customers.

Protection against unfair competition

826. The possible claims of a person whose rights have been violated or threatened are contained in section 2988 of the Civil Code. Such a person may seek the perpetrator to refrain from competing unfairly or to remove the defective state, and he/she may also request adequate satisfaction, compensation for damage and restitution of unjust enrichment.

827. In addition, according to section 2989(2) of the Civil Code, if a claimant is a consumer and he/she seeks the perpetrator to refrain from competing unfairly or to remove a defective state or compensation for damage, there is a switch in the burden of proof for claims based on: (i) section 2976 of the Civil Code (general clause); (ii) section 2977 of the Civil Code (misleading advertising); (iii) section 2978 of the Civil Code (misleading identification of goods and services); (iv) section 2979 of the Civil Code (misleading advertising and misleading identification of goods and services); (v) section 2980 of the Civil Code (comparative advertising); (vi) section 2981 of the Civil Code (creating a likelihood of confusion) and (vii) section 2987 of the Civil Code (threat to health or the environment). This means that in those cases the alleged perpetrator must prove that he/she did not compete unfairly (or eventually that he/she did not cause harm due to unfair competition).

828. However, not only a person whose rights have been violated or threatened may seek those claims. In the cases mentioned in the previous paragraph (i.e., in the cases in which the claim is based on section 2976 of the Civil Code to 2981 of the Civil Code and on section 2987 of the Civil Code, plus on section 2987 of the Civil Code), the right to have the violator refrain from competing unfairly or remove a defective state may also be asserted by a legal person entitled to defend the interests of competitors or customers.[445]

829. In connection with civil proceedings, it is important to mention that the initiation of proceedings which seek to refrain or remove a defective state in the matters of protecting rights violated or threatened by unfair competition prevents the commencement of other proceedings by other potential claimants against the same defendant which would seek the same remedies and which would be based on the

445. Section 2989(1) of the Civil Code, which implements Directive 2009/22/EC of the European Parliament and of the Council of 23 Apr. 2009 on injunctions for the protection of consumers' interests.

same merits.[446] The opinion in a final judgment which decided in the cases mentioned in section 83(2) of the Civil Procedure Code is binding not only to the parties of the proceeding but also to other persons entitled against the defendant for the same claims from the same act or condition.

830. Last but not least, section 2990 of the Civil Code provides that '[a] person whose right has been threatened or violated by an unlawful restriction of competition has the rights set out in section 2988'. This provision implements the possibility of private enforcement of antitrust law in the Civil Code.

446. Section 83(2) of Act No. 99/1963 Coll., Civil Procedure Code, as amended.

Chapter 5. Financial System

§1. The CNB Within the Czech System of Banks

831. The Central Bank of the Czech Republic (the 'CNB'), which is the supervisor of the Czech financial market and the Czech resolution authority, was established under the Constitution of the Czech Republic and carries out its activities in compliance with Act No. 6/1993 Coll., on the CNB, as amended (the 'CNB Act') and other regulations. The primary objective of the CNB is to maintain price stability. The CNB is a part of the European System of Central Banks and contributes to the fulfilment of its objectives and tasks. It is also a part of the European System of Financial Supervision and cooperates with the European Systemic Risk Board and with European Supervisory Authorities (*see* section 2 paragraph 1 of the CNB Act).

832. In accordance with its primary objective, the CNB sets monetary policy (*see* section 2 paragraph 1 letter (a) of the CNB Act). It also functions as supervisor of the banking sector, the capital market, the insurance industry, pension funds, credit unions, electronic money institutions and certain other institutions (*see* section 44 paragraph 1 in connection with section 2 paragraph 1 letter (d) of the CNB Act). In order to undertake its tasks, the CNB processes and generates statistical information (*see* section 42 paragraph 1 of the CNB Act).

§2. Monetary Policy

833. According to the Czech Constitution and the CNB Act, CNB's primary goal is to maintain price stability. Without prejudice to its primary objective, the CNB also supports the general economic policies of the Czech Government.[447] The CNB influences price stability mainly by making changes to the monetary conditions using its instruments, especially key interest rates (*see* section 23 of the CNB Act). The monetary policy decisions of the CNB Bank Board are based on the current macroeconomic forecast and an assessment of risks to its fulfilment.[448]

§3. Financial Stability

834. In addition to maintaining price stability and promoting sustainable economic development, the activities of the CNB also include overseeing payment systems and acting as a lender of last resort. Section 2 paragraph 2 letter (e) of the CNB Act explicitly requires the CNB to set '*macroprudential policy by identifying, monitoring and assessing risks jeopardising the stability of the financial system and, in*

447. The CNB may only support the government's policies to such an extent which does not interfere with its primary goal (*see* s. 2 para. 1 of the Czech National Bank Act).

448. For further information, *see also* the section on monetary policy at: https://www.cnb.cz/en/monetary-policy/.

order to prevent or mitigate these risks, contribute by means of its powers to the resilience of the financial system and the maintenance of financial stability; where necessary, it must cooperate with the relevant state authorities in setting macroprudential policy'. In relation to the activities above, the CNB also submits a financial stability report, which includes a macroprudential policy strategy, to the Chamber of Deputies (one of the houses of the Czech Parliament) once a year.[449] The key preconditions for achieving this objective are price stability and sound development of financial institutions, which are attained by means of monetary policy instruments and financial sector supervision.[450]

835. The CNB regularly monitors and analyses developments in all areas, which may influence financial stability. The main interest of the CNB is not to maintain the stability of an individual financial institution but of the financial sector as a whole.

§4. Financial Market Supervision

836. Since the CNB acts as a supervisory authority of banks and other financial institutions, it supervises the whole banking sector, the capital market, pension funds, the insurance industry, credit unions, etc.[451] To protect the environment of the financial sector in the Czech Republic (and potentially the rest of the EU), the CNB does not only provides ground rules and guidelines for the financial sector; it is also authorized to issue penalties for failure to comply with these regulations (provided that such regulations are legally binding).[452]

837. Under section 16 paragraph 3 of Act No. 256/2004 Sb., Coll, on Capital Markets, the CNB publishes 'regulated information' sent by issuers of listed securities and other obliged entities. Depending on the nature of the information received by the CNB, said information may be either published online or published as a part of annual reports and semi-annual reports, notifications of major holdings or of proportion of voting rights, inside information, manager's transactions, etc. The CNB is also obliged to publish data on significant net short positions in shares in accordance with Regulation (EU) of the European Parliament and of Council No. 236/2012 on short selling and certain aspects of credit default swaps.

§5. Banks

838. Apart from being subject to EU legislation, banks registered in the Czech Republic are mainly governed by Act No. 21/1992 Coll., on Banks, as amended (the

449. *See* s. 3a of the Czech National Bank Act.
450. For further information, *see also* the section on monetary policy at: https://www.cnb.cz/en/monetary-policy/.
451. All categories of institutions supervised by the CNB are stated in s. 44 para. 1 of the Czech National Bank Act.
452. The CNB's authority to issue penalties is stated in s. 46b of the Czech National Bank Act.

'Act on Banks'), which sets some of the ground rules for bank regulation in the Czech Republic. The Act on Banks, in section 1 paragraph 1, defines a bank as a legal entity having its registered office in the Czech Republic, founded as a joint-stock company, which: (i) accepts deposits from the public, (ii) provides loans, and (iii) has been granted a banking licence to carry on the activities referred to above.[453] These activities may also be carried on by foreign banks through branches, provided that they have obtained the required licence (*see* section 1 paragraph 6 of the Act on Banks). A bank may not carry on business activities other than those permitted in its licence. This shall not apply to activities carried on for another entity, provided that they are associated with safeguarding its operation and the operation of other banks, financial institutions and ancillary services undertakings controlled by the bank.

839. Pursuant to section 1 paragraph 3 of the Act on Banks, a bank may, in addition to the above-mentioned activities, also carry out the following activities, provided that it is duly authorized to do so in its licence:

(a) investing in securities for its own account;
(b) financial leasing;
(c) money transmission services;
(d) issuing and administering means of payment, e.g., credit cards and travellers' cheques;
(e) providing guarantees;
(f) opening letters of credit;
(g) collecting payments;
(h) providing investment services pursuant to a special legal rule, where the licence specifies the principal investment services and activities and ancillary investment activities the bank is authorized to carry on and the investment instruments in relation to which they may be carried on pursuant to a special legal rule;
(i) money broking;
(j) acting as a depository;
(k) bureau-de-change activities;
(l) providing banking information;
(m) trading for its own account or for the account of clients in foreign exchange and gold;
(n) renting safety deposit boxes;
(o) activities directly associated with accepting deposits from the public and providing loans.

---

453. Generally, on banking regulation, *see*, e.g., Liška, P., Elek, Š., Marek, K. Bankovní obchody. Praha. Wolters Kluwer, 2014, Smutný, A., Pihera, V., Sýkora, P., Cuník, T. Zákon o bankách. Komentář. 2. vydání. Praha. C. H. Beck, 2019, Bakeš, M., Karfíková, M., Kotáb, P., Marková, H. a kol. Finanční právo. 6. upravené vydání. Praha. C. H. Beck, 2012, pp. 53 et seq., Liška, P. Bankovní tajemství a povinnost mlčenlivosti. Obchodněprávní revue. 2016, Vol. 8, No. 9, pp. 241 et seq. or Liška, P. Zproštění povinnosti mlčenlivosti podle zákona o bankách. Bulletin Advokacie. 2020, Vol. 2020, Nos 1–2, pp. 37 et seq.

§6. LICENCE

840. Each bank regulated by the Act on Banks must always be authorized to procure the above-mentioned services by a licence provided by the CNB. For a bank to obtain the said licence, the following must be submitted to the CNB. Primarily, a draft of the bank's articles of association must be submitted with the licence application. The minimum amount of registered capital shall be CZK 500,000,000, which must comprise pecuniary contributions in at least this amount. The CNB shall set forth in a decree the essential elements of the licence application. Pursuant to section 4 of the Act on Banks, other specific conditions must also be met:

(a) the bank's capital and other funds must be of transparent and unexceptionable origin, sufficient amount and appropriate structure;
(b) the capital must be paid up in full;
(c) persons having a qualifying holding[454] in the bank must be trustworthy and competent to exercise shareholder rights in the bank's business activities;
(d) the persons who are nominated for executive managerial positions in the bank with which are associated the powers and responsibilities laid down in the articles of association must have sufficient trustworthiness, competence and experience;
(e) the bank must have in place the technical and organizational prerequisites for pursuing its proposed activities and a functional and effective management and control system and organizational structure of the bank, including information on controlling persons and financial holding companies and mixed financial holding companies in the group;
(f) the bank must have a programme of operations proceeding from its proposed strategy of activities and based on realistic economic calculations and clearly shows the activities that the bank intends to carry out;
(g) any group of entities having close links with the bank must be transparent;
(h) the close links within the group referred to in subparagraph (g) must not impede the exercise of supervision in the state within whose territory the group referred to in subparagraph (g) has close links;
(i) there must be no legal or factual impediment to the exercise of supervision;
(j) the registered office of the future bank must be within the territory of the Czech Republic.

841. If the bank manages to duly provide the CNB with such information and documentation, and all other relevant conditions are met, a licence is granted, and the bank is allowed to legally operate its business activities (to the extent specified by the licence).

454. Under the Act on Banks, a qualified holding is understood as a direct or indirect holding in an entity's capital or voting rights, or a sum thereof, which represents 10% or more, or which makes it possible to exercise a significant influence over its management.

§7. Other Financial Market Entities

842. Corresponding to the regulations applied in the EU, the respective Czech Act No. 256/2004 Coll., on Business Activities on the Capital Market (the 'Capital Market Business Act'), acknowledges the following categories of persons analysed in greater detail below: (i) market operator; (ii) investment firm; (iii) investment intermediary; (iv) tied agent; and (v) management company.

§8. Market Operators

843. Under Czech law, investment securities can be offered both publicly and privately. A public offer (meaning a notice to a wider range of persons about the securities offered and the conditions of their purchase) requires a prospectus. The prospectus is a mandatory part of the public offer, and it includes information for assessing the security offered, such as what rights are attached to it, and information about the assets of the person issuing the securities or profits and losses of the issuer.[455] The prospectus has to be made available and approved by the CNB, which shall do so if the prospectus contains all the mandatory information (*see* section 36c of the Capital Market Business Act). Thereafter, the prospectus is usually published on the website of the seller of the security.

844. Issued securities may be further traded on the secondary market. The securities market can be imaginatively divided into stock exchanges and over-the-counter markets. The regulated market (i.e., the stock exchange) is organized by legal entities authorized by the CNB, so-called Market Operators. There are currently only two regulated Market Operators in the Czech Republic:

(a) Burza cenných papírů Praha, a.s. (Prague Stock Exchange); and
(b) RM-SYSTÉM, česká burza cenných papírů a.s. (RM-SYSTÉM Czech Stock Exchange).

§9. Investment Firm

845. An investment firm is a legal entity that, on the basis of a licence issued by the CNB, is authorized to provide principal investment services (*see* section 5 paragraph 1 of the Capital Market Business Act). However, not all the entities that provide investment services have to possess an investment firm licence.[456] Apart from

455. The prospectus is mainly regulated by ss 34 et seq. of the Capital Market Business Act as well as by the provisions of Regulation (EU) 2017/1129 of the European Parliament and of the Council, of 14 Jun. 2017 on the prospectus to be published when securities are offered to the public or admitted to trading on a regulated market, and repealing Directive 2003/71/EC.

456. For example, a foreign person who is authorized by the supervisory authority of another EU Member State to provide investment services may provide investment services in the Czech Republic without an investment firm licence issued by the Czech National Bank under conditions specified in s. 25 of the Capital Market Business Act.

providing investment services, an investment firm may also undertake other business activities. Pursuant to section 6a paragraph 2 of the Capital Market Business Act, such business activities may consist solely in providing other services on the financial market, in particular, activities relating to building savings, mortgage or other loans, supplementary pension savings, or supplementary pension savings or insurance insofar as they consist of mediation or other procurement activity or consultancy, rental of safety deposit boxes, foreign exchange activities and non-cash foreign currency transactions, and financial market educational activities.

846. An entity that intends to be an investment firm has to fulfil several conditions prior to applying for a licence. These conditions are mainly supposed to protect individual investors as well as the whole capital market. For example, the investment firm's minimum registered capital needs to amount to at least EUR 730,000 unless the investment firm is a bank, or its investment services are limited (*see* section 8a paragraph 1 of the Capital Market Business Act). Moreover, the Capital Market Business Act further establishes minimum requirements for the statutory body of each investment firm, e.g., a statutory body is to be composed of at least two persons who have to be able to invest a reasonable amount of time to ensure the financial well-being of the investment firm (*see* section 10 of the Capital Market Business Act).

§10. Investment Intermediaries and Tied Agents

847. An investment firm may carry out its activities not only directly but also through other business entities, such as investment intermediaries and tied agents. In order to protect clients, these persons are subject to the same demands on trustworthiness, expertise and manner of dealing with clients as the investment firms. The range of investment services that investment intermediaries and tied agents can perform is narrower than that of an investment firm (in principle, they only receive and transmit orders and provide investment advice). Neither investment intermediaries nor tied agents may accept money from customers. An investment intermediary and a tied agent must, like an investment firm, be registered with the CNB (*see* section 32a of the Capital Market Business Act).

848. An investment intermediary is an intermediary between an investment firm or a collective investment fund manager on the one hand and a client on the other. It may carry out its activities in person, by a tied agent or with the assistance of employees. The tied agent shall represent either an investment firm, an investment intermediary or an investment company authorized to provide investment services (*see* section 29 of the Capital Market Business Act).

Chapter 6. Consumer Law

§1. General Observations

849. In accordance with EU law, the Czech Republic's consumer protection policy has certain defined priorities, which include the following:[457], [458]

(a) the safety of goods and services;
(b) protection of consumer economic interests;
(c) ensuring market surveillance;
(d) enforcement of consumer rights;
(e) emphasis on legislative activities in the field of consumer protection;
(f) cooperation with consumer associations;
(g) consumer information and education; and
(h) support for self-regulation.

850. Czech Consumer Protection law can be found in different codes and statutes. The Czech Republic implemented the main definitions and general principles of consumer contracts within the Civil Code and laid down specific statutes, namely in the Consumer Protection Act, Act on Safety of Goods, Credit Consumer Act and Czech Trade Inspection Act.

851. The Consumer Protection Act incorporates relevant European Union legislation and is a follow-up to the applicable European Union regulations. It governs the conditions under which relations between consumers and traders can be established and also the scope of public administration in the area of consumer protection, consumer associations or other legal entities established for consumer protection, as well as the out-of-court settlement of consumer disputes. The main areas of the Consumer Protection Act include fairness of sale, prohibition of unfair commercial practices, disclosure and labelling, organized events and out-of-court settlement of consumer disputes.

852. The purpose of the Act on Safety of Goods is to ensure, in accordance with European Union Law, that products placed on the market or put into circulation are safe for consumers in terms of safety and health. Thus, the Act on Safety of Goods particularly imposes obligations upon producers, importers and distributors in relation to ensuring product safety, defines the supervisory authorities responsible for monitoring compliance with the law, lays down procedures for inspections of product safety at country borders, and defines the basic legal framework for ensuring the

---

457. Generally on Czech consumer law, *see*, e.g., Moravec, T., Pastorčák, J. Spotřebitel a podnikatel na dynamicky se rozvíjejícím trhu. Praha. C. H. Beck, 2019, Polišenská, P. Cestovní smlouva jako spotřebitelská smlouva a její vztah ke spolucestujícím osobám. Soukromé právo. 2019, Vol. 7, No. 10, pp. 28 et seq., Bednář, S., Dočekalová, L. Evropská ochrana spotřebitelů na digitálním trhu v českém podání. Právní rádce. 2019, Vol. 27, No. 10, pp. 40 et seq. or Hulmák, M. Ochrana spotřebitele v rozkazním řízení. Právní rozhledy. 2019, Vol. 27, Nos 15–16, pp. 515 et seq.
458. Ministry of Industry and Trade: Consumer Policy Priorities for 2015–2020. Available at: https://www.mpo.cz/dokument158801.html.

functioning of the European information system, RAPEX, as it concerns information on the occurrence of dangerous non-food products in the Czech Republic.

853. The Credit Consumer Act incorporates relevant European Union legislation and is a follow-up to the applicable European Union regulations. It governs the activities of certain persons authorized to grant and facilitate consumer credit, imposes rights and duties when granting and facilitating consumer credit, and regulates the powers of administrative bodies in the related area.

854. The Czech Trade Inspection Act regulates the position of the Czech Trade Inspection Authority and defines its competence, and also determines the authorization of its employees in inspection activities. The Czech Trade Inspection Authority inspects natural and legal persons who offer, sell, supply or market products, offer or provide services or perform other activities pursuant to the CTIA. The Czech Trade Inspection Authority further imposes fines and other measures pursuant to the CTIA or a special legal regulation, generalizes the findings of the inspection and publishes the results thereof in order to prevent infringements.

§2. Representation of Consumer Interests

855. Consumers in the Czech Republic are represented at the national government level by the *Ministry of Trade and Industry of the Czech Republic* (*Ministerstvo průmyslu a obchodu České republiky*) ('Ministry'). The Ministry coordinates the implementation of consumer policy priorities and, in cooperation with other ministries, organizations and associations, evaluates their ongoing performance. The Ministry also, subject to legal conditions, gives related persons a mandate to settle out-of-court consumer disputes.

856. The Ministry further cooperates with *non-governmental and non-profit organizations* (NGO/NGOs), whose main objective is consumer protection. Their activities are financially supported by the state through subsidized support for the implementation of selected projects which mainly serve consumer interests. Their cooperation has been enhanced on the principle of a common platform, namely the 'Consumer Advisory Committee' between consumer organizations, on the one hand, and representatives of the administrative bodies and business representatives, on the other. The list of consumer organizations which are members of the Consumer Advisory Committee includes:

(a) dTEST, o.p.s
(b) Sdružení českých spotřebitelů, z.ú.
(c) Generation Europe
(d) Asociace občanských poraden
(e) Sdružení obrany spotřebitelů Moravy a Slezska, z. s.
(f) Sdružení obrany spotřebitelů – Asociace, z. s.

857. NGOs having a legitimate interest under national law in protecting consumers are entitled to engage public authorities to initiate their supervision of protecting consumers' interests. The public authorities receiving such complaints shall inform the NGOs when processing their initiatives without undue delay, but no later than two months after receiving them. The NGOs can also bring an action for an injunction in the public interest on behalf of consumers.

858. There is also a new system of so-called *Consumer Ombudsman.*[459] The Consumer Ombudsman is not a new official or other public authority but rather a system that, with the help of contact points at Trade Licensing Offices and their cooperation with non-governmental and NGOs, enables deceived and abused consumers, especially seniors, effectively, fast and free of charge to claim their consumer rights.

859. The Consumer Ombudsman was introduced to address 'the burning problem of unfair sales in the case of so-called sales demonstrations promptly'. In many cases, goods are sold, or services are offered using unfair commercial practices. Consumers are forced to buy goods they do not really need. Moreover, goods are often considerably overpriced. The Consumer Ombudsman is, therefore, not a new official, but 'the better use' of the existing network of municipal Trade Licensing Offices.

860. Thanks to this system, the consumer is able to contact one of the Trade Licensing Offices free of charge, where a simple entry form is filled in, creating a case which is further processed locally by the nearest NGO. This organization then advises and represents consumers free of charge. At the same time, the system makes it possible to control the seller concerned by the authorities. Consumers can also choose to contact the NGO directly and, where appropriate, use templates which are published on the Ministry's websites.

§3. Consumer Information

861. The seller[460] is obliged to duly inform consumers about the characteristics of the products sold or the nature of the services provided, about the use and maintenance of the product and about the dangers arising from its improper use or maintenance, as well as about any risks associated with the provided services. The seller is obliged to ensure that this information is contained in the enclosed written instructions and is comprehensible if it is necessary with regard to the nature of the

459. Ministry of Industry and Trade: Consumer Ombudsman. Available at: https://www.mpo.cz/cz/ochrana-spotrebitele/spotrebitelsky-ombudsman/.

460. EU legislature adopted a particularly broad notion of the term 'trader', which refers to 'any natural or legal person' who carries out a gainful activity and does not exclude from its scope either bodies pursuing a task of public interest or those which are governed by public law (*see* Judgment of European Court of Justice of 3 Oct. 2013, Zentrale zur Bekämpfung unlauteren Wettbewerbs, C-59/12, ¶32).

product, the manner and time of its use. The seller cannot be relieved of this obligation by reference to the fact that the manufacturer, importer or supplier did not provide them with necessary or correct information (*section 9 of the CPA*).

862. The information provided by the seller to the consumer must be given in Czech. The individual information may be provided in the form of symbols (pictograms), which shall be understandable, legible and complete. In the case of the sale of products using symbols (pictograms), the seller is obliged to explain them to the consumer or to provide access to an explanation on request (*section 11 of the CPA*).

863. When selling products or providing services by electronic means via the website, the seller is obliged to inform the consumer in advance in a clear manner whether there are any restrictions on the supply of products or services and what payment methods are accepted (*section 11a of the CPA*). The seller is obliged to inform the consumer in accordance with price regulations about the price of the products or services sold by clearly labelling the product with the price or by otherwise making the information about the prices of the products or services available (*section 12 of the CPA*).

864. The seller must ensure that the products it sells are clearly and comprehensibly marked with:

(a) the manufacturer's or importer's identification and, where appropriate, the supplier's identification and, where the nature of the product or the form of sale so requires, the product name, weight, quantity or size and proportions, and, if appropriate, other particulars necessary for the product's identification or use; and
(b) details of the materials used in its main parts (*section 10 of the CPA*).

865. If it is necessary to follow special rules in using a thing, especially if the use is guided by instructions, the seller is obliged to inform the consumer about such provisions unless these are generally known rules.

866. If the products sold cannot be labelled directly, the seller must mark them visibly and comprehensibly with the required data and characteristics in another appropriate manner. If it is not possible or expedient to label such products due to their nature, the seller is obliged to provide this information truthfully at the request of the consumer or authorities supervising compliance with the provisions of the Consumer Protection Act, or to substantiate it. There are also some exceptions for the labelling of some special products and for the information obligation. The seller may not remove or change the product designation or any other data provided by the manufacturer, importer, or supplier.

867. The seller must also clearly inform the consumer in advance when selling used or modified products, defective products or products whose performance is otherwise restricted. Such products must be sold separately from other products. Objects which are not for sale must not even be stored in the place where such products are sold.

868. The seller is further obliged to duly inform consumers about the scope, conditions and method of exercising the right from defective performance together with information on where the complaint can be raised.

869. The seller shall inform the consumer in a clear, understandable and easily accessible manner about the out-of-court consumer dispute resolution body that is materially competent for the type of offered, sold, provided or mediated product or service. The information shall also include the websites of said body. If the seller operates a website, it shall also include this information on the website. Where the contract concluded between the seller and the consumer refers to general terms and conditions, the information on out-of-court dispute settlement shall also be included in these general terms and conditions. The seller shall provide the consumer with this information in paper form or on another durable medium (*section 14 of the CPA*).

870. The seller shall, at the consumer's request, inspect or demonstrate the product, if the nature of the product and the form of sale so permit. The seller is also obliged to issue to the consumer at his/her request a written confirmation of the obligations arising from defective performance (*section 15 of the CPA*).

871. If the service is not provided while the consumer is waiting, the seller is obliged to give him/her a written confirmation that the order has been received. The confirmation must include the designation of the subject of the service, its scope, quality, price for service performance and the date thereof.

872. At the consumer's request, the seller is normally obliged to issue a receipt of purchase of the product or service, stating the date of sale of the product or service, which product or service it is and at what price the product was sold or service provided, together with the seller's identification data containing the name and surname or the name or business name, or the name of the seller, its identification number. When selling products with subsequent delivery, the document must also include the destination and date of delivery. Similarly, when selling used or prepared products, defective products or products whose performance is otherwise restricted, these shall be clearly indicated in the document as well (section 16 of the CPA).

§4. Safety of Goods and Services

873. The safety of goods is governed by EU law and by the Act on Safety of Goods at the national level. A safe product is a product which under normal or reasonably foreseeable conditions of use, for the duration specified by the manufacturer or for the duration of its usual shelf life, does not present a risk or only the minimum risks compatible with the product's use which can be considered acceptable and consistent with a high level of protection for the safety and health of persons (*section 3 of the ASG*). To assess the safety of a product, the following must be particularly taken into account:

(a) the characteristics of the product, its useful life, composition, packaging, instructions for assembly and installation, availability, instructions for use, including specification of the environment in which it is to be used, labelling warnings, instructions for maintenance and disposal and other information provided by the manufacturer; this information must always be provided in the Czech language;
(b) the effect of the product on other products, where it is assumed that it will be used with other products;
(c) the presentation of the product;
(d) the categories of consumers at risk when using the product, in particular, children and persons with reduced mobility and orientation.

874. Generally, except in some special cases, a product is considered to be safe if it conforms to the requirements of special legislation, which transposes the requirements of European Union Law and specifies the health and safety requirements. The product must satisfy these requirements in order to be placed on the market.

875. A product placed on the market must include documentation and be labelled in the manner and to the extent specified under the law. Accompanying documentation includes documents necessary for accepting and using the goods. The product labelling provides consumers with relevant information to enable them to assess the risk inherent in a product or with information related to product safety (*section 4 of the ASG*).

876. If the product's characteristics meet the safety requirements, but a certain form of usage may present a risk, the producer or distributor marketing the product must warn of the danger in the accompanying documentation if the risk is not immediately obvious. At the same time, these persons must specify any parts of the product that may pose a hazard and describe how the product should be safely used. It is also necessary to realize that the presence of warnings does not exempt the producer or distributor from compliance with the other safety requirements for the product.

877. In order to ensure high protection of consumers in terms of safety of goods, the Act on Safety of Goods broadly defines who is to be considered a producer (*section 5(1) of the ASG*):

(a) a person resident in the Czech Republic or in any other Member State of the European Union that has produced a final product, as well as any other person

presenting himself/herself as the manufacturer by affixing his/her name, trademark or other distinctive marks on the product, or the person who reconditions the product;
(b) the manufacturer's authorized representative as a person empowered in writing by the manufacturer if the manufacturer is not resident in the Czech Republic or in another Member State of the European Union;
(c) an importer, in the absence of the manufacturer's authorized representative resident in the Czech Republic or another Member State of the European Union; or
(d) other professionals in the supply chain insofar as their activities may affect the safety of the product characteristics.

878. A 'distributor' is defined as any professional in the supply chain whose activities do not affect the safety characteristics of the given product (section 5(2) of the ASG).

879. Producers may only market safe products. Distributors, on the other hand, may not market any product if they are aware or may expect on the basis of their information and professional knowledge that the product does not meet product safety requirements. Producers must also take samples of marketed products and test them for safety, in all cases where necessary to reduce existing risks.

880. Producers are further obliged to adopt measures to stay informed about the safety of their products after they have been marketed or put into circulation. If a producer or distributor finds that a product is unsafe, they must inform consumers accordingly and recall the unsafe product from the market to prevent it from being distributed, sold or displayed. Producers or distributors must enable any person who owns or holds an unsafe product to return it to them at their expense. If a producer or distributor does not fulfil this obligation and life, health or property are at risk, the competent authority may order the destruction of the product in addition to imposing a fine on the person who failed to recall the product from the market at his/her own expense.

881. If a producer or distributor has marketed an unsafe product, they must notify the competent authority immediately after discovering the fact. The producer and distributor must cooperate with the competent authority on measures adopted to eliminate or reduce any risks inherent in the unsafe product. In the case of a serious risk whose effects are imminent or whose effects are not imminent but may pose a serious risk to consumer safety and consequently require rapid action, the notification must include at least (section 5(9) of the ASG):

(a) a detailed identification of the relevant product or product series;
(b) a full description of any risks inherent in the product;
(c) any available information important for tracking the product;
(d) a description of measures adopted to prevent risks to the consumer.

882. The distributor participates in activities related to assuring the safety of marketed products, in particular, by providing information about any risks related to the products. It must keep and provide written information necessary for tracking the origin of the product and cooperate during action taken by manufacturers, competent authorities and those adopting the security measures (section 5(10) of the ASG).

§5. Quality of Goods and Services

883. The seller is obliged to:

(a) sell products in the correct weight, scale or quantity and enable the consumer to check the accuracy of those particulars;
(b) sell products and provide services in the prescribed, approved or otherwise stated quality or, if the quality is not prescribed, approved or stated, in the usual quality;
(c) sell products and provide services at prices negotiated in accordance with price regulations[461] and correctly charge prices when selling products or providing services;
(d) when selling products, use meters that meet the requirements set out in a special legal regulation regulating the field of metrology.[462]

884. If the goods do not reach the required quality, the consumer has the right to defective performance, which depends on the severity, extent and frequency of the defect.

§6. Consumer Contracts

885. General rules for concluding contracts between entrepreneurs and consumers are laid down by the Civil Code, which, therefore, represents a guarantee of fundamental consumer protection when contracting with professionals. As the European Court of Justice highlighted: '*(…) in relation to a trader, the consumer is in a weaker position, in that he/she must be deemed to be less informed, economically weaker and legally less experienced than the other party to the contract*'.[463]

886. If the contents of a contract allow different interpretations, the interpretation which is most favourable to the consumer has to be used. Similarly, stipulations in the contracts which derogate from the statutory provisions on consumer protection are disregarded, e.g., stipulation where a consumer waives a special right conferred upon him/her by a statute (*section 1812 of the Civil Code*).

---

461. Act No. 526/1990 Coll., on Prices, as amended.
462. Act No. 505/1990 Coll., on Metrology, as amended.
463. Judgment of European Court of Justice of 3 Oct. 2013, Zentrale zur Bekämpfung unlauteren Wettbewerbs, C-59/12, ¶35.

887. All of an entrepreneur's communications with a consumer must be made clearly and understandably in the language in which the contract is concluded. If the dealings of the parties aim at concluding a contract and these facts are not evident from the context, the entrepreneur must, sufficiently in advance before the contract is concluded or before the consumer makes a binding offer, provide the consumer with (*section 1811 of the Civil Code*):

(a) the entrepreneur's identity or his/her phone number, email address or other contact information;
(b) the designation of the goods or service, and a description of their main characteristics;
(c) the price of the goods or service, or the method of calculation thereof, including all taxes and fees;
(d) the method of payment and the method of supply or performance;
(e) the costs of supply, and if these costs cannot be calculated in advance, an indication that they may be subsequently charged;
(f) information on the rights arising from defective performance, as well as the rights arising from a guarantee and other conditions for those rights to be asserted;
(g) information indicating the period of the obligation and the conditions for the extinction of the obligation where a contract is concluded for an indefinite period;
(h) information on the functionality of digital content, including technical protection measures, and
(i) information on the hardware and software interoperability with digital content of which the entrepreneur is aware or where he/she can be reasonably expected to have been aware thereof.

888. To meet the information obligation, it may be sufficient for only certain of a product's main characteristics to be given and for the trader to refer in addition to its website, on condition that on that site there is essential information on the product's main characteristics, price and other terms.[464]

889. The entrepreneur is not obliged to provide the above-mentioned information to the consumer in the case of contracts concluded for the purpose of dealing with the matters of everyday life if the mutual performance is to be provided immediately after the contract is concluded, and in the case of contracts concluded for the supply of digital content if supplied on a tangible medium.

890. According to the Civil Code, stipulations which establish, contrary to the requirement of proportionality, a significant imbalance in the rights or duties of the parties to the detriment of the consumer, are presumed to be prohibited (*section*

464. Judgment of the European Court of Justice dated 12 May 2011, Ving Sverige, C-122/10, ¶54.

1813 of the Civil Code). This is not the case of stipulations on a subject of performance or price if they are provided to the consumer clearly and understandably. The prohibition, in particular, applies to stipulations which (*section 1814 of the Civil Code*):

(a) exclude or limit the rights of the consumer arising from defective performance or compensation for harm;
(b) oblige the consumer to perform while the entrepreneur becomes obliged to perform only when a condition depending on his/her will is met;
(c) allow the entrepreneur not to surrender to the consumer what the consumer surrendered to the entrepreneur, even where the consumer fails to conclude or withdraws from the contract;
(d) entitle the entrepreneur, but not the consumer, to withdraw from the contract for no reason;
(e) entitle the entrepreneur to terminate an obligation for no reason which deserves special consideration without an appropriate notice period;
(f) irrevocably oblige the consumer to perform under conditions with which he/she had no opportunity of becoming familiar before the contract was concluded;
(g) allow the entrepreneur to change the rights or duties of the parties at his/her discretion;
(h) postpone the determination of the price up until the time of the performance;
(i) allow the entrepreneur to raise the price without giving the consumer the right to withdraw from the contract in the case of a significant increase in the price;
(j) exclude or hinder the consumer's right to file an application or use other procedural remedies, or oblige the consumer to assert his/her right exclusively before an arbitration court or an arbitrator who is not bound by the legal regulations on the protection of consumers;
(k) pass on the consumer the burden of proof that the entrepreneur has fulfilled his/her duty imposed on him/her by the provisions of the contract for the provision of financial services; or
(l) exclude the consumer's right to determine which obligation is to be paid from the performance provided as a matter of priority.

891. The most important thing for the consumer is that disproportionate stipulations are disregarded unless they are invoked by the consumer himself/herself (*section 1815 of the Civil Code*).

§7. Distance Contracts and Contracts Negotiated Away from Business Premises

892. When an entrepreneur exclusively uses at least one communication means which allows a contract to be concluded without the simultaneous physical presence of the parties ('distance contract') or when a contract is negotiated away from business premises, there are some special rules aiming at higher consumer protection that have to be followed and which impose more obligations upon entrepreneurs.

893. First of all, it has to be mentioned that the entrepreneur is obliged, well in advance before the contract is concluded or before the consumer makes a binding offer, also communicate to the consumer the following information (*section 1820 of the Civil Code*):

(a) the costs of the means of distance communication if they differ from the basic rate;
(b) information on the duty to pay an advance or similar payment, if required;
(c) in the case of a contract stipulating recurrent performance, the shortest period for which the contract will bind the parties;
(d) in the case of a contract concluded for an indefinite period or one which stipulates recurrent performance, information on the price or the manner of its determination for one billing period, which is to be always one month if the price remains constant;
(e) in the case of contracts concluded for an indefinite period or those which stipulate recurrent performance, information on all taxes, fees and the costs;
(f) if the right of withdrawal may be exercised, the conditions, time limit and procedures necessary to assert such a right, as well as the withdrawal form, whose elements are provided by an implementing legal regulation;
(g) information specifying that in the case of withdrawal, the consumer will bear the cost of returning the goods and, in the case of a distance contract, the cost of returning the goods if, given their nature, the goods cannot be returned by ordinary mail;
(h) information on the duty to pay a proportional part of the price in the case of withdrawal from a contract concerning services which have already begun to be provided;
(i) information specifying that the consumer may not withdraw from the contract; and the conditions under which his/her right of withdrawal from the contract is extinguished, where the law permits;
(j) an indication of the existence, manner and conditions of out-of-court settlement of consumer complaints, including information on whether a controlling body or state supervision body may be approached with such a complaint.

894. In the case of doubt, the entrepreneur must prove that he/she provided the consumer with the information which he/she is required to provide.

895. A concluded contract must also contain information communicated to the consumer before it was concluded. This information may be changed only if it is expressly stipulated by the parties. A concluded contract must thus be consistent with the information communicated to the consumer before it was concluded; otherwise, the contents of the contract, which are more favourable to the consumer, is applicable (*section 1822 of the Civil Code*).

896. If a contract concerns the provision of services, the entrepreneur can start performing his/her duty within the time limit for withdrawal from the contract only at the express request of the consumer, with such request to be made in writing (*section 1823 of the Civil Code*).

897. If a contract is negotiated over the phone, the entrepreneur shall, at the beginning of the call, provide the consumer with basic information about himself/herself and with the purpose of the call. A consumer using electronic means must be allowed to check and change all the input information which he/she entered in the order before he/she places it. Where a consumer places an order through a means of distance communication, the entrepreneur is obliged to use a means of distance communication to immediately acknowledge its receipt. However, this is not the case of a contract which is concluded exclusively by the exchange of electronic mail or equivalent individual communication. Further, if a contract is concluded through electronic means, the entrepreneur shall, in addition to the text of the contract, provide the consumer with the text of the standard commercial terms.

898. If a contract is negotiated away from an entrepreneur's usual business premises, the entrepreneur shall provide the consumer with the above-mentioned information, which has to be given before the contract is concluded in writing. A contract negotiated away from business premises also includes a contract concluded (*section 1828 of the Civil Code*):

(a) within the entrepreneur's usual business premises if it was concluded immediately after the entrepreneur approached the consumer outside of these premises; and
(b) during a package tour organized by the entrepreneur for the purpose of promoting and selling goods or providing services.

Withdrawal from a distance contract and a contract negotiated away from business premises

899. A consumer has the right to withdraw from a contract within fourteen days. This time limit starts on the date of conclusion of the contract, and in the case of:

(a) a contract of sale, from the date of the takeover of the goods;
(b) a contract concerning several kinds of goods or the supply of several parts, from the date on which the last supply of goods is taken over; or
(c) a contract concerning a regular recurrent supply of goods, from the date on which the first supply of the goods is taken over (*section 1829 of the Civil Code*).

900. However, if the consumer has not been advised of his/her right to withdraw from a contract before it is concluded, the consumer may withdraw from the contract within one year and fourteen days from the beginning of the time limit for withdrawal. On the other hand, if the consumer has been advised of his/her right of withdrawal within this time limit, the fourteen-day time limit for withdrawal commences on the date on which the consumer was advised.

901. If the entrepreneur allows a consumer to withdraw by completing and dispatching a standard withdrawal form on a website, he/she is obliged to provide the consumer with a confirmation of its receipt in writing without undue delay.

902. If a consumer withdraws from a contract, he/she shall, without undue delay and no later than fourteen days after the withdrawal, dispatch or hand over to the entrepreneur the goods received from him/her. If a service has already been provided to the consumer, he/she incurs no duty towards the entrepreneur thereunder. The entrepreneur may only require the consumer to pay the costs provided by law (*section 1831 of the Civil Code*).

903. If a consumer withdraws from a contract, the entrepreneur shall, without undue delay and no later than fourteen days after the withdrawal, return to the consumer, in the same way, all funds, including the costs of supply, which the entrepreneur received from the consumer under the contract. The entrepreneur may return to the consumer the received funds in another way only with the consent of the consumer, and only if the consumer incurs no additional costs thereby. If a consumer has chosen a supply method other than the cheapest supply method offered by the entrepreneur, the entrepreneur is allowed to return the consumer the costs of supply in the amount corresponding to the cheapest supply method offered (*section 1832 of the Civil Code*).

904. The entrepreneur shall pay the consumer the costs of returning the goods if he/she did not inform the consumer about the duty to bear these costs before the contract was concluded. If a consumer withdraws from a contract of sale, the entrepreneur is obliged to return the funds received from him/her only after (not any time before) the consumer has handed over the goods to the entrepreneur or proved to him/her that the goods were dispatched to him/her.

905. The consumer is liable to an entrepreneur only for the reduction in the value of the relevant goods which he/she caused by handling the goods in a manner other than that which is necessary with regard to the goods' nature and characteristics about which he/she was informed by the entrepreneur in advance (*section 1833 of the Civil Code*).

906. If a consumer withdraws from a contract for services and the entrepreneur, at the express request of the consumer, begins to perform before the end of the time limit for withdrawal from the contract, the consumer shall pay the entrepreneur a part of the agreed price proportional to the performance provided until the time of withdrawal from the contract. If the agreed price is excessive, the consumer shall pay the entrepreneur a part of the price proportional to the market value of the performance provided.

907. The entrepreneur has to, at his/her own cost, take over the goods from the consumer at the latter's household if the consumer withdraws from a contract negotiated away from business premises, the goods were supplied to the consumer's household at the time the contract was concluded, and the nature of the goods does not allow them to be dispatched by usual mail.

908. On the other hand, the consumer may not withdraw from a contract (*section 1837 of the Civil Code*):

(a) for services if they were performed with his/her prior express consent before the end of the time limit for withdrawal and the entrepreneur informed the consumer before concluding the contract that he/she shall thereby lose the right of withdrawal;
(b) for the supply of goods or services whose price depends on fluctuations of the financial market which are beyond the control of the entrepreneur and which may occur during the time limit for withdrawal;
(c) for the supply of alcoholic beverages which can only be supplied after thirty days and whose price depends on fluctuations of the financial market which are beyond the control of the entrepreneur;
(d) for the supply of goods which were customized or personalized;
(e) for the supply of goods subject to rapid decay, as well as goods which were irreversibly mixed with other goods after supply;
(f) for repair or maintenance work carried out at the place designated by the consumer at his/her request;
(g) for the supply of sealed goods which were unsealed after supply by the consumer and which are not suitable for return due to hygiene reasons;
(h) for the supply of audio or video recordings or computer software whose original seal was unsealed after supply;
(i) for the supply of newspapers, periodicals or magazines;
(j) for accommodation, transport, catering or leisure activities where the entrepreneur provides the performances at a specific date;
(k) concluded at a public auction in accordance with the statute governing public auctions; or
(l) for the supply of digital content which is not supplied on a tangible medium if it was supplied with the prior express consent of the consumer before the time limit for withdrawal and the entrepreneur informed the consumer before concluding the contract that he/she shall thereby lose his/her right of withdrawal.

909. If the entrepreneur has supplied a thing to the consumer without the consumer's order and if the consumer assumed the possession thereof, he/she is considered to be a possessor in good faith. The consumer is not obliged to give anything back to the entrepreneur at his/her own expense or even inform him/her thereof (*section 1838 of the Civil Code*).

910. The special rules for distance contracts and contracts negotiated away from business premises are not applicable to contracts (*section 1840 of the Civil Code*):

(a) concerning the provision of social services, social housing, childcare and support for persons who are permanently or temporarily in an emergency situation;
(b) concerning the provision of health care;

(c) concerning betting, gaming or lottery;
(d) concerning the creation, transfer or extinction of a right to an immovable thing and the lease of an apartment;
(e) concerning the construction of a new building and substantial reconstruction of a building;
(f) for a package tour;
(g) for the supply of foodstuffs, beverages or other goods intended for everyday consumption supplied to the consumer's household or another place designated by the consumer;
(h) for the carriage of a person;
(i) concluded by means of automatic vending machines or automated commercial premises; or
(j) concluded with the provider of a publicly available electronic communications service for the use of, and by a payphone or concluded for a single connection of the consumer by phone, fax or internet.

§8. Organized Events

911. A seller who intends to sell products or provide services, or promote or offer them as part of an organized event, is obliged to notify the Czech Trade Inspection Authority, at least ten days before the organized event takes place, about the following (*section 20 of the CPA*):

(a) the address of the place where the sale of the products, provision of service, promotion or offer thereof will take place;
(b) the date of the organized event, including its expected timetable;
(c) identification of the product or service being promoted, offered, sold or provided in the context of the organized event, indicating the price at which such products or services will be offered to consumers at the event without taking into account any discounts individually negotiated with the consumer for the event;
(d) a copy of the invitation to participate in the organized event.

912. An organized event means an event addressed to a limited number of consumers who have been invited to it in an addressed or unaddressed manner and during which products are sold, services provided or promoted or offered, irrespective of whether transportation of persons is also a part of the event. If there is an event organized solely for the purpose of tasting, consumption and sale of tasting products, the special rules for organized events are not applicable to these events, as well as in case of events organized solely for the purpose of individual conclusion of an insurance contract, supplementary pension insurance, investment service or trade in the market for investment instruments.

913. The seller who sells products or provides services under an organized event cannot request or accept performance corresponding to the purchase price of the offered product or service or part thereof during this event or before the expiry of a period of seven days after the conclusion of the contract. The prohibition is also applicable to advance payments or any other charges.

§9. Unfair Commercial Practices

914. Unfair commercial practices are defined in the Consumer Protection Act which implements relevant EU law (namely Directive 2005/29/EC of the European Parliament and of the Council of 11 May 2005 concerning unfair business-to-consumer commercial practices in the internal market). A commercial practice is considered to be unfair if it is contrary to the requirements of professional care and substantially distorts or is capable of substantially distorting the economic behaviour of the consumer to which it is intended or to which it is exposed in relation to the product or service (*section 4 of the CPA*). If a commercial practice is aimed at a particular group of consumers, it is assessed by the average member of that group. The use of unfair commercial practices before, during and after the purchase decision is strictly prohibited. In particular, unfair commercial practices are deemed misleading conduct, misleading omission and aggressive commercial practice.

915. A commercial practice is generally considered misleading if it contains factually inaccurate information and is, therefore, false, which leads or may lead the consumer to make a purchase decision that he/she would otherwise not have taken. Also, a commercial practice containing truthful information can be considered misleading if it leads or may lead the consumer to make a purchase decision that he/she would not otherwise have made if it in any way misleads or is likely to mislead the consumer as to (*section 5 of the CPA*):

(a) the existence and nature of the product or service;
(b) the main features of the product or service, such as availability, benefits, risks, performance, composition, accessories, after-sales service and complaint handling, the manufacturing process and date of manufacture or delivery, method of delivery, fitness for use, options for use, the quantity, specification, geographical or commercial origin, expected results of their use or results, and tests or controls carried out;
(c) the extent of the seller's obligation, business practice motive and the nature of the sales process, statement or symbol relating to the direct or indirect sponsorship or approval of the seller or product or service;
(d) the price or method of calculating the price or the existence of a specific price advantage;
(e) need for service, spare part, replacement or repair;
(f) the nature, characteristics and rights of the seller or his/her representative, such as his/her identity and property, competence, status, approval, association or relationship, industrial, commercial or intellectual property rights or his/her awards and promotions; or
(g) the rights of the consumer, including the right to substitute delivery or refund of the purchase price arising from rights arising from the defective performance or the risk to which it may be exposed.

916. The benchmark to be used for a misleading commercial practice is that of the average consumer, who is reasonably well informed and reasonably observant and circumspect, taking into account social, cultural and linguistic factors.[465]

917. Even a commercial practice which leads or may lead to the situation that the consumer makes a purchase decision that he/she would otherwise not have made has to be regarded as misleading if, in a factual context, taking into account all its features and circumstances, it involves:

(a) any marketing of a product or service, including comparative advertising, which leads to confusion with another product or service or which gives rise to confusion with the trademark, trade name or other distinguishing marks of another seller; or
(b) failure to comply with a clear commitment contained in the code of conduct to which the seller has demonstrably committed itself.

918. A misleading omission is established by a commercial practice which, in its material context and taking into account all its features, circumstances and media constraints, omits to give the essential information that the consumer needs to make a purchase decision, and thereby causes or is likely to cause the consumer to make a decision on the purchase that he/she would not have otherwise made. It should also be considered as a misleading omission if the seller conceals or provides the essential information in an unclear, incomprehensible or ambiguous manner or in an inappropriate time and it leads or may lead the consumer to make a purchase decision that he/she would otherwise not have taken (*section 5a of the CPA*).

919. For instance, commercial practices are always considered misleading if the seller:[466]

(a) declares that it has undertaken to comply with certain rules of conduct or those rules of conduct have been approved by a particular body, although this is not the case;
(b) wrongly uses a quality mark or other similar mark;
(c) declares that it, or its product or service, has been granted an approval certificate or authorization, although this is not the case;
(d) with the intention of promoting another product or service, offers to buy a product or service for a certain price and then refuses to show it to the consumer or refuses to accept an order or delivery of the product or service within a reasonable time;
(e) falsely states that the product or service will be offered for a limited time only or that it will be offered for a limited time only under certain conditions in order to induce the consumer to make an immediate decision without giving him/her reasonable time to make an informed decision;

465. Judgment of the European Court of Justice of 26 Oct. 2016, Canal Digital Danmark, C611/14, ¶39.
466. Annex No. 1 to the Consumer Protection Act.

(f) claims or gives the impression that the sale of a product or service is permitted, even if it is not; or
(g) mentions as a priority the rights which the consumer derives directly from the law.

920. An aggressive commercial practice means, on the other hand, a practice which, in its factual context and taking into account all of its features and circumstances, significantly deteriorates or may significantly deteriorate the consumer's freedom of choice or behaviour in relation to the product or service by harassing or coercing, thereby causing or likely to cause the consumer to make a purchase decision that he/she would otherwise not have made.

921. During the assessment of whether a commercial practice is aggressive, the following has to be taken into account (*section 5b of the CPA*):

(a) the timing, location, nature or duration of the commercial practice;
(b) the manner of conduct, its threatening or offensive nature;
(c) whether there is a conscious use of the consumer's unfavourable situation, which leads to a deterioration of the consumer's judgment, to influence his/her decisions in relation to the product or service;
(d) whether there is a disproportionate non-contractual obstacle imposed by the seller for the exercise of his/her consumer rights, including the exercise of the right to terminate the contract or to change a product or service or to change the seller; or
(e) whether there is a threat of unlawful conduct.

922. For instance, commercial practices are always considered aggressive if the seller:[467]

(a) gives the impression that the consumer cannot leave the establishment or place without concluding a contract;
(b) personally visits the consumer in his/her place of residence, even though the consumer has called on him/her to leave his/her place of residence and not return;
(c) repeatedly makes unsolicited offers to the consumer by telephone, facsimile, electronic mail or other means of distance transmission;
(d) requires the consumer, when exercising the right conferred by the insurance contract, to produce documents which cannot be regarded as justified or do not respond to correspondence when assessing the legitimacy of a claim, to deter the consumer from exercising the rights under the contract;
(e) encourages children, through advertising, to purchase or persuade an adult to purchase the goods or services offered;

467. Annex No. 2 to the Consumer Protection Act.

(f) requires the consumer to pay immediately or to defer payment for goods or services that he/she has supplied, even if the consumer has not ordered them, or requests the return or retention of unsolicited products;
(g) declares that if the consumer does not purchase the product or service, this will endanger his/her business, his/her job or existence; or
(h) gives a false impression that the consumer will win or wins a prize if he/she acts in a certain way, although in reality, there is no such prize or he/she incurs expenses.

§10. Alternative Dispute Resolution

923. The Consumer Protection Act lays down an out-of-court settlement system for resolving consumer disputes (also referred to as 'ADR' – alternative dispute resolution), which represents a faster and alternative way of resolving disputes than court proceedings. Under the Consumer Protection Act, consumers have the right to an out-of-court settlement in the case of sales contracts or service contracts, with the exception of contracts concluded in the field of health services provided by healthcare professionals in order to provide healthcare, including prescribing, dispensing and supplying medicines and medical devices; in the field of non-economic services of general interest; with public or higher education providers. The initiation of an out-of-court settlement is without prejudice to the parties' right to seek protection of their rights and legitimate interests through legal proceedings.[468]

924. The following entities are involved in the system: the Czech Telecommunications Office, the Energy Regulatory Office, the Financial Arbitrator, the Czech Trade Inspection Authority, as well as entities that have requested it, have fulfilled legal obligations, and are authorized by the Ministry of Industry and Trade. So far, the following entities have been entrusted with the out-of-court settlement of consumer disputes: the Czech Bar Association, the Association of Czech Consumers, z.ú., and the Ombudsman's Office of the Czech Insurance Association, z.ú. Out-of-court consumer dispute resolution entities must be linked to a European online consumer dispute resolution platform. The platform aims to help consumers resolve consumer disputes which are primarily related to the cross-border purchase of goods and services online.[469]

468. Ministry of Industry and Trade: Alternative Dispute Resolution – ADR. Available at: https://www.mpo.cz/en/consumer-protection/alternative-dispute-resolution-adr/.
469. https://ec.europa.eu/consumers/odr/main/index.cfm?event=main.home2.show&lng=CS.

Selected Bibliography

Adámková, K., Spolkové a nadační právo. Brno: Masarykova univerzita, 2008.

Andreisová, L., Působení správní rady v monistické struktuře akciové společnosti. Obchodní právo. 2014, Vol. 23, No. 8, pp. 314 et seq.

Balasczyk, B., Privatization in Post-Communist Countries. Varšava: Center for Social and Economic Research, 1996.

Babchuk, L.A., Kahan, M. Adverse Selection and Gains to Controllers in Corporate Freezeouts. In Morck, Randall K. Concentrated Corporate Ownership. Chicago: University of Chicago Press, 2000.

Bakeš, M. a kol. Finanční právo, 5. vydání. Praha. C. H. Beck, 2009.

Bakeš, M., Karfíková, M., Kotáb, P., Marková, H. a kol. Finanční právo. 6. upravené vydání. Praha. C. H. Beck, 2012.

Balcarová, A., Nový zákon o spotřebitelském úvěru. Právní rozhledy. 2017, Vol. 25, No. 8, pp. 272 et seq.

Balýová, L., Péče řádného hospodáře ve volených orgánech obchodních korporací ve světle rekodifikace. Obchodněprávní revue, 2014, Nos 7–8, pp. 212 et seq.

Bednář, S., Dočekalová, L., Evropská ochrana spotřebitelů na digitálním trhu v českém podání. Právní rádce. 2019, p. 32. Vol. 27, No. 10, pp. 40 et seq.

Bejček, J., Některá úskalí racionality obchodních podmínek. Právní rozhledy. 2015, Vol. 23, No. 18, pp. 611 et seq.

Bejček, J., Praktické problémy distribučních dohod. Právní rozhledy. 2011, Vol. 19, No. 18, pp. 643 et seq.

Bejček, J., Principy odpovědnosti statutárních a dozorčích orgánů kapitálových společností. Právní Rozhledy, 2007, No. 17, pp. 613 et seq.

Bejček, J., Soukromoprávní ochrana slabšího obchodního partnera. Bulletin advokacie. 2015, Vol. 2015, Nos 7–8, pp. 24 et seq.

Bejček, J., Zprostředkování. Obchodněprávní revue. 2015, Vol. 7, No. 9, pp. 241 et seq.

Berle, Adolf A., Means, Gardiner C., The Modern Corporation & Property. New Jersey: Transaction Publishers, 2009. Tenth Printing.

Bělohlávek, A. J. a kol. Komentář k zákonu o obchodních korporacích. Plzeň: Aleš Čeněk, 2013.*Bělohlávek, A.J.:* Arbitration in the Czech Republic, in Arbitration Journal, 7 February 2019.

Bělohlávek, A.J., Zákon o rozhodčím řízení a o výkonu rozhodčích nálezů. Komentář. Praha. C. H. Beck, 2012.

Blümelová, K., Nový občanský zákoník rozšíří možnosti factoringu (rozhovor s Tomášem Morávkem). Právní rádce. 2013, Vol. 21, No. 10, pp. 74 et seq.

Bodlák, F., Správní rada akciové společnosti v České republice a Itálii. Obchodněprávní revue. 2015, Vol. 7, No. 3, pp. 65 et seq.

Bohumil, S., Teorie a praxe dluhopisů I. Praha. Vysoká škola ekonomická v Praze, 2013.

Borkovec, A., Akciová společnost a rozptýlené vlastnictví. Praha: Leges, 2014.

Borsík, D., Péče řádného hospodáře a pravidlo podnikatelského úsudku bez legend. Obchodněprávní revue, 2015, Nos 7–8, pp. 193 et seq.

Brada, J., Krabec, T. Regulatorní aspekty spotřebitelského úvěrového financování v ČR pohledem law and economics. Obchodněprávní revue. 2019, Vol. 11, Nos 7–8, pp. 169 et seq.

Broulík, J., Pravidlo podnikatelského úsudku a riziko. Obchodněprávní revue. 2012, Vol. 4, No. 6, pp. 161 et seq.

Bříza, P., Břicháček, T., Fišerová, Z., Horák, P., Ptáček, L., Svoboda, J., Zákon o mezinárodním právu soukromém. Komentář. 1. vydání. Praha: C. H. Beck, 2014.

Ctibor, J., Horáčková, I. Franchising. Praha. Wolters Kluwer, 2017.

Ctibor, J., Zelená, I. Kdy se z franšízanta stává zaměstnanec. Právní rádce. 2020, Vol. 28, No. 1, pp. 46 et seq.

Čada, K., K některým otázkám moderní české judikatury v oblasti práv k technickým řešením. Acta MUP. 2015, Vol. 6, No. 2, pp. 59 et seq.

Čáp, Z., Jahelka, P., Josková, L., Hejda, J., Vaněčková, V. Zákon o obchodních korporacích. Výklad jednotlivých ustanovení včetně návaznosti na české a evropské předpisy. 1. vydání, Praha: Linde Praha a.s., 2013.

Čech, P., Akcie po rekodifikaci. Právní rádce. 2012, Vol. 20, No. 10, pp. 34 et seq.

Čech, P., Akcie ve víru rekodifikace aneb nevtělené, zaknihované a kusové akcie v návrhu zákona o obchodních korporacích. Obchodněprávní revue. 2011, No. 10, pp. 294 et seq.

Čech, P., Ke svéprávnosti právnické osoby a postavení člena statutárního orgánu při jednání za ni (nejen) v situaci zájmového střetu. Právní rozhledy. 2016, Vol. 24, Nos 23–24, pp. 835 et seq.

Čech, P., Péče řádného hospodáře a povinnost loajality. Právní rádce, 2007, No. 3, pp. 4 et seq.

Černá S., Štenglová, I., Pelikánová, I. a kol. Právo obchodních korporací. 1. vydání. Praha: Wolters Kluwer, 2015.

Černá, S., Štenglová, I., Pelikánová, I. A Dědič J., Obchodní právo: podnikatel, podnikání, závazky s účastí podnikatele. Praha: Wolters Kluwer, 2016.

Černá S., Plíva, S. a kol. Podnikatel a jeho právní vztahy. 1. vydaní. Praha: Univerzita Karlova v Praze, Právnická fakulta, 2013.

Černá, S., K právům, která lze spojit s akcií. Obchodní právo. 2016, Vol. 25, No. 3, pp. 82 et seq.

Černá, S., O akciích s rozdílnou vahou hlasů v budoucím českém akciovém právu. Obchodněprávní revue. 2012, Vol. 4, Nos 7–8, pp. 193 et seq.

Černá, S., ed. Obchodní korporace a ochrana slabší strany. Praha. Wolters Kluwer, 2017.

Černá, S., O nepravých a pravých kusových akciích. Obchodněprávní revue. 2014, Vol. 7, No. 5, pp. 129 et seq.

Černá, I., Lze Akcionářům odejmout zákonem přiznaná práva, aneb kdy přestává akcie být akcií? Bulletin advokacie. 12/2017. p. 17.

Chaloupková, H., Holý, P., Urbánek, J., Mediální právo. Komentář. Praha. C. H. Beck, 2019.

Chalupa, I., Reiterman, D., Holý, V., Obchodní korporace. Obecná část. Základy soukromého práva V. Praha: C. H. Beck, 2015.

Chalupa, I., Reiterman, D., Holý, V., Obchodní korporace. Přeměny a obchodní rejstřík. Základy soukromého práva VI. Praha: C. H. Beck, 2016.

Charvát, R., Stěžejní judikatura Soudního dvora EU v oblasti průmyslových vzorů. Právní rozhledy. 2014, Vol. 22, Nos 23–24, pp. 829 et seq.

Chloupek, V., Hartvichová, K. a kol. Patentový zákon. Komentář. Praha. C. H. Beck, 2017.

Dallas, Lynne L., Short-Termism, the Financial Crisis, and Corporate Governance. The Journal of Corporation Law, 2011, Vol. 37, pp. 264 et seq.

David, M., K povaze rozhodčí smlouvy podruhé a jinak. Bulletin advokacie. 2011, Vol. 2011, No. 10, pp. 27 et seq.

Dědek, O., Kupónová privatizace a rozvoj kapitálového trhu v Československu. Praha: Ekonomický ústav Československé akademie věd, 1992.

Dědič, J., Nenápadné výhody kusových akcií. Online. Patria.cz, 2012.

Dědič, J. a kol. Obchodní zákoník. Komentář. Díl III. Praha: Polygon, 2002.

Dědič, J., Lasák, J., Monistický systém řízení akciové společnosti: výkladové otazníky (1. část). Obchodněprávní revue. 2013, Vol. 5, No. 3, pp. 65 et seq.

Dědič, J., Lasák, J., Monistický systém řízení akciové společnosti: výkladové otazníky (2. část). Obchodněprávní revue. 2013, Vol. 5, No. 4, pp. 97 et seq.

Dědič, J., Štenglová, I., Kříž, R., Čech, P., Akciové společnosti. 7., přepracované vydání. Praha. C. H. Beck, 2012.

Dědič, J. Šuk, P., Nad novelou zákona o obchodních korporacích (aneb sporné otázky nové úpravy zaměstnanecké participace). Obchodněprávní revue. 2017, No. 4, pp. 97 et seq.

Deverová, L., Nový občanský zákoník – zvýšení odpovědnosti orgánů právnických osob. Svět neziskovek, 2012.

Divišová, K., Hejda, J., Prosser, M., Vaněčková, V., Akciová společnost podle nového zákona o obchodních korporacích 2014. Olomouc: ANAG, 2014.

Dočkal, T., Koričanská, M., Šedina, P. a Vrba, M., Hurychová, K., ed. Postavení podnikatele v závazkověprávních vztazích: kolektivní monografie. Praha: Všehrd, 2014.

Doleček, M., Pravomoc soudů ve vztahu k rozhodčímu řízení. Bulletin advokacie. 2018, Vol. 2018, No. 9, pp. 40 et seq.

Doležal, T., Patentovat či nikoliv? Právní a morální dilemata spojená s komerční využitelností výstupů výzkumu na lidských embryonálních kmenových buňkách. Právní rozhledy. 2012, Vol. 20, No. 18, pp. 640 et seq.

Dvořák, T., K některým otázkám obchodního rejstříku. Právní rozhledy. 2001, Vol. 9, No. 2, pp. 77 et seq.

Dvořák, T., Osobní obchodní společnosti ve světle rekodifikace českého obchodního práva. Praha: Wolters Kluwer ČR, 2012.

Dvořák, J. a Knidl, M., ed. Pocta Martě Knappové k 80. narozeninám. Praha: ASPI Publishing, 2005.

Dvořák, J., Švestka, J., Zuklínová, M. a kol. Občanské právo hmotné I. Obecná část. Praha: Wolters Kluwer, 2013.

Dvořák, T., Akciová společnost. Praha: Wolters Kluwer, 2016.

Eliáš, K., K pojetí dispozitivního práva v občanském zákoníku. Bulletin Advokacie. 2015, No. 9, pp. 13 et seq.

Estrin, S., Nuti, D., Uvalic, M., The Impact of Investment Funds on Corporate Governance in Mass Privatization Schemes: Czech Republic, Poland and Slovenia. Londýn: London Business School, 2000.

Fairfax, Lisa M., The Uneasy Case for the Inside Director. Iowa Law Review, 2011, Vol. 96, pp. 127 et seq.

Frinta, O., Smlouva o přepravě osoby v novém soukromém právu. Praha. Wolters Kluwer, 2018.

Gelter, M., Dark Side of Shareholder Influence: Managerial Autonomy and Stakeholder Orientation in Comparative Corporate Governance. Harv. Int'l J. L., 2009, Vol. 50, pp. 129 et seq.

Gilson, R.J., Whitehead, Ch.K. Deconstructing Equity: Public Ownership, Agency Costs, and Complete Capital Markets, Columbia Law Review, 2008, Vol. 108, pp. 231 et seq.

Greenfield, Kent. The Failure of Corporate Law. Chicago: The University of Chicago Press, 2006.

Hajn, P. Když nevíme, jak právně vymezit 'know-how'. Obchodněprávní revue. 2010, Vol. 2, No. 11, pp. 313 et seq.

Hamerník, P., Regulace veřejné podpory profesionálnímu sportu jako příklad vyvažování zájmů na periferii práva EU. Právník. 2017, Vol. 156, No. 8, pp. 686 et seq.

Havel, B., Synergie péče řádného hospodáře a podnikatelského úsudku. Právní Rozhledy, 2007, No. 11, pp. 412 et seq.

Havel, M., Štenglová, I., Dědič, J., Jindřich, M. a kol Zákon o veřejných rejstřících právnických a fyzických osob. Komentář. Praha. C. H. Beck, 2015.

Hájková, A., Nebuželská, M., Pavlok, P., Spolky a spolkové právo. Praha: C. H. Beck, 2015.

Hálová, M., Právní povaha kontrolních činností při kontrole veřejné účelové podpory poskytované na řešení projektů výzkumu, experimentálního vývoje a inovací. Právník. 2015, Vol. 154, No. 11, pp. 895 et seq.

Hámorská, A., Povinnost členů orgánů obchodních korporací jednat s péčí řádného hospodáře po rekodifikaci. Obchodněprávní revue, 2012, No. 9, pp. 250 et seq.

Hásová, J. Moravec, T., Insolvenční řízení. Vydání druhé. Praha: C. H. Beck, 2018.

Hásová, J., Moravec, T. a kol. Insolvenční zákon, 3. vydání. Praha: C. H. Beck, 2018.

Hendrych, D. a kol. Právnický slovník. Praha: C. H. Beck, 2009.

Hexner, A. a Matas, M., Nabývání svéprávnosti nezletilými a nepříznivé důsledky současné právní úpravy (část I). Soukromé právo. 2018, Vol. 6, No. 5, pp. 9 et seq., Vol. 6, No. 6, pp. 7 et seq.

Hobza, M., Zprostředkování uzavření smluv týkajících se investičních nástrojů ve světle rozsudku Khorassani. Obchodněprávní revue. 2019, Vol. 11, No. 2, pp. 36 et seq.

Holman, R., Transformace české ekonomiky: V komparaci s dalšími zeměmi střední Evropy. Praha: Centrum pro ekonomiku a politiku, 2000.

Horáček, R., Čada, K., Hajn, P., Práva k průmyslovému vlastnictví. 3. vydání. Praha. C. H. Beck, 2017.

Hrádek, J., Předsmluvní odpovědnost: Culpa in contrahendo. Praha. Auditorium, 2009.

Hrádek, J., Smlouvy o přepravě v občanském zákoníku. Komentář. Praha. C. H. Beck, 2017.

Hrádek, J., Vymezení smluvních typů přepravních smluv po rekodifikaci. Obchodněprávní revue. 2017, Vol. 9, Nos 7–8, pp. 198 et seq.

Hulmák, M. a kol Občanský zákoník V. Závazkové právo. Obecná část (§ 1721–2054). Komentář. 1. vydání. Praha: C. H. Beck, 2014.

Hulmák, M. a kol. Občanský zákoník VI. Závazkové právo. Obecná část (§ 1721–2054). Komentář. Praha. C. H. Beck, 2014.

Hulmák, M., Ochrana spotřebitele v rozkazním řízení. Právní rozhledy. 2019, Vol. 27, Nos 15–16, pp. 515 et seq.

Hurdík, J., Kogentnost a dispozitivnost ustanovení nového občanského zákoníku o právnických osobách. Ke vzájemné použitelnosti ustanovení o nadacích a nadačních fondech, Právní rozhledy, 2014, No. 7, pp. 229 et seq.

Hurychová, K., Zásada rovného zacházení se všemi akcionáři – k významu ustanovení § 244 odst. 2 ZOK. Obchodněprávní revue. 2015, Vol. 7, No. 10, pp. 285 et seq.

Hynčicová, K., Jak bude fungovat monistický systém správy a.s.? Právní rádce. 2013, Vol. 21, No. 6, pp. 6 et seq.

Jandová, L., Šlauf, P., Svejkovský, J., Pojištění v novém občanském zákoníku. Komentář. Praha. C. H. Beck, 2014.

Jankanič, D., Předložení pojistné smlouvy jako podmínka pro uzavření smlouvy na plnění veřejné zakázky. Veřejné zakázky. 2018, Vol. 2018, No. 1, pp. 46 et seq.

Janoušek, M., Ochrana slabší smluvní strany v občanském zákoníku. Praha. C. H. Beck, 2018.

Janoušková, A., Rozsah a limitace odpovědnosti za ukončení vyjednávání o smlouvě bez spravedlivého důvodu. Právní rozhledy. 2016, Vol. 24, Nos 23–24, pp. 807 et seq.

Jensen, M., C.; Meckling, W.H., Theory of the Firm: Managerial Behaviour, Agency Costs and Ownership Structure. Journal of Financial Economics, 1976, Vol. 3, No. 4, pp. 305 et seq.

Ježek, T., Privatizace české ekonomiky: její kořeny, metody a výsledky. Praha: Vysoká škola ekonomická, 2006.

Ježek, T., Zrození ze zkumavky: svědectví o české privatizaci 1990–1997. Praha: Prostor, 2007.

Josková, L., Budou mít akciové společnosti lepší dozorčí rady? (K účasti žen ve vedení společností). Obchodněprávní revue. 2013, Vol. 5, Nos 7–8, pp. 203 et seq.

Josková, L. a kol. Likvidace obchodních společností. Praha: C. H. Beck, 2017.

Josková, L. Likvidátor a statutární orgán kapitálové společnosti v likvidaci. Obchodněprávní revue. 2017, Vol. 9, No. 3, pp. 70 et seq.

Kadečka, S., Neoprávněné odběry elektřiny (jako jeden z aktuálních problémů energetické legislativy). Právní rozhledy. 2010, Vol. 18, No. 17, pp. 610 et seq.

Kasl, F., Obhajitelnost softwarových patentů. Revue pro právo a technologie. 2017, Vol. 8, No. 16, pp. 25 et seq.

Kincl, M., Veřejná podpora v příkladech a poznámkách. Praha. Wolters Kluwer, 2017.

Kindl, J., Kartelové a distribuční dohody: teorie a praxe. Praha. C. H. Beck, 2009.

Kindl, M., Na co nezapomínat při sjednávání rozhodčí smlouvy. Bulletin advokacie. 2018, Vol. 2018, No. 9, pp. 29 et seq.

Kislingerová, E., Richter, T., Smrčka, L. et al. Insolvenční praxe v České republice v období 2008–2013. 1. vydání. Praha: C. H. Beck, 2013.

Klein, Š., Zákonný manželský majetkový režim z komparativního hlediska. Ad Notam. 2017, Vol. 23, No. 6, pp. 3 et seq.*Kočenda, E., Lízal, L.* Český podnik v české transformaci 1990–2000. Praha: Academia, 2003.

Kolektiv autorů. Corporate governance. Praha: Wolters Kluwer, 2015.

Konečná, P., Vliv nového pojetí společného jmění manželů na exekuční řízení z pohledu manžela povinného. Komorní listy. 2015, Vol. 7, No. 2, pp. 10 et seq.

Kopcová, M., Moderní funkce ochranných známek a jejich vliv na posouzení konfliktu ochranné známky s obchodní firmou v judikatuře SDEU. Právní rozhledy. 2019, Vol. 27, No. 8, pp. 282 et seq.

Kopp, K. Bartošík, M.; Minařík, J., Právní úprava malé privatizace. Ostrava: MONTANEX, 1991.

Kotásek, J., Pihera, V., Pokorná J., Právo cenných papírů. Praha. C. H. Beck, 2013.

Kovařík, Z., Směnka a šek v České republice. 6., přeprac. a dopl. vyd. Praha. C. H. Beck, 2011.

Kovařík, Z., Zákon o omezení plateb v hotovosti ve vztahu ke směnce a šeku. Právní rozhledy. 2005, Vol. 13, No. 7, pp. 234 et seq.

Kovařík, Z., Zákon směnečný a šekový. Komentář. 6., dopl. vydání. Praha. C. H. Beck, 2014.

Kozák J., Brož, J. Dadam A., Stanislav A., Strnad Z., Zrůst L., Žižlavský M. Insolvenční zákon. Komentář. 5. vydání. Praha: Wolters Kluwer ČR, 2019.

Kožiak, J. Obchodní firma v novém občanském zákoníku. Brno: Masarykova univerzita, 2013.

Kožiak, J., Pravidlo podnikatelského úsudku v návrhu zákona o obchodních korporacích (a zahraničních právních úpravách). Obchodněprávní revue, 2012, No. 4, pp. 108 et seq.

Kožušník, R., Povinná písemná forma spotřebitelských smluv o úvěrovém financování. Soudce. 2016, Vol. 18, No. 6, pp. 25 et seq.

Krausová, A., Patentové právo a jeho strategické využití. Revue pro právo a technologie. 2013, Vol. 4, No. 7, pp. 27 et seq.

Krtoušová, L., Péče řádného hospodáře: odpovídá britskému konceptu duty of care, skill and diligence? Obchodněprávní revue, 2013, No. 10, pp. 277 et seq.

Kříž, R., Několik poznámek k přeměně cenných papírů na zaknihované cenné papíry. Obchodněprávní revue. 2017, Vol. 6, No. 6, pp. 161 et seq., pp. 26 et seq.

Kučera, Z., Mezinárodní právo soukromé. 5. vydání. Brno: Doplněk, 2001.

Kuklík, J., Znárodněné Československo: Od znárodnění k privatizaci – státní zásahy do vlastnických a dalších majetkových práv v Československu a jinde v Evropě. Praha: Auditorium, 2010.

Kyzlinková, Š. Intraunijní arbitráž: Veřejná podpora jako možný limit vykonatelnosti rozhodčího nálezu. Obchodněprávní revue. 2016, Vol. 8, No. 6, pp. 169 et seq.

Lasák, J., With Love from the Heart of Europe: New Rules for Czech Joint-Stock Companies. European Business Organization Law Review, Vol. 18, No. 1, pp. 94 et seq.

Lasák, J., Akciová společnost na prahu rekodifikace: základní novinky. Obchodněprávní revue. 2012, No. 2, pp. 46 et seq.

Lasák, J., O limitech lidské představivosti: glosa k akciím bez hlasovacího práva (jiným než prioritním). Právní rozhledy. 2017, Vol. 25, No. 2, pp. 58 et seq.

Lasák, J., Dědič, J., Pokorná, J., Čáp, Z. a kol. Zákon o obchodních korporacích. Komentář. 2. vydání. Praha: Wolters Kluwer, a.s., 2021. .

Lavický, P.a kol. Občanský zákoník I. Obecná část. Komentář. 1. vydání. Praha: C. H. Beck, 2014., pp. 51 et seq., pp. 1651 et seq.

Lavický, P. a kol Občanský zákoník I. Obecná část (§ 1-654). Komentář. 1. vydání, Praha: C. H. Beck, 2014.

Linhart, A., Meze předsmluvní odpovědnosti podle o. z. a výkladová praxe soudů. Bulletin advokacie. 2017, Vol. 2017, No. 3, pp. 29 et seq.

Lisse, L., Know-how v českém právním řádu. Právní rozhledy. 2003, Vol. 11, No. 10, pp. 503 et seq.

Liška, P., Bankovní tajemství a povinnost mlčenlivosti. Obchodněprávní revue. 2016, Vol. 8, No. 9, pp. 241 et seq.

Liška, P., Nad institutem bankovní záruky. Právní rozhledy. 2007, Vol. 15, No. 18, pp. 651 et seq.

Liška, P., Některé (staro)nové otázky správy a řízení akciových společností. Soukromé právo, 2016, No. 12, pp. 5 et seq.

Liška, P., Zproštění povinnosti mlčenlivosti podle zákona o bankách. Bulletin Advokacie. 2020, Vol. 2020, Nos 1–2, pp. 37 et seq.

Liška, P., Elek, Š., Marek, K., Bankovní obchody. Praha. Wolters Kluwer, 2014.

Lojda, J., Nákladní list a elektronický nákladní list podle Úmluvy CMR. Obchodněprávní revue. 2013, Vol. 5, No. 5, pp. 157 et seq.

Lojda, J., Rozsah a způsob použití Úmluvy CMR. Obchodněprávní revue. 2014, Vol. 6, No. 4, pp. 121 et seq.

Makarius, V., Rozhodčí smlouvy v mezinárodním obchodě: prevence, plánování a rˇízení sporu v mezinárodním obchodě. Praha. C. H. Beck, 2015.

Mancelová, S., Loajalita a péče řádného hospodáře v akciové společnosti. Praha: C. H. Beck, 2015.*Marek, K.* K některým smlouvám příkazního typu. Bulletin Stavební právo. 2019, Vol. 22, No. 2, pp. 35 et seq.

Marek, K., Ke smlouvě o obchodním zastoupení. Daně a právo v praxi. 2016, Vol. 2016, No. 2, pp. 40 et seq.

Marek, K., Leasingová smlouva. Právní rádce. 2009, Vol. 17, No. 4, pp. 16 et seq.

Marek, K., Leasingová smlouva, smlouva o koupi najaté věci. Komorní listy. 2012, Vol. 4, No. 2, pp. 28 et seq.

Marek, K., Problémy realizace nové úpravy smlouvy o zprostředkování a smlouvy komisionářské. Bulletin advokacie. 2014, Vol. 2014, No. 6, pp. 17 et seq.

Marek, K., a Žváčková L. Obchodní podmínky, obchodní zvyklosti a vykládací pravidla. Praha: ASPI-Wolters Kluwer, 2008.

Marek, R., Ježek, V., Cenné papíry v novém občanském zákoníku. Komentář. Praha. C. H. Beck, 2013.

Marek, T., Franchisingová smlouva perspektivou některých institutů práva duševního vlastnictví. Právní fórum. 2012, Vol. 9, No. 8, pp. 377 et seq.

Maršíková, J., et al. Insolvenční zákon s poznámkami, judikaturou, nařízením Evropského parlamentu a Rady (EU) č. 2015/848 a prováděcími předpisy. 3. aktualizované vydání. Praha: Leges, 2018.

Mates, P., a Šemík, K. Nad zákonem o veřejných rejstřících aneb nihil novi sub sole. Bulletin advokacie. 2014, Vol. 2014, Nos 1–2, pp. 39 et seq.

Matula, Z., Culpa in contrahendo. Praha. Wolters Kluwer ČR, 2012.

McCahery, Joseph A., Vermeulen, Erik P., Corporate Governance of Non-listed Companies. New York: Oxford University Press, 2008.

Mejstřík, M., Czech investment funds as a part of financial sector and their role in privatization of the economy. Praha: Univerzita Karlova, 1994.

Melzer, F., Dispozitivní a kogentní normy v novém občanském zákoníku. Právní rozhledy. 2013, No. 7, pp. 253 et seq.

Melzer, R, Tégl P. a kol. Občanský zákoník. III. Velký komentář. 1. vydáni. Praha: Leges, 2014.

Mišúr, P., Evropský parlament: Produkty získané biologickými procesy nesmějí být patentovatelné. Obchodněprávní revue. 2019, Vol. 11, No. 10, pp. 263 et seq.

Moravec, T., Pastorčák, J., Spotřebitel a podnikatel na dynamicky se rozvíjejícím trhu. Praha. C. H. Beck, 2019.

Munková, J., Kindl, J., Svoboda, P., Soutěžní právo. 2. vydání. Praha: C. H. Beck, 2012.

Muroň, J., Malá privatizace. Praha: Panorama, 1991.

Neubauer, J., Veřejná podpora bankám ve světle směrnice o ozdravných postupech a řešení krize na finančním trhu. Obchodněprávní revue. 2018, Vol. 10, No. 3, pp. 73 et seq.

Němec, L., Investování po evropsku: Nová úprava nabídne i SICAV a SICAR. Právní rádce, 2013, No. 4, pp. 41 et seq.

Němec, L., Murár, F., Zaknihované akcie – nová podmínka pro účast ve veřejných zakázkách. Veřejné Zakázky. 2016, No. 3, pp. 34 et seq.

Pauknerová, M., Kolizněprávní úprava obchodních společností. Právní rozhledy, 2005, No. 7, pp. 244 et seq.

Pavelcová, A., Autorská směrnice: nejasnosti převažují. Právní rádce. 2019, Vol. 27, No. 5, pp. 66 et seq.

Pecková, A., Vliv institutu užitného vzoru dle německé předlohy ve vybraných mimoevropských zemích. Acta MUP. 2018, Vol. 9, No. 2, pp. 5 et seq.

Pelikán, V., Likvidace podniku. Praha: Grada, 2011.

Pelikán, M., K některým otázkám předsmluvní odpovědnosti v praxi. Obchodněprávní revue. 2017, Vol. 9, No. 5, pp. 129 et seq.

Pelikán, R., Kogentní a dispozitivní ustanovení v novém zákonu o obchodních korporacích. Obchodněprávní revue. 2012, No. 9, pp. 246 et seq.

Pelikán, R., Právní subjektivita. Praha: Wolters Kluwer ČR, 2012.

Pelikánová, I., Černá, S. a kol. Obchodní právo. Společnosti obchodního práva a družstva. II. díl, Praha: ASPI, 2006.

Petr, M., Vztah českého a unijního soutěžního práva. 1st edition. Prague: C. H. Beck, 2018.

Pihera, V., Investiční fond. Vyměřování teritoria. Obchodněprávní revue. 2017, Vol. 9, No. 9, pp. 241 et seq.

Pilátová, J., Likvidace obchodních společností. Olomouc: ANAG, 2014.

Pilík, V., Ke vztahu úplaty a náhrady nákladů za obstarání podle smluv příkazního typu. Obchodněprávní revue. 2019, Vol. 11, No. 5, pp. 121 et seq.

Pilík, V., Komisionářská smlouva. Bulletin Stavební právo. 2018, Vol. 21, No. 1, pp. 7 et seq.

Pilík, V., Pojetí a úprava ochrany právní osobnosti právnických osob v občanském právu. Právní rozhledy. 2016, Vol. 24, Nos 13–14, pp. 457 et seq.

Pilík, V., Smlouva o zprostředkování. Právní rozhledy. 2018, Vol. 26, No. 17, pp. 573 et seq.

Plíhal, T., Porušování povinnosti zakládat řádně listiny do sbírky listin jako důvod pro zrušení právnické osoby s likvidací soudem. Bulletin advokacie. 2014, Vol. 2014, Nos 1–2, pp. 46 et seq.

Plíva, S., Přibyl, Z., Socialistické organizace. 2. přeprac. vyd. Praha. Státní pedagogické nakladatelství, 1976.

Pokorná, J., Vzpomínka na hospodářské právo. CPVP – Časopis pro právní vědu a praxi. 2019, Vol. 27, No. 100, pp. 107 et seq.

Pokorná, J., Holejšovský, J., Lasák, J., Pekárek, M. a kol. Obchodní společnosti a družstva. Praha: C. H. Beck, 2014.

Pokorná, J., Večerková E., Levická T. a Dudová J., Ochrana spotřebitele proti nekalým obchodním praktikám podnikatelů. Praha: Wolters Kluwer, 2017.

Polišenská, P., Cestovní smlouva jako spotřebitelská smlouva a její vztah ke spolucestujícím osobám. Soukromé právo. 2019, Vol. 7, No. 10, pp. 28 et seq.

Polišenská, P., Hrabalová, M., Perejdová A., Právo cenných papírů: výběr z důležitých soudních rozhodnutí v právu cenných papírů za období let 2002 až 2015. Praha. Wolters Kluwer, 2016.

Pospíšil, P., Kdo může uzavírat rozhodčí smlouvu?. Bulletin advokacie. 2010, Vol. 2010, No. 12, pp. 34 et seq.

Přikryl, V., Čechová, J., Pojistná smlouva a její základní znaky. Právní rozhledy. 2018, Vol. 26, No. 10, pp. 364 et seq.

Příkazská, M., Překvapivá ujednání v obchodních podmínkách a jejich důsledky. Právní rozhledy. 2017, Vol. 25, No. 12, pp. 419 et seq.

Psutka, J., Společné jmění manželů. Praha: C. H. Beck, 2015.

Pullmannová, H., Název podnikatele jako věc a převod práv k němu se vztahujících. Obchodní právo. 2019, Vol. 28, No. 10, pp. 2 et seq.

Pullmannová, H., Právo k obchodnímu jménu zahraničního podnikatele na území České republiky v mezinárodních souvislostech. Právní rozhledy. 2020, Vol. 28, No. 6, pp. 216 et seq.

Pullmannová, H., Vztah a limity používání obchodního jména a ochranné známky v judikatuře SDEU. Právní rozhledy. 2018, Vol. 26, No. 19, pp. 649 et seq.

Rejmont, V., Další závazky ze smluv příkazního typu (komise, obchodní zastoupení). Účetnictví. 2016, Vol. 2016, No. 1, pp. 49 et seq.

Richter, T., Insolvenční právo. 2. vydání. Praha: Wolters Kluwer ČR, 2017.

Richter, T., Insolvenční zákon: od vládního návrhu k vyhlášenému znění. In: Právní rozhledy 21/2006, p. 765.

Richter, T., Kuponová privatizace a její vlivy na správu a financování českých akciových společností. Praha: Univerzita Karlova, 2005.

Roe, M., Gordon, J.N., Convergence and Persistence in Corporate Governance. Cambridge: Cambridge University Press, 2004.

Ronovská, K., Vitoul, V., Bílková, J., Nové spolkové právo v otázkách a odpovědích. Praha: Leges, 2014.

Řezníček, D., Vykonatelnost a výkon rozhodčích nálezů. Bulletin advokacie. 2018, Vol. 2018, No. 9, pp. 43 et seq.

Řezníčková, M., Franchising: podnikání pod cizím jménem. 3. vyd. Praha. C.H. Beck, 2009.

Sadecký, L., Odmítnutí podpisu rozhodčího nálezu rozhodcem s vazbou na jeho odlišné stanovisko. Obchodní právo. 2020, Vol. 29, No. 2, pp. 16 et seq.

Salač, J., Autorská a průmyslová práva z pohledu zaměstnance a zaměstnavatele. Práce a mzda. 2019, Vol. 67, Nos 7–8, pp. 25 et seq.

Selucká, M., a kol. Koupě a prodej: nový občanský zákoník, společná evropská právní úprava prodeje. Praha. C. H. Beck, 2013.

Skálová, J., Účetní a daňové souvislosti zákona o obchodních korporacích. Praha: Wolters Kluwer, 2015.

Smrčka, L., Plaček, J., Schönfeld, J., Louda, L., Insolvenční řízení (očekávání, realita a budoucnost insolvenčního zákona). 1. vydání. Praha: Kamil Mařík – Professional Publishing, 2016.

Smutný, A., Pihera, V., Sýkora, P., Cuník, T., Zákon o bankách. Komentář. 2. vydání. Praha. C. H. Beck, 2019.

Sprinz, P., Úvěrové financování v insolvenčním řízení: mechanika uzavření a povaha pohledávek. Právní rozhledy. 2019, Vol. 27, Nos 15–16, pp. 526 et seq.

Sprinz, P., Jirmásek, T., Řeháček, O., Vrba, M., Zoubek, H. et al., Insolvenční zákon. Komentář. 1. vydání. Praha: C. H. Beck, 2019.

Ständer, K., Juřica, A., Komanditní společnost s podíly vtělenými do cenného papíru podle české a německé úpravy. Obchodněprávní revue, 2013, No. 4, pp. 105 et seq.

Steiner, M., Zásada 'pacta sunt servanda' jako součást ústavního pořádku. Soudní rozhledy. 2002, Vol. 8, No. 2, pp. 39 et seq.

Svoboda K., Smolík P., Levý J., Šínová R., a kol. Občanský soudní řád. Komentář. 2. vydání. Praha. C. H. Beck, 2017.

Szmuda, J., Účast zaměstnanců na volbě členů dozorčí rady v akciové společnosti: (stále) nevyřešení otázky. Obchodněprávní revue. 2016, Vol. 8, No. 5, pp. 143 et seq.

Šlejharová, M., Vybrané projevy ochrany 'slabší strany' z pohledu civilního práva procesního. Bulletin advokacie. 2018, Vol. 2018, Nos 7–8, pp. 46 et seq.

Šovar, J., Mikula, O., O komanditní společnosti na investiční listy. Obchodněprávní revue, 2014, Nos 11–12, pp. 305 et seq.

Šovar, J., Králík, A., Beran, J., Doležalová, D., a kol. Zákon o investičních společnostech a investičních fondech. Praha: Wolters Kluwer, 2015.

Šovar, J., Úvaha nad některými aspekty práva nedržícího vlastníka na vydání zaknihovaných cenných papírů. Obchodněprávní revue, No. 3/2015, C. H. Beck, p. 81.

Špačková, M., Zásada rovného zacházení se všemi akcionáři. Obchodněprávní revue. 2016, Vol. 8, No. 1, pp. 1 et seq.

Špička, M., Stahují se nad emisemi korporátních dluhopisů mračna? Právní rádce. 2018, Vol. 24, No. 3, pp. 36 et seq.
Štenglová, I., Havel, B., Cileček, F., Kuhn, P., Šuk, P., Zákon o obchodních korporacích. Komentář. 2. vydání. Praha. C. H. Beck, 2017.
Švestka, J., Dvořák J., Fiala, J. a kol Občanský zákoník (zák. č. 89/2012 Sb.). Komentář. Svazek I (obecná část). Praha: Wolters Kluwer ČR, 2020.
Štenglová, I., Havel, B., Cileček, F., Kuhn, P., Šuk, P., Zákon o obchodních korporacích. Komentář. 2. vydání. Praha: C. H. Beck, 2017.
Štenglová, I., Dědič, J., Tomsa, M., a kol. Základy obchodního práva. Praha: Leges, 2014, pp. 51 et seq.
Šuk, P., Čech, P., Právo obchodních společností v praxi a pro praxi (nejen soudní). Praha: Polygon, 2016.
Švejnar, J., Česká republika a ekonomická transformace ve střední a východní Evropě. Praha: Academia, 1997.
Telec, I., Tůma, P., Autorský zákon, Komentář. Praha. C. H. Beck, 2019.
Tichý, L., Pipková P. J., Balarin, J., Kupní smlouva v novém občanském zákoníku. Komentář. Praha. C. H. Beck, 2014.
Tomšík, V., Proces ekonomické transformace v zemích střední a východní Evropy. Praha: Vysoká škola ekonomická, 1999.
Tříska, D., Kupónová privatizace: sborník textů. Praha: CEP Centrum pro ekonomiku a politiku, 2002.
Uminský, P., Účetní a daňové souvislosti faktoringu. Daně a právo v praxi. 2012, Vol. 2012, No. 12, pp. 25 et seq.
Valouch, P., Leasing v praxi, 5. aktualizované vydání. Praha. GRADA Publishing, a.s., 2012.
Večeřa, J., Ochrana spotřebitele v České republice a Evropské unii. Praha: Leges, 2013.
Veličková, A., Úskalí nabývání vlastních akcií. Právní rádce. 2019, Vol. 27, No. 6, pp. 52 et seq.
Vlachová, B., Rozhodčí nález jako exekuční titul. Komorní listy. 2017, Vol. 9, No. 3, pp. 20 et seq.
Vychopeň, J., Veřejná obchodní společnost z právního, účetního a daňového pohledu. Daně a právo, 2014, No. 11, pp. 2 et seq.
Vymazal, L., Ochrana spotřebitele a její meze v obchodním závazkovém právu. Obchodněprávní revue. 2010, Vol. 2, No. 2, pp. 35 et seq.
Winterová, A., Macková, A. et al. Civilní právo procesní. Část druhá: Řízení vykonávací, řízení insolvenční. 1. vydání. Praha: Leges, 2015.
Zbránek, M., Leasing a zásada poctivého obchodního styku. Bulletin advokacie. 2010, Vol. 2010, No. 5, pp. 33 et seq.
Zibner, J., Akceptace právní osobnosti v případě umělé inteligence. Revue pro právo a technologie. 2018, Vol. 9, No. 17, pp. 19 et seq.
Zibner, J., Otázky odpovědnosti umělé inteligence za zásah do autorského práva. Revue pro právo a technologie. 2019, Vol. 10, No. 20, pp. 65 et seq.
Zima, P., K možnosti analogické aplikace ustanovení o obchodním zastoupení na franšízové smlouvy. Obchodněprávní revue. 2017, Vol. 9, No. 10, pp. 289 et seq.

Selected Bibliography

Zvára, M., Nabytí podílu od neoprávněného ve společnosti s ručením omezeným na základě smlouvy o převodu podílu. Obchodněprávní revue. 2017, Vol. 9, Nos 7–8, pp. 193 et seq.

Index

The numbers here refer to paragraph numbers.

Index

www.ingramcontent.com/pod-product-compliance
Ingram Content Group UK Ltd.
Pitfield, Milton Keynes, MK11 3LW, UK
UKHW020137290926
15471UKWH00003B/537

9 789403 502267